An Anthropology of the
European Union

An Anthropology of the European Union

Building, Imagining and Experiencing the New Europe

Edited by
Irène Bellier and Thomas M. Wilson

Oxford • New York

First published in 2000 by
Berg
Editorial offices:
150 Cowley Road, Oxford, OX4 1JJ, UK
838 Broadway, Third Floor, New York, NY 10003-4812, USA

Berg is an imprint of Oxford International Publishers Ltd.

Library of Congress Cataloging-in-Publication Data
A catalogue record for this book is available from the Library of Congress.

British Library Cataloguing-in-Publication Data
A catalogue record for this book is available from the British Library.

ISBN 1 85973 324 7 (Cloth)
1 85973 329 8 (Paper)

Typeset by JS Typesetting, Wellingborough, Northants
Printed in the United Kingdom by Biddles Ltd, Guildford and King's Lynn

Contents

Acknowledgements   vii

List of Contributors   ix

1   Building, Imagining and Experiencing Europe:
         Institutions and Identities in the European Union
         Irène Bellier and *Thomas M. Wilson*   1

**Part I Institutions, Politics and Society at the Core of the
European Union**

2   Virtual Europe
         Marc Abélès   31

3   The European Union, Identity Politics and the Logic of Interests'
         Representation
         Irène Bellier   53

4   Debating Europe: Globalization Rhetoric and European Union
         Unemployment Policies
         Gilbert Weiss and *Ruth Wodak*   75

5   Surrogate Discourses of Power: The European Union and the
         Problem of Society
         Douglas R. Holmes   93

Part II Belonging and Identity in the European Union

6   European Citizenship, Citizens of Europe and European Citizens
         Catherine Neveu   119

7   Agendas in Conflict: Nation, State and Europe in the Northern
         Ireland Borderlands
         Thomas M. Wilson   137

Contents

8 Not Simple At All: Danish Identity and the European Union
   Richard Jenkins   159

9 Boundaries at Work: Discourses and Practices of Belonging in the
   European Space Agency
   Stacia E. Zabusky   179

Index   201

Acknowledgements

This book began as an invited session of the Society for the Anthropology of Europe at the 1996 annual meetings of the American Anthropological Association in San Francisco. We would like to thank all who participated in that session, as well as the program committee of the SAE that year, as led by Jane Nadel-Klein, SAE program chair. We also thank Robert Harmsen of Queen's University Belfast for his linguistic advice. Irène Bellier wishes to thank Susan Carol Rogers of the Institute of French Studies of New York University for her support while she was a Visiting Professor in autumn 1995, and for her commitment to developing scientific exchanges between French and American anthropologists. Thomas Wilson wishes to thank Tony R. Judt and Jair Kessler of the Remarque Institute of New York University for their collegial and financial support while he was a Visiting Fellow there in autumn 1998. Finally, we gratefully acknowledge the debt we owe to Kathryn Earle of Berg Publishers, whose sound advice and good cheer encouraged and sustained us in this truly transnational enterprise.

List of Contributors

Marc Abélès is research director at the National Centre for Scientific Research in France (CNRS), Head of the Laboratoire d'Anthropologie des Institutions et des Organisations Sociales (LAIOS). He has published extensively on Ethiopia, France and the European Union. Among his books are *Anthropologie de l'Etat* (1990), *La vie quotidienne au Parlement Européen* (1992), *En attente d'Europe* (1996). His current research is on American Foundations and Philanthropy.

Irène Bellier is a political anthropologist affiliated to the LAIOS, at the National Centre for Scientific Research in France (CNRS). Author of *El Temblor y la Luna* (1991) on gender in Amerindian society, and *L'Ena comme si vous y étiez* (1993) on French corporate identities and State power-training, she conducted research and published extensively on bureaucratic and multicultural institutions in the European Union. She is currently co-ordinating an academic and research network between the European and the Indian Unions.

Douglas Holmes teaches social anthropology at the University of Otago in New Zealand. He is the author of *Integral Europe: Fast-Capitalism, Multiculturalism, Neofascism* (2000) and *Cultural Disenchantment: Worker Peasantries in Northeast Italy* (1989). His current research deals with Central Bankers in the US, Japan, and the EU and how they conceptualize their engagement with society.

Richard Jenkins trained as a social anthropologist at the Queen's University of Belfast, and the University of Cambridge, and has done research in Northern Ireland, England, Wales and Denmark. Among his books are *Social Identity* (1996), *Rethinking Ethnicity* (1997) and *Questions of Competence* (1998). He is Professor of Sociology at the University of Sheffield.

Catherine Neveu is a political anthropologist, affiliated to the LAIOS, at the National Centre for Scientific Research in France (CNRS). She conducted research in London (*Communauté, Nationalité et Citoyenneté. De l'autre côté du miroir, les Bangladeshis de Londres* (1993)) and in Northern France (*Espace public et engagement politique* (1999)) and has published extensively on the anthropology of citizenship.

Gilbert Weiss holds a PhD in Sociology from the University of Vienna. He is research associate at the University's Research Centre on Discourse, Politics, Identity, where he is heading a project on 'European Union discourses on unemployment'. He has published several articles in this field.

Thomas M. Wilson is Senior Lecturer in European Studies at The Queen's University of Belfast, and has conducted anthropological research in Ireland, the United Kingdom and Hungary. He is the co-author of *Borders: Frontiers of Identity, Nation and State* (1999) and co-editor of *Border Identities* (1998). His current research is on European policy in Northern Ireland, and he is one of the founders of QUB's new Centre for International Borders Research (CIBR).

Ruth Wodak is Professor of Linguistics at the University of Wien. Awarded the Ludwig Wittgenstein Prize in 1996, she established a Research Centre on Discourse, Politics, Identity, which is now affiliated with the Austrian Academy of Sciences. Author of *Disorders of Discourses* (1996) and *Decision Making in Organizations: Recontextualization as Transformation of Meanings* (forthcoming), she has published extensively on gender, anti-Semitism and racism.

Stacia E. Zabusky received her PhD in Cultural Anthropology from Cornell University, and is the author of *Launching Europe: An Ethnography of European Cooperation in Space Science* (1995). She is currently working on an ethnographic study of European expatriate women in the Netherlands.

Building, Imagining and Experiencing Europe: Institutions and Identities in the European Union

Irène Bellier and Thomas M. Wilson

The issues of culture and identity have long been marginal aspects of the general scholarship of the European Union (EU). Until recently, most academic studies of the EU have treated the thorny problems of local and national identities, loyalties, traditions, ideologies and affiliations as secondary concerns to the more important projects of creating, sustaining, and understanding the EU as a political and economic entity and system. But the importance of the roles which national and other cultures play in the processes of 'Europe-building' (a phrase often used to refer to the strengthening of the institutions of the EU and to the expansion of its membership), and in Europeanization (which is a much wider and perhaps more important process connoting the role of European culture in the integration of disparate European communities and societies), has not gone unnoticed by social scientists. This attention has been generated by what some believe was the shock inflicted on political insiders, government leaders, journalists and academics by the initial Danish rejection of the Maastricht Treaty on European Union. Recently a number of sociologists and political scientists have recognized the need for more studies of European culture and identity, as they are related to European integration (Hedetoft 1994: 1–2; see also Landau and Whitman 1997). In fact one leading scholar, in his critique of academic European Studies in North America, has specifically called for more involvement by anthropologists and other social scientists in research in cultural and political integration (Tarrow 1994; see also Hedetoft 1994).

Missing from these welcome calls by our cognate disciplines for anthropological attention to the development of the EU and to the processes of Europeanization and European integration is a clear understanding of what anthropologists have already achieved in these regards, and the research designs which they have established and will continue to develop in the future. The simple point is that the anthropology of the EU and of European integration is very much alive and well, on both sides of the Atlantic, and in at least three different anthropological traditions.

In fact, the contributors to this book have worked in varying degrees within the professional and intellectual traditions of American, British and French anthropology. While French anthropology has for a long time been associated with structuralism, studies of non-Western societies, and cultural anthropology, a significant turn has been undertaken by a number of scholars since the 1980s. These studies focus on what has been called 'new objects' in France and the wider Europe, and they have contributed to the construction of the conceptual paradigm of 'anthropologie du proche'. Simultaneously, there has been a radical shift within French political anthropology to the examination of political and bureaucratic institutions as well as social and economic organizations. American anthropologists in recent years have increasingly problematized their approaches to culture and identity, as part of their efforts to distance themselves from some methods and theories which placed them in positions of authority and power, albeit often unconsciously. American applied anthropologists have continued within their evolving sub-discipline to investigate policy makers, institutions, and impact at all levels of politics and society. British anthropology has also begun to explore policy making as a new arena of political and social organization within their ethnographic analyses 'at home' and abroad. As can be seen in our structuring of this volume, one of the central motifs in the analysis of culture and identity in Europe today is that of 'belonging'. Among the primary arenas in which this is now being explored are local, state and supranational institutions. We expect that there are scholars in all of the EU member states working in their and other national traditions and in languages other than English and French who are tackling the issues of European integration, culture and identity. We are also hopeful that this volume will delineate common areas of concern among us all, and open up new opportunities for dialogue.

Thus, this collection brings together various case studies to illustrate extant anthropological research in the issues of culture and identity within the EU. As such it serves as both a reminder of the prior anthropology of the EU, as well as a profile of emergent anthropological research initiatives and agendas. Its focus is on the EU as both a political project and object. It seeks to delineate the ways in which culture acts to distinguish or to obscure EU institutions, policies, leaders, ideologies, and values in the daily lives of people who live in the peripheries and localities of the EU as well as those at the centres of EU decision-making. The contributors to this volume also demonstrate ways in which culture frames perceptions of the 'Europe' of the EU and its project of Europeanization. In this regard nationalism and national identities function at every level of the EU in ways which sometimes complement, and sometimes oppose, the goals of EU decision-makers, government leaders, and civil servants in EU institutions and in the institutions of member states and regions. Although national identities are flourishing throughout the member states of the EU, special attempts have also been made at the EU level to clarify and promote the notion of a common European identity. It is not the intention of the contributors to this volume to reify European culture and identity. Rather the aim is to explore the meanings which are given to the concepts of European and national identities both within the institutions of the EU and beyond their formal limits, as these impinge upon EU structures.

European identity is being shaped within the EU, in part around a typology of European features which has been called 'a European model of society' by the Forward Studies Unit of the European Commission.[1] This model's features include similar family structures, the democratic distribution of power, and freedom of individuals vis à vis the state. In other instances, the Commission and other EU institutions construct different, more general, and in some ways more powerful models of European identity, which have remained undefined within the institutional context of the EU but which converge around the notion of a 'shared common interest'. European identity is also finding expression outside of the EU, in the notion of a common 'European external identity', based on the developing role of the EU as a solitary entity in international relations on the continental and world stages. It is the role of EU institutions in the production and perception of common or shared European identity, both within and outside of the EU, which is one of the primary concerns of this volume.

It is perhaps prudent to clarify here, however, what we mean by the term 'European Union'. In the first instance the 'EU' is the formal institutional system of economic and political integration which is based on international treaties agreed by the current 15 member states (Belgium, France, Germany, Italy, Luxembourg, the Netherlands, Denmark, Ireland, the United Kingdom, Spain, Portugal, Greece, Austria, Finland, and Sweden). The 'EU' also denotes the institutions set up under these treaties. Foremost among these institutions are the Commission, which provides administrative leadership and policy initiatives to the EU, the Council, composed of the member states delegations in what amounts to a policy-making role, and the Parliament, made up of directly-elected representatives who serve in informational and oversight roles. But the 'EU' also refers to the wider evolving social system within the 15 member states in which there is very little which is unaffected by EU legislation, even though much of the EU's involvement in peoples' everyday lives occurs principally through national administrative channels.

In this introduction we seek to review themes in the anthropology of the EU which has preceded us, and to explore ways in which anthropology can clarify how the EU and its various institutions and policies are understood and experienced in a variety of localities within its borders. We also examine the usefulness of anthropological perspectives on culture and identity for the analysis of the processes of Europe-building and Europeanization, especially regarding the imaginings needed for social integration to be achieved along with the EU's driving forces of economic and political integration. Anthropological methods and practice offer insights into the ways in which culture and identity are problematized within EU institutions, and they clarify how EU institutions, policies and agendas produce new forms of European culture and identity, as well as affect some old ones.

Anthropological Approaches

There have been anthropological studies of the EU from a variety of perspectives for some time now, and their numbers as well as the general anthropological interest in the EU are growing. In an effort to bring these anthropological viewpoints to the attention of other social scientists, in disciplines such as politics, public administration and economics, which have long been more associated than anthropology with the study of the development of the EU, they have been characterised by Wilson as the study of the EU 'from above' and 'from below' (1998; see also Hedetoft 1994). Although this schema may be a useful starting point in the characterization and categorization of social anthropological studies of EU institutions, policies, and symbols, it may obscure the dimensions of the EU as an object, as a process, or, in the sense of the creation of the economic and political union of its member states, as an objective. From above and below implies some sort of Platonic ideal, in which anthropologists, and other social scientists who employ this popular metaphor for studying large political and social institutions, like the state, approach an entity from opposite directions but never reach their goal, never actually study it, or only devise strategies to study its outline or its manifestations in the lives of people removed from its core or its head. In this sense it is as if anthropologists just observe the observers, those who distinguish a monolithic EU from afar.

In fact, any categorization or overview which implies an anthropological distance from the organizations and people of the EU risks exoticizing anthropological research in the EU, and does a disservice to many anthropologists who have worked very hard over the years to understand EU decision-makers, committees, cliques, factions, and political parties, all within the context of their homes, families, national backgrounds and political cultures. Still other anthropologists have investigated the role of European institutions in the dissemination of the ideals, policies and practices of the EU, which includes their impact on national and regional governments, businesses, and communities. But analyses such as these aside, there remains the vexing situation that the EU, as a set of institutions, ideas and behaviours, is extremely difficult to approach with the standard, tried and true methods of social anthropology.

This is because the EU is not only a collection of political and bureaucratic institutions, nor simply an umbrella organization for the articulation of member state policies, but it is an arena of cultural relations (Wilson 1993), an entity creating and recreating its own culture, its own sets of representations and symbols.

Recurrent efforts within the EU to create symbols and representations of the EU owe much to the fact that the European project is evolving through on-going negotiations among multiple and changing partners in a completely open-ended system. The EU's goals of European integration and unification may appear to be self-evident to some, but to our contributors as well as other scholars of these processes such goals are extremely problematic, even among the EU leaders who are often seen from a distance to be a homogeneous group of committed idealists, futurists, and Europhiles. In truth, for them, for us, and for most Europeans, the EU is an indistinct entity, a contradictory conglomeration of words and actions, of symbols and policies, of intrusive and liberating values. 'Always seen as a means to realize some ill-defined community, the EU is increasingly an end in itself. However, this circularity — the EU as both cause and effect of itself – begs the fundamental question of what it in fact is' (Borneman and Fowler 1997: 488).

There are of course many correct answers to this question, as there would be to questions of 'What is France?' or 'What is Britain?' But beyond textbook answers regarding the history and functions of European institutions and laws, the responses to the question 'What is the EU?' must perforce be much more confused, contradictory and problematic than any response to queries about the nature of one nation or state, precisely because the EU as an object and a project has no modern historical antecedent, and no cultural template or political form with which people have become comfortable through long-standing enculturation. The task at hand for anthropologists who study the evolution of local and national European societies is not to label the form of institutional arrangements which the EU develops (for example, as a federal union, an intergovernmental body, or a supranational entity). Rather, it is to describe and analyze the cultural articulations between local, regional, national and EU levels, and to inform both insiders and outsiders alike about the EU's structures and functions.

Perceptions of the organs and activities of the EU diverge considerably throughout the member states, depending on a host of factors, including the important ones of national, regional and local culture and identity. While the EU is perceived in places like Britain to be a centralized bureaucratic monster, in other places like Spain, and even in the European Parliament, it is considered to be retarded by its decentralized and poorly staffed institutions, especially in the Commission.[2] In fact, the institutions of the EU can be more fruitfully approached as sets of self-representations too complex to be easily reduced to one image or one symbol. In reality, although such institutions as the European Commission, the European Parliament, and the European Court of Justice are all headquartered in European capitals, they do not always share the same capitals, nor are all the sections of one institution always together in one city. This decentralization is matched by the relatively few bureaucrats who work for these institutions. There are only about 20,000 officials working in EU institutions, 80 per cent of whom are in the Commission. This bureaucracy is small indeed when compared to the administration of capital cities of member states alone, which in Paris is made up of around 40,000 people and in Lisbon is approximately 22,000. In fact, the EU is a rather diffused set of political actors and institutions.

The anthropological problems of approach to the EU are exacerbated by the methodological problems of participant observation, based on long-term ethnographic field research. Because of the anthropological intention to immerse the researcher within the total lives of a community, it is very difficult to study political institutions, and the many 'communities' which give them definition and meaning, during office hours, and within the physical constraints of office blocks, committee rooms, and airport lounges. In this sense the anthropology of EU institutions and identities shares much with all anthropological studies of culture and power, where ethnographers attempt to 'study up' (cf. Nader 1974; Wolf 1974) by tracing the lines of differential access to wealth and political power from local communities to the wider arenas of economics and politics in regions and states. In their attempts to pursue networks of wealth and influence in the EU, anthropologists face grave difficulties in gaining access to powerful institutions and people, and they are confronted by daunting, abundant and critical apparatuses of information in the media and among other academic disciplines. Furthermore they must negotiate their way among extremely knowledgeable respondents and audiences whose own models of culture and identity create remarkable dialectics of method and theory within an anthropologist's field experience (see Rogers 1997).

These difficulties in anthropological approach notwithstanding, the EU can and should be studied by anthropologists precisely because it, like many other sets of political institutions and identities, is simultaneously both cultural object and project. It is a structure of government and administration and a field of social relations with particular political, economic, social and cultural goals, which increasingly has had as its objectives the integration, harmonization and 'ever closer union' of member states and societies. This project of defining and expanding a new public space in Europe is also one of building a new cultural space, a process which is largely ignored by many of its architects and critics because of their focus on the political and economic forms the 'New Europe' will take.

This inattention to the cultures and identities of European integration is surprising, since much of the political debate about the European Union's future – as in the intergovernmental widening vs the federal deepening – rests squarely on a foundation of the state as the principal political actor and model. In fact, although the EU is a political entity with no clear prescriptive framework, its leaders and elites borrow heavily from the models of nation and state building, precisely because many do not know how to escape intellectually and linguistically from the dominant model of the nation state. This is a problem shared by many scholars of the social sciences, such as political scientists, who Schmitter (1996: 25) suggests use a vocabulary 'contaminated by the (usually implicit) assumption that, whatever the actors or the actions, they are taking place within the confines of a sovereign nation state or of an interstate system formed by such units'.

The EU project entails an almost continuous redefinition of the EU's relations with its member states and its putative citizens, and an on-going reconstruction of its own identity. As a result, European officials and governmental representatives should heed the problems encountered by most nation states, which historically and in today's world have sought, and in large part failed, to forge relatively homogeneous nations out of multiple cultural diversities. The fact that European elites have not fully recognized that the divisive issues of political, economic and social inclusion and exclusion are the legacy of every European state seems evident in the ways they have approached the same issues as 'European' concerns. The European project has developed within the linguistic and conceptual boundaries which establish state, nation and nation state as referents for European political structures, and which leave to the member states the lion's share of inventing the models by which European membership, citizenry and identity will evolve.

It is because of the constraints which nation and state-building place on the evolution of the EU project that the voluminous literature on nationalism may have much to tell us of the difficulties of culture and identity which face the EU. Borrowing from Benedict Anderson (1991), we wonder how and where the majority of the people of the EU will begin to 'imagine' their joint community of Europe, and whether the disparate forms of European identity which exist today, some of which are the concerns of this volume's contributors, can ever be integrated into an identification with and support of EU institutions, policies and ideals? This is not to say that there is not already in existence strong, and perhaps competing, imaginings of European identity. Certainly the European Commission is an important force in all forms of Europeanization, and it and its supporters have some clear and strongly voiced beliefs in European identity, beliefs linked to identi-fication and affiliation with the EU project as shaped by the Commission. Yet the European identity to be found in the Commission does not appear as a single coherent reference but as a complex modality of identification idealistically undertaken for professional purposes. While a corporate European identity is often demonstrated by their attitudes and patterns of communication, the various cultures and identities of the Commission's officials temper and alter the strongest tenets of Europeanism in their daily lives. European civil servants have different ways of 'thinking European'. This results in a pattern of identification with the European project which leaves immense areas of uncertainty, because of its reactive role in regard to other agents in the production of areas of European culture (Bellier 1997a: 96).

If the engineers of the EU, and here we refer specifically to government leaders and EU civil servants, must depend on the institutional structures of the states to forge a European Union, and if they also must rely on their own ideological models of the nation-state to construct their building blocks of a new Europe, then we suggest that the methods which anthropologists have utilized to study the nation and the state might be used to explore the roles of the EU in the everyday lives of its citizens and residents. While it is true that overall anthropological studies of nation and state in Europe have been a mixed bag, there have been notable achievements (such as Schneider et al. 1972; Blok 1974; Cole and Wolf 1974; Boissevain 1975; Schneider and Schneider 1976; Grillo 1980; Wolf 1982; Borneman 1992; Verdery 1995) upon which to build a new anthropology of the EU. In addressing the EU, anthropologists must define new approaches to studying the complex relationships between institutions, identities, cultures and societies. Among these approaches are the analysis of official discourses and languages and the ways they map new territories for political action (for a range of anthropological views on institutional semantics, see *Ethnologie Française* 1999); processes of hybridization (Bellier 1999); multiculturalism and the consequences of changing referents for the development of political cultures (Abélès 1996b); and the emergence of new temporalities and forms of representations in leading institutions (Abélès 1999). These studies resonate with similar attempts made by anthropologists beyond Europe to reconsider the relationships between place, culture and power (Gupta and Ferguson 1997) and between globalization, migration, and new technologies (Appadurai 1997).

Our contributors to this volume present a variety of perspectives which show that, much like nations are built and imagined, and the institutions and policies of the state are experienced by its people, the models of imagining, building and experiencing the Europe of the EU are fruitful ways to focus anthropologists, and other social scientists, on culture and identity in the EU. It is the guiding principle of this volume in fact that anthropologists have been and continue to be in premier positions to chart cultural change in the EU precisely because they recognize that the EU is much more than an economic market and political organization. The EU is creating its own culture, which we see as sets of institutions, behaviours, and ideas which often coincide with, and often contradict, national and other forms of local culture, but which have, as one very important result, the shaping of identities throughout Europe, and the identities of Europe outside its boundaries. Anthropological studies of the EU in the recent past, and as represented in this volume, have much to offer to the understanding of how the culture of the EU is experienced, which is integral to any process of building and imagining the Europe of the EU.

Boundaries of Institutions, Disciplines and Identities

A new Europe is being built in the European Union. The processes of Europeanization are as much about the legitimization of the EU's institutions and agenda as they are about the creation, recognition and acceptance of new forms of European identity (see Wallace 1997: 16). In fact these processes of building and imagining Europe are inextricably linked, dialectically related components of the EU's project. As such the boundaries between institution building in the EU and the fostering of one or many European identities, through the EU's and others' efforts to establish common bonds of history, experience and culture, are not hard and fast. Building and imagining Europe are flip sides of the same coin. While 'building Europe' implies the growth and strengthening of EU institutions, it also suggests the expansion of the EU's membership, a widening of the European club which some member states hope or fear will mean a dilution of the EU's institutional and legislative authority.

Whatever direction the future EU takes, it will entail a great deal of wrangling in each of the member states over issues of national identity, sovereignty, and power, which will reverberate throughout Europe's regions, some of which seek more power within their states. Battles over future EU competencies will also be battles for the loyalties of Europe's citizens, who heretofore have been first and foremost 'national' citizens. As a result, the social and economic discrepancies between men and women, the rights of minorities formerly oppressed because of their sexual preference, the legal statuses of stateless and nomadic peoples, such as the Rom, and the role of political and economic refugees to the EU will all be part of national and European debates about citizenship. While governments will continue to negotiate the defence of national interests, Europeans may also enjoy the convenience and safety of the wider identity of 'European citizen', which might allow more space for the recognition and validation of their minority racial, ethnic, and political identities. Anthropologists have pointed out for some time that identities are never better perceived than in places and times of encounter with their 'others', within real and metaphorical frontiers. The frontiers between European identities and national identities have been and will continue to be extremely problematical concerns to the EU and member states.

In today's world the boundaries of our academic disciplines appear just as permeable and transient as those of European states and social identities. Since the Second World War anthropologists have increasingly turned their theories, methods and models to the structures and ideologies of the state, in the developed as well as the less developed worlds. As a result of the growing interest among anthropologists in the organs and policies of modern states, anthropologists have taken to the study of institutions at local, regional, national and international levels of action. As part of this endeavour, anthropologists have examined institutions in terms of their internal structures, their cultures of organisation, their roles in wider institutions, their relations to other organs of power and influence, their impact on the communities which they serve, and their roles as producers of ideas and ideologies (see, for example, Abélès 1990; Bellier 1993; Herzfeld 1987, 1992; Holmes 1993; Marcus 1986, 1992; Rabinow 1989; Varenne 1993).

From an anthropological viewpoint, the institutions of the EU and other supranational agencies, such as NATO (North Atlantic Treaty Organization) and the European Space Agency (ESA), are microcosms, constituting very small worlds within the states which house them and give them charters for action, but they are also as complex as the global world which gives them definition too (Bellier 1997b). As political and cultural microcosms they are not simple reductions of scale. As powerful political institutions they are the places where a 'new world' is designed and where traditional practices, ideas and concepts are giving birth to new ones. It is in this sense that they function as European melting pots, as suggested by Jean Monnet in his reference to the 'laboratory of Europe' (1975: 441) and as chronicled in the ESA (Zabusky 1995).

In fact, the macro and the micro perspectives are so closely interrelated within the confines of these institutions that anthropologists must always cross the borders which seemingly separate these institutions from the other people and institutions of which they are a part. What happens inside the walls of these structures of government cannot be separated from what happens outside, regardless of how well an organization protects itself by limiting access to it by all except those properly authorized. Their actions and rhetoric of inclusion and exclusion have important effects beyond their doors, in ways expected and intended, but often in ways which are surprising and unintentional. Thus the anthropologist must place European institutions within fields of political and social relations in order to make these bodies' roles in building and maintaining Europe comprehensible. This entails two tasks. One is the identification of the institution at its boundaries, by marking its internal and external limits through the delineation of the structure and function of the organization. The second way considers its actors, members and 'inhabitants' within their own micro and macro social fields. In other words, anthropologists must simultaneously study institutional relations with other political structures, as well as the political and other networks of the people who work in these institutions, networks which often extend far beyond the institutional framework. Through this dual effort a more complete topography can be constructed of the fields of social and political action and allegiance among the leaders and staffs of European institutions, as one way to delineate their notions of belonging, experiencing and imagining an evolving EU.

Anthropologists must pay attention to the raison d'être of an EU institution, and must not be limited to what other social scientists might call its rationality and efficiency. Overall, the raison d'être of European institutions is to build unity, albeit from their different viewpoints, and according to the procedures and practices associated with their place within the political fields of EU administration. Their officials, civil servants, leaders and representatives, along with their corresponding partners, their opposite numbers, in other European and national institutions, manipulate a variety of ideologies to justify the legitimacy of the European project, a legitimacy which consolidates their own position within their institutions. But such justification is both facilitated and made more difficult because the project is incomplete. Nevertheless, for many the future Europe of the EU is desirable regardless of how controversial, ineluctable and contested it is. European institutions are operating as if they were establishing something whose form everyone agrees, which to some must be some type of a European state. In fact, the European Commission is an institution whose performance, ideology, and modes of integration are such that it can be considered as the 'avant garde' of a new society in the making. At the least the Commission projects an image of what a multicultural organization is like within the global context of Europeaness.

Our goal in this volume is to transcend the EU institution as an object, in order to understand the roles which culture and identity play in the institution, as well as the roles the institution plays as an agent of political and cultural change. Each of the institutions of the EU, in fact, are multicultural entities attempting to transcend the narrow limits of their bureaucratic portfolios in order to achieve something greater, even if at this stage the full dimensions of the Europe they are building are unclear and European governance is difficult to understand (Kohler-Koch 1997). Thus our perspective on the European institution treats it as a process as much as a political organization.

This point raises a number of controversial issues, among which is the fact that one European institution, the Commission, functions as a 'scapegoat' in many of the discourses of national political actors. This puts great pressure on the Commission and its officials, but it also puts them in an important, if not crucial, role in any process of Europeanization. If we accept that such an institution is a microcosm of a number of political and social entities, in and across the member states, and one which maintains special links among these entities within the global society, then we can from the anthropological point of view develop a cultural analysis of its 'inhabitants', their ideas, language, actions, social links and strategy of reproduction.

This perspective has sustained the approach of a number of scholars who have worked in the European Commission (Abélès et al 1993; Bellier 1997a; McDonald 1993, 1997; Ross 1993; Shore 1993; Shore and Black 1992), in the European Parliament (Abélès 1992, 1993; Holmes 1993), and in the European Space Agency (Zabusky 1995). Their intention was not simply to exemplify a new way of life in a sort of protected middle ground of Eurocracy, in the interstices of the EU, but to explore areas where something 'new' was happening in terms of cultural definitions and political projections. European institutions generate their own meanings about their own roles, but also contribute to the overall construction of meaning in the European project, a process significant among elites as well as in the everyday lives of Europeans everywhere. Through examining EU institutional discourse (as evidenced in Weiss and Wodak's contribution to this volume) anthropologists have explored the conception of Europe at the core of the EU, a multicultural world with a great deal of cross-cultural discussion on sovereignty, community, identity and consciousness, but one with a very light symbolic superstructure. This world is forward-looking, precisely because its engineers and its critics, including anthropologists, must disconnect from the analysis of the reciprocal impact of tradition on modernity in order to understand the cultural relations which frame the EU's open-ended political and economic projects. In this regard, Weiss and Wodak demonstrate in their contribution to this volume how globalization rhetoric is invoked to proclaim a European identity distinct from other 'global players', such as the USA and Japan.

As a result, anthropological observations have had to expand to include what surrounds, emanates from, and feeds into the EU's institutions. The various societies of Europe sustain European institutions, either directly or through their national governments, but they also tend to react strongly to the many changes which are introduced by EU institutions and programmes, depending on the ways in which national and European officials and representatives identify the problems and adopt solutions for building the future (Wilson 1996).

It is important to emphasize here that the core issues of culture, economics and politics which frame the evolving European project are not just the concern of its leading architects in EU and national capitals. They are the stuff of daily life among all Europeans, including many who live beyond the borders of the EU itself. In this volume we privilege two perspectives on these core issues, approaches which are linked and interdependent, and which result in different research emphases, i.e. an institutional approach and a local community approach. In fact, the study of the impact of the EU on local communities has been a long-standing interest in anthropology. Ethnographers have chronicled a number of local and national reactions to EC and EU policies, among farmers in Sicily (Giordano 1987), Ireland (Shutes 1991, 1993; Wilson 1989), and Spain and the Netherlands (Jurjus 1993); among fishermen in Spain (LiPuma and Meltzoff 1989, 1994) and Ireland (Dilley 1989); and among a variety of concerned citizens and communities across the EU (for example, in Corsica (Jaffe 1993), Spain and France (McDonogh 1993), and Ireland (Sheehan 1991)). All of these anthropological studies of institutions and political fields, at the EU's core and periphery, from below, in the middle and from above, contribute to a fuller picture of culture and identity in the everyday lives of the EU's people. They, along with the contributions to this collection, offer some insight on the ways in which the 'Europe' of the EU is being built, imagined and experienced in a variety of levels and in a variety of places of European society and politics.

Building Europe

European societies pre-date the institutional Europe of the EU, and as such constitute the basis of a number of ideas about Europe, including those which postulate a common European identity which is not linear or homogeneous.

> Modern Europe is the fruit of a perpetual metamorphosis: from Europe of the states to Europe of the nation-states, from Europe of the balance of powers to Europe of deregulation and outburst, from merchant Europe to industrial Europe, from Europe of the Apogee to Europe of the Abyss, from Europe master of the world to Europe region under control. So its identity is not defined despite metamorphosis but *within* metamorphosis. (Morin 1990: 71, editors' translation)

One thing that is clear in this history of metamorphosis is that while states were defining boundaries, governance and sovereignty, they also developed a shared resistance to Europe being united under the hegemony of a single state or political master. As a result most attempts to define European identity as either common or contested view Europe as a culture area, or as an area of diverse cultures. Such perspectives may or may not run counter to the prevailing views of the EU, or Western Europe, as a political space. The cultural viewpoint allows us to consider that social, economic, and political organisations legitimate certain processes of institution building. This is the foundation of the whole category of Western society, or Occidentalism, which rests on liberal democracy, division of power, democratic representation, free elections, and so on. Within this political framework, a historical perspective enables us to understand how nation states emerged with strong cultural and linguistic boundaries, helping to build precise definitions of national identity and citizenship (see, for example, Bhabha 1990; Dumont 1983; Mauss 1974; Noiriel 1991).

The 'New Europe', i.e. the new institutional Europe, is a product of its time, brought into existence by a generation of politicians who are now called 'the founding fathers of Europe'. They conceptualized the dynamic required to overcome nationalist passions and decided on precise steps and measures to produce an economic interdependence and national convergence, to stimulate unity through consensus, and to reshape nationalism through liberalism. The European project has matured as it has been progressively deepened and widened through the incorporation of more and more countries. But the experience of European integration does not end for its many civil servants, Commissioners and Members of Parliament as a matter internal to the EU. Among the architects of EU integration and union are those who deal with the rest of the world, many of whom wish to use their experience of Europe-building to help build other regional trading blocs and political entities. This is noticeable in the framing of European relations with the African-Caribbean-Pacific countries during the course of renegotiating the Lomé Convention, as well as in EU relations with Mercosur (the common market of South America's southern cone) or with the South Asian Association for Regional Cooperation. This developing model of regional integration is of interest to anthropologists because its goals of unification, harmonization and integration, key processes in the context of Europe-building, require an alteration in the core political values which previously were defined within the frame of nation states.

The complex and sophisticated processes of EU institutional development have progressively affected the organization of each member state. Member state populations are sometimes suspicious of Eurocrats because of the latter's independence and commitment to the European project. The radical modernity of these elites may also produce suspicion among people who believe that they should know exactly what is going on in the virtually transparent world of the capitals of the EU. Ironically, much of this world is rendered opaque because its dimensions escape most ordinary citizens. As suggested by Abélès (this volume), to conceive Europe one should forget about the notion of achieving an end result of integration and talk instead of harmonization as an indefinite quest whose accomplishment is forever postponed, a process inextricably linked to the structural incompleteness of Europe.

The EU, in fact, seems to be a Faustian object, which, once created, is endowed with its own dynamic which cannot be controlled by any one member state, or even necessarily by the majority of member states. The distrust of the autonomy and independence accorded to such EU institutions as the European Commission, which has been exacerbated by the Commission's resignation in 1999, is also the result of the changes in political scale throughout Europe. The displacing of some policy making from local and national levels to the supranational has had a considerable impact on the perception of EU institutions in the member states. Much of this is negative even if the EU has propounded a doctrine of subsidiarity (wherein the EU proposes that social and political issues be dealt with at the political level closest to them). This principle, a focus of the contributions to this volume by Abélès and Holmes, allows for non-hierarchical relations between the EU and national, regional and local communities. It was introduced in the early 1980s but only became formally inscribed in the Maastricht Treaty of European Union in 1993. As Holmes observes, however, such a principle not only encompasses the institutional development of an increasingly federal EU, it also provides the substance of an intricate moral discourse to sustain the European project and its relations with existing diversities.

The social and political distinctions are often unclear between, on the one hand, those involved in EU institutions, their constituencies and their cultures, and, on the other hand, those outside of these institutions. This is partly due to the fact that it is not a standard social divide or an ethnic opposition. Nonetheless it seems to reflect the relation (and potential conflict) between the technocrats and political leaders in power (the elites who inscribe themselves in a 'community of practice'), on the one hand, and those people defined by their residence, culture, work, and local, regional, and national identities. But because of this obscure line between those who work in the institutions and 'others', and because the European project is multi-dimensional and gives support to the recognition of other social categories beyond the strictly political, there are many ways in which peoples' responses to institutional Europe might be studied. Such categories are projected in official discourses which are the product of processes of selection within European institutions. These address specific groups, such as 'women' and 'youth', through particular programs and policies which seek to change, improve, and regulate their conditions of involvement in the European project. European institutions also often intend to build or to reinforce new social and political categories such as 'citizens', to delineate a new political space in Europe, and 'consumers', to both give credence to and to criticize the idea of the 'market' as the guiding force behind EU integration. And even when EU institutions seek only to accomplish a finite, set task, as in the case of the scientists and engineers mobilized to develop space technology, they also build new social categories which affect the relations between institutions and the EU's population. From these processes it is clear that the project of a united Europe very often creates a stark contrast between what occurs under the labels of professionalism and policy within the EU's institutions, and what relates to issues of citizenship, national identity, and feelings of belonging among European individuals, in their localized contexts.

In fact, we suggest that any discussion of 'European institutions and identities' requires special attention not only because of the surface incongruity between the two words 'institutions' and 'identities', but because of the nature of the European project itself, which is not explicitly about the creation, definition, monitoring and evolution of European cultures and identities. But creating and moulding culture and identity is precisely what the EU is doing, and we contend that it cannot succeed in its other pursuits unless it succeeds in these areas, because of the feedback relations between its political and economic projects on one hand and its cultural infrastructure on the other. The building of the EU is not only a process of harmonization and integration, but one of legitimization, in which the structures and aims of the EU must find approval and meaning among its people.

Europe-building changes people's lives and environment in a number of ways and the notion of building carries various meanings (for a review of metaphors in EU official discourse, see Shore 1997). It can be understood as establishing or expanding a new form and dimension where nothing previously existed. This is the easiest definition of a new Europe, with little need to consider the historical reasons which give rise to the emergence of a new shape. While it is an attempt to suppress the causes of war that led to a world conflagration 60 years ago, the

Europe of the EU is as much a thing of the future as it is a thing of the past. Only a very strong political commitment to some form of integration and a sophisticated apparatus to sustain a platform of dialogue could replace the fragile equilibrium of the nation states.

'Building Europe' also refers to an open-ended ontology. It is not like a nation state, it is not oriented towards a spatial dimension, its limits are more political than geographical, it is evolving in size and philosophy. As such, it creates enthusiasm for the dynamics it introduces, but it can also bring despair to many, for different reasons. Small farmers suffer from the Common Agricultural Policy because its reforms favour large-scale producers and the industrial farm lobbies. Unemployed people, through some unions and political representatives, attribute the economic crises which marginalize them in their national contexts to the evolution of a free-market Europe. And how despairing will some governments be if their applications to the EU club are declined or postponed indefinitely? Will they continue to strengthen civil society, democracy and market economics? The EU rests on centripetal dynamics which lead toward cohesion, harmonization, and political dialogue, but it still has to master centrifugal forces which are operating at the social and political level, introducing areas of exclusion (for instance, in labour markets and among non-Europeans) and reviving nationalist political parties. In this regard building Europe is as much about a state of mind, an aspiration and an ethos as it is about concrete programmes.

From this perspective, we should consider another meaning of 'building'. Step by step, the EU has been defined by treaties, rules, public policies, and programmes. In fact, this is the basis of the controversial visibility of institutional Europe. Community law is primary law in every member state, and its definition is of considerable importance for day-to-day life throughout the EU. This is especially evident at the core of the EU, because Community law cannot be analytically isolated from the conditions of its negotiation between EU institutions, a process in which interest groups, regional associations, and other lobbies play a role (see Bellier's chapter in this volume). The new social morphology of power is based on political and economic compromises which were not foreseen in the early days of the Community as a necessary tool of decision-making, but which now impose themselves as a necessary condition for the actualization of the EU's project. In the EU, the emphasis has been put on the means to reduce political divergence between the nation-state governments in order to bring peace and tolerance, guarantee a better future, and create the conditions for a sort of collective happiness. Europeans are often reminded that Europe was born from the ashes of barbarism, as evidenced in the EU's recent reaction to the presence of a far-right party in Austria's new coalition government. As such, the new European cohesion should be an exemplary model for the rest of the world, even though it is also an example of 'an unidentified political object' ('*un objet politique non identifié*'), as described by Jacques Delors, the former president of the European Commission (see Abélès, this volume). Which brings us back to the point that building Europe is a metaphor of construction in which the end product is in dispute, with the smaller feats of engineering required to get there also being contested because of a lack of agreement about the reasons, methods and functions of the building itself. Thus 'building Europe' is also a matter of 'imagining Europe'.

Imagining Europe

Institutional discourses have a direct impact on the construction of European identity, inside and outside the institutions' boundaries. But to what extent is European identity influenced by European officials' definitions of their own identities? This question raises the issue of methodology, of how anthropologists record and analyse the nature of officials' statements, discourses and narratives, and the context in which the officials (as interlocutors) and the institutions (as public and official viewpoints) inscribe themselves. It also invites anthropologists to undertake another exploration inside European institutions, to analyse the meaning of European identity for the people whose European life is defined by status, personal commitment or professional assignment. To many people outside of the core EU institutions, as well as to many within them, the European officials of the Commission, the civil servants of the Council, the members of the European Parliament, and the engineers and technicians of the European Space Agency are the new 'true Europeans'. They are essential parts of the process of building Europe, metaphorically called 'architects' or more often 'experts' and 'engineers', who often have a clear idea of what Europe means in terms of cultural and linguistic self- and collective definitions. Stacia Zabusky in her contribution to this volume qualifies their belonging to a European context with the suggestive expression of 'boundaries at work', reminding us that although the EU has suppressed the national borders between its member states feelings of belonging have not been diminished. She also reminds us that ethnographic analysis of European integration often takes place in the frame of an institution, in this case a scientific agency where people must acknowledge but transcend many boundaries of identity in order to work together.

For those people who work in EU institutions, converting a national being into a European one, jumping into a multicultural if not Babelian world, is not as simple as might be suggested by the word 'Eurocrat', which is often used pejoratively to refer to the agents of the European Commission and other EU institutions. The European Commission is the 'laboratory' where officials, recruited from all the member states, commit themselves to serve 'Europe', thus taking a position on the future which might affect their perception of their national identity. Being a multicultural place par excellence, the European Commission is the place where incongruent social and cultural systems redefine their relative positions. Abélès and Bellier suggest that a 'cultural compromise' is being negotiated in the professional workplace, thus establishing the basis for a 'political culture of the compromise' (1996). Because of the recognition that national stereotypes interfere with demonstrations of linguistic flexibility and cultural tolerance among civil servants, what increasingly concerns most officials are the forms of dialogue, such as political dialogue between government representatives, institutional dialogue between European and national institutions, and the administrative and consultative dialogues which have been established between different parts of Europe and the EU (see Weiss and Wodak, this volume, and Morin 1990). Such dialogue is made necessary by EU officials' linguistic and cultural diversity. No idea or expression can be taken for granted within the EU institutions. It has to be explained, clarified, and conceptually transparent in order for it to be appropriated by its interlocutors so that it might circulate and contribute to the definition of policy. But this is also a contested issue within institutions because of the time which this process entails within these multilingual arenas, which yet again calls into question the capacity of the EU institutions to build their much advocated transparency.

This process at the level of the Commission's services leads to an interesting movement of conversion in which 'strangers' become colleagues (Bellier 1997a), when after some time the perception of the newcomer as a national being in the office is overcome, when they start sharing the same conceptual space. In a related process, officials working in other EU institutions and in national and regional governments become 'partners' (but not 'colleagues') to Commission officials through the dialogues which develop between them. Moreover, in Commission social practice, linguistic choices, patterns of behaviour and professional attitudes cannot be determined by, or judged from, a single reference point, and are proving to be expressions of a European pluralism. In fact, they introduce a dynamic that changes the terms of reference, not only for the insiders who finally get used to the uncertainty of the rules of the game, but for the outsiders who might be seen as the profane in the presence of a 'secret society'.

Although some outsiders may choose to denounce the opaque language and structures of some of the organs of the EU, for example, in the Commission, this would not be an accurate assessment of all the peoples and institutions of the EU. The cultural diversity of the whole organization militates against a world closed in on itself, or cut off entirely from its grass-root realities. More people are becoming involved in Europe-building each year as a consequence of the ongoing moves to widen the EU, on the one hand, and of the evolving patterns of policy making and consultative process on the other hand. Officials and national political representatives from the new member states introduce new linguistic and other cultural practices among their EU peers. Non-governmental actors, such as lobbyists and consultants, bring new voices, new practices, and new perceptions to what amounts to an ever-adapting EU institutional culture. Changes in both the national composition and professional background of EU officials contribute to a permanent environment of criticism, as demonstrated in the changes introduced by the United Kingdom in the institutional practices and in the political framework of the EU. However, despite this dynamic pattern of cultural mix, there still remains the institutional will for more transparency, which so far has not mitigated the complexity of the European policy and decision-making processes, nor changed the fact that only a few practitioners seem to exert some influence and to manage if not orchestrate the circulation of information. In this context, it is important for anthropologists and other observers to pay attention to the critical balance at the core of the European project between the theorization of Europe by the policy makers and national representatives and the management of changes by the technicians and experts.

Acknowledging that Europe is commonly held to be suffering from a 'democratic deficit', Bellier in her chapter analyses the consequences of what she calls the 'logics of interests' fed by the institutional recognition of the diversity of the social and economic actors. Liberal democracies are based on the principle of democratic representation whose definition has changed historically. In the EU today, representation is changing locus, from Parliament, which has adopted the role of an 'agora', to the lobbies, where precise, concrete, and partial interests are being pushed by new representatives. A critical moment in Europe-building is developing, wherein the *engrenage* referred to by Abélès (1996a: 33–41) is significantly limiting the margins of manoeuvre for national governments. 'National interests', whose defence were at stake at the beginning of the European Common Market, thus sustaining the moral and political sources of national identification among national civil servants, are now challenged by the affirmation of many other categories of interests whose fields of application range from the 'global world' of transnational cultures and companies to the 'local world' of regional, sectoral, and community interests.

Of course, the ideas of Europe as represented in the Europeanizing processes of the EU are not exempt from contradictions. In this regard, Holmes in his chapter engages the radical discourse on 'Europe' by examining two intellectual traditions, French social modernism and European social catholicism, which have sustained political integration. From the French social modernists, the EU has inherited respect for universal principles as well as a technocratic, largely elitist, tradition. From social catholicism, European thinkers have extracted the theory of 'subsidiarity', conveniently susceptible to flexible interpretation and contest. The strength of this concept relies on its potential to simultaneously sustain 'pluralism' and 'solidarity' for the creation of a 'community' or a 'union', not just a market. From these two traditions emerges a view of a society and political economy in which pluralism is a fundamental condition, which rests on hierarchy and social differentiation. Solidarity remains the basis for attaining ideological pluralism and promoting the notion of 'common good'. But this is also a limiting factor in the European project, for the modernist discourse of Europe finds the idiosyncratic character of cultural difference unmanageable. The issue of cultural diversity, says Holmes, defies institutional scrutiny save when it is framed in commercial terms as in the case of the business practices of the media.

Holmes also reinforces our point that the EU is a space which is built and imagined in processes which are simultaneously political and cultural. The institutions of the EU, which are staffed by political and technocratic elites and functionaries, are important to these processes, but they are not the only places where Europe's construction and identification are experienced as crucial aspects of daily life. Europe is being built not only from the top down, but from the bottom up, a fact which continues to invite anthropological investigation.

Experiencing Europe

The interplay of national, entrepreneurial, and local interests, as represented by civil servants or others (consultants, advocates, lobbyists, corporate agents, and a wide variety of local and regional representatives) affects the construction and perception of European identity and the definition of a new political and cultural space within the EU. Various mechanisms, according to Wilson in his chapter, filter the implementation of EU programmes in member states. As a result some state structures keep alive different forms of nationalism and regionalism, which to some extent run counter to the fostering of common forms of European identity and affiliation, and may even subvert the seemingly uncontentious goals of a 'Europe without Frontiers'.

In the case of the Northern Ireland borderlands, an area of strongly felt national identities, nationalism inhibits political and economic integration between the Irish and British states. EU actions to alleviate the problems of generations of ethno-nationalist struggle at and across this border are articulated and experienced, in local terms, as projections of state policies, and are accepted, resisted, or even rejected on these terms. This situation, due in part to the centralization of the Irish and British states, calls into question the interplay of the EU and the member states in the enhancement or constraint of many national, regional and local identities. This creates an ambivalence towards the EU which resonates throughout Europe, whether it be in the halls of power in Brussels, or in a small community in distant Denmark, where Jenkins in his chapter has chronicled that debates about the future Europe of the EU have also been debates about 'Danish-ness', in which Danish national identity simultaneously serves as support for pro- and anti-EU camps.

Such seeming contradictions are hardly surprising. Depending on local and national political cultures, and the centralized (for example, in France and the UK) or decentralized (for instance, in Spain and Germany) nature of the state, regionalism and nationalism are growing simultaneously, using Europe as a ladder to reach power. As Abélès observes in his contribution to this collection the impact of Europe in terms of harmonization, and the way European political practice begins to influence the national approaches to politics, reveal that, as an emerging political object, the EU deeply affects a very old and maybe obsolete perception of territorial identity. This would mean that deterritorialized Europe, virtual Europe, does not change people's identity, but brings them to a completely new perspective on their own traditions. Even if there is no word in the political vocabulary to satisfactorily qualify the Europe of the EU (is it postnational, supranational, postetatic, or multigovernmental?), it appears that Europe as an emerging form creates significant changes in our conception of politics and of identity.

In this context, the construction of a European citizenship is a key process in the future building, imagining and experiencing of the EU, as outlined in Neveu's chapter in this volume. Once the symbolic level of harmonizing European passports and defining the EU citizens' queue in EU airports has been reached, there remains the conversion of a 'national' being into a European citizen. The question before the EU, and critical to the success of its projects of Europeanization, is how malleable are the cultures of Europe in the quest for harmonization, unification and integration? How manageable are the differences of languages and cultures in order to give a concrete reality to the four freedoms of circulation (of people, goods, information and capital) that legitimate the Single Market? While it is clear that ideas flow more readily thanks to the new technologies of communication, that capital circulates more freely than once it did (with the expectation that more barriers will come down if the 'Euro-land' of the common currency expands), and that services can be more easily traded throughout the EU, the issue of circulating people is a difficult one.

Opening borders certainly facilitates commerce, tourism, cross-cultural encounters, professional migration, and regional identification as a substitute to national identification in a variety of locales in the larger context of a European system. But the question remains of what citizenship will mean in the EU, and what meanings it will have for European individuals. The question is twofold: one aspect refers to the contents of citizenship, as it is received and transformed by the people of the EU, while the other aspect is its supranational definition, its legal and administrative role as decided and disseminated at and above the level of the member states. Will a European citizen be a true member of a polity beyond his or her state, entitled to political and social rights and responsibilities which may be distinct from those offered and allowed in member states but which will integrate the diverse peoples of Europe? Or will EU initiatives in this regard result in a 'virtual citizen', sandwiched between the other qualifications of 'worker' and 'consumer'?

Free circulation in Europe will only become a reality for workers through radical changes in market labour regulations, in which slogans of flexibility seem to be replacing, at least for a time, the older notions of 'solidarity'. What is at stake is the possibility for individuals to project themselves into and over the mental and geographical territories in which they were born, to imagine themselves as being in commune with other Europeans in affective associations which transcend the instrumental institutions and relations which heretofore have cemented the parts of the EU together. But diverse individuals and groups are experiencing these new processes of Europeanization differently. Elites, workers, the unemployed and the disenfranchized are not evolving in the same ways and at the same rate. As European citizens they may share the same legal space but they definitely diverge in their roles in the building and articulation of the new cultures of the EU. The New Europe of the EU is in fact a variety of new Europes, and the more that the EU does to achieve total harmonization and integration among the institutions, peoples, cultures and identities of its member states the more potential there will be for a proliferation of these overlapping and competing imagined, constructed and experienced layers of Europe.

Warnings about the creation of a 'virtual citizen' are simultaneously warnings about 'virtual Europeans', in and outside of European institutions, as well as within and beyond the halls of academe. This volume's essays not only problematize the dangers inherent in fostering essentialized notions of European institutions and identities, in what might very well be construed as a 'virtual anthropology of Europe', but it also seeks to interrogate, if only implicitly, the often divergent perspectives in a variety of anthropological approaches to the EU. We do not seek to camouflage or erase the differences which exist in these approaches, but rather to place them side by side, allowing them to speak for themselves, so that differences and disjuncture, along with similarities and agreement, might result in a creative tension that will produce insights on the evolution of EU institutions and identities.

Notes

The editors would like to thank Douglas Holmes, Susan Carol Rogers, and Stacia Zabusky for their close and critical reading of earlier versions of this introduction.

1. The Forward Studies Unit, the think tank of the Commission, is a small unit attached to the President, with a clearly defined mission of conducting studies

on issues such as growth and unemployment, equal opportunities, governance, social models, and culture. It employs Commission civil servants, national experts, and interns, and produces analyses and recommendations.
2. Perceptions in the European Parliament about the European Commission and other institutions are contained in the Resolution on the Green Paper on Relations between the EU and ACP countries, A4-0274/97.

References

Abélès, M. (1990), *Anthropologie de l'Etat*, Paris: Armand Colin.
—— (1992), *La Vie Quotidienne au Parlement Européen*, Paris: Hachette.
—— (1993), 'Political Anthropology of a Transnational Institution: The European Parliament', *French Politics and Society*, 11 (1): 1–19.
—— (1996a), *En attente d'Europe*, Paris: Hachette.
—— (1996b), 'Le rationalisme à l'épreuve de l'analyse', in J. Revel (ed.), *Jeux d'échelles, la micro-analyse à l'expérience*, Paris: Gallimard – Le Seuil.
—— (1999), 'Avec le temps', *Critique*, 620–1: 42–60.
Abélès, M. and Bellier, I. (1996), 'Du compromis culturel à la culture politique du compromis', *Revue Française de Science Politique*, 46 (3): 431–56.
Abélès, M., Bellier, I. and McDonald, M. (1993), *An Anthropological Approach to the European Commission*, Brussels: European Commission.
Anderson, B. (1991 (1983)), *Imagined Communities: Reflections on the Origin and Spread of Nationalism*, London: Verso.
Appadurai, A. (1997), *Modernity at Large, Cultural Dimension of Globalization*, Oxford: Oxford University Press.
Bellier, I. (1993), *L'ENA comme si vous y étiez*, Paris: Editions du Seuil.
—— (1995), 'Moralité, langue et pouvoirs dans les institutions européennes', *Social Anthropology*, 3 (3): 235–50.
—— (1997a), 'The Commission as an Actor: An Anthropologist's View', in Helen Wallace and Alasdair R. Young (eds), *Participation and Policy-making in the European Union*, Oxford: Clarendon Press.
—— (1997b), 'Une approche anthropologique de la culture des institutions', in M. Abélès and H.P Jeudy (eds), *Anthropologie du Politique*, Paris: A. Colin.
—— (1999), 'Le lieu du politique, l'usage du technocrate: hybridation à la Commission Européenne', in V.Dubois and D. Dulong (eds), *La question technocratique. De l'invention d'une figure aux transformations de l'action publique*, Strasbourg: Presses Universitaires de Strasbourg.

Bhabha, H. (1990), 'DissemiNation: Time, Narrative and the Margins of the Modern Nation', in H. Bhabha (ed.), *Nation and Narration*, London: Routledge.

Blok, A. (1974), *The Mafia of a Sicilian Village, 1860-1960*, Oxford: Basil Blackwell.

Boissevain, J. (1975), 'Introduction: Towards a Social Anthropology of Europe', in Jeremy Boissevain and John Friedl (eds), *Beyond the Community: Social Process in Europe*, The Hague: Department of Educational Science of the Netherlands.

Borneman, J. (1992), *Belonging in the Two Berlins*, Cambridge: Cambridge University Press.

Borneman, J. and Fowler, N. (1997), 'Europeanization', *Annual Review of Anthropology*, 26: 487–514.

Cole, J.W. and Wolf, E.R. (1974), *The Hidden Frontier*, London and New York: The Academic Press.

Dilley, R. (1989), 'Boat Owners, Patrons and State Policy in the Northern Ireland Fishing Industry', in H. Donnan and G. McFarlane (eds), *Social Anthropology and Public Policy in Northern Ireland*, Aldershot: Avebury.

Dumont, L. (1983), *Essai sur l'individualisme, une perspective anthropologique sur l'idéologie moderne*, Paris: Editions du Seuil.

Ethnologie Française (1999), *Les mots des institutions*, 1999 (4), PUF.

Giordano, C. (1987), 'The "Wine War" Between France and Italy: Ethno-anthropological Aspects of the European Community', *Sociologia Ruralis*, 27: 56–66.

Grillo, R.D. (1980), 'Introduction', in R.D. Grillo (ed.), *'Nation' and 'State' in Europe: Anthropological Perspectives*, London: Academic Press.

Gupta, A. and Ferguson, J. (1997), 'Culture, Power, Place: Ethnography at the End of an Era', in A. Gupta and J. Ferguson (eds), *Culture, Power, Place: Explorations in Critical Anthropology*, Durham: Duke University Press.

Hedetoft, U. (1994), 'National Identities and European Integration "From Below": Bringing People Back In', *Journal of European Integration*, 17 (1): 1–28.

Herzfeld, M. (1987), *Anthropology Through the Looking-glass: Ethnography in the Margins of Europe*, Cambridge: Cambridge University Press.

—— (1992), *The Social Production of Indifference: Exploring the Symbolic Roots of Western Bureaucracy*, Oxford: Berg.

Holmes, D. (1993), 'Illicit Discourse', in G. Marcus (ed.), *Perilous States: Conversations on Culture, Politics and Nation*, Chicago: University of Chicago Press.

Jaffe, A. (1993), 'Corsican Identity and a Europe of Peoples and Regions', in Thomas M. Wilson and M. Estellie Smith (eds), *Cultural Change and the New Europe: Perspectives on the European Community*, Boulder and Oxford: Westview Press.

Jurjus, A. (1993), 'Farming Styles and Intermediate Structures in the Wake of 1992', in Thomas M. Wilson and M. Estellie Smith (eds), *Cultural Change and the New Europe: Perspectives on the European Community*, Boulder and Oxford: Westview Press.

Kohler-Koch, B. (1997), 'Organized Interests in European Integration: The Evolution of a New Type of Governance?', in H. Wallace and A. Young (eds), *Participation and Policy Making in the European Union*, Oxford: Clarendon Press.

Landau, A. and Whitman, R.G. (eds) (1997), *Rethinking the European Union: Institutions, Interests and Identities*, London: Macmillan.

LiPuma, E. and Meltzoff, S.K. (1989), 'Toward a Theory of Culture and Class: An Iberian Example', *American Ethnologist*, 16 (2): 313–34.

—— (1994), 'Economic Mediation and the Power of Associations: Toward a Concept of Encompassment', *American Anthropologist*, 96: 31–51.

McDonald, M. (1993), 'The Construction of Difference: An Anthropological Approach to Stereotypes', in Sharon Macdonald (ed.), *Inside European Identities*, Oxford: Berg.

—— (1997), 'Identities in the European Commission', in Neill Nugent (ed.), *At the Heart of the Union*, London: Macmillan.

McDonogh, G.W. (1993), 'The Face Behind the Door: European Integration, Immigration, and Identity', in Thomas M. Wilson and M. Estellie Smith (eds), *Cultural Change and the New Europe: Perspectives on the European Community*, Boulder and Oxford: Westview Press.

Marcus, G. (1986), 'Contemporary Problems of Ethnography in the Modern World System', in J. Clifford and G. Marcus (eds), *The Poetics and Politics of Ethnography*, Berkeley: University of California Press.

—— (1992), 'A Broad(er)side to the Canon, Being a Partial Account of a Year of Travel among Textual Communities in the Realm of Humanities Centres, and Including a Collection of Artificial Curiosities', in G. Marcus (ed.), *Rereading Cultural Anthropology*, Durham: Duke University Press.

Mauss, M. (1974), 'Note sur la notion de civilisation', in E. Durkheim and M. Mauss (eds), *Oeuvres, vol. 2. Representation collectives et diversite des civilisations*, Paris: de Minuit.

Monnet, J. (1975), *Mémoires*, Paris: Fayard.

Morin, E. (1990 (1987)), *Penser l'Europe*, Paris: Folio, Gallimard.

Nader, L. (1974), 'Up the Anthropologist – Perspectives Gained from Studying Up', in D. Hymes (ed.), *Reinventing Anthropology*, New York: Vintage.

Noiriel, G. (1991), 'La question nationale comme objet de l'histoire sociale', *Genèse*, 4: 72–94.

Rabinow, P. (1989), *French Modern*, Chicago: The University of Chicago Press.

Rogers, S.C. (1997), 'Explorations in Terra Cognita', *American Anthropologist,* 99 (4): 717–19.

Ross, G. (1993), 'Sidling into Industrial Policy', *French Politics and Society,* 11 (1): 20–44.

Schmitter, P.C. (1996), 'Some Alternative Futures for the European Polity and Their Implications for European Public Policy', in Yves Meny, Pierre Muller and Jean-Louis Quermonne (eds), *Adjusting to Europe: The Impact of the European Union on National Institutions and Policies,* London: Routledge.

Schneider, J. and Schneider, P. (1976), *Culture and Political Economy in Western Sicily,* New York: Academic Press.

Schneider, J., Schneider, P. and Hansen, E. (1972), 'Modernization and Development: The Role of Regional Elites and Noncorporate Groups in the European Mediterranean', *Comparative Studies in Society and History,* 14: 328–50.

Sheehan, E.A. (1991), 'Political and Cultural Resistance to European Community Europe: Ireland and the Single European Act', *Socialism and Democracy,*13: 101–18.

Shore, C. (1993), 'Inventing the "People's Europe": Critical Approaches to European Community "Cultural Policy"', *Man* 28: 779–800.

—— (1997), 'Metaphors of Europe: Integration and the Politics of Language', in Stephen Nugent and Cris Shore (eds), *Anthropology and Cultural Studies,* London: Pluto.

Shore, C. and Black, A. (1992), 'The European Communities and the Construction of Europe', *Anthropology Today,* 8 (3): 10–11.

Shutes, M. (1991), 'Kerry Farmers and the European Community: Capital Transitions in a Rural Irish Parish', *Irish Journal of Sociology,* 1: 1–17.

—— (1993), 'Rural Communities Without Family Farms? Family Dairy Farming in the Post-1993 EC', in Thomas M. Wilson and M. Estellie Smith (eds), *Cultural Change and the New Europe: Perspectives on the European Community,* Boulder and Oxford: Westview Press.

Tarrow, S. (1994), *Rebirth or Stagnation? European Studies after 1989,* New York: Social Science Research Council.

Varenne, H. (1993), 'The Question of European Nationalism', in Thomas M. Wilson and M. Estellie Smith (eds), *Cultural Change and the New Europe: Perspectives on the European Community,* Boulder and Oxford: Westview Press.

Verdery, K. (1995), *National Ideology under Socialism,* Berkeley: University of California Press.

Wallace, H. (1997), 'Introduction', in H. Wallace and A. Young (eds), *Participation and Policy Making in the European Union,* Oxford: Clarendon Press.

Wilson, T.M. (1989), 'Large Farms, Local Politics, and the International Arena: The Irish Tax Dispute of 1979', *Human Organization,* 48 (1): 60–70.

—— (1993), 'An Anthropology of the European Community', in T.M. Wilson and M.E. Smith (eds), *Cultural Change and the New Europe: Perspectives on the European Community*, Boulder and Oxford: Westview Press.

—— (1996), 'Sovereignty, Identity and Borders: Political Anthropology and European Integration', in L. O'Dowd and T.M. Wilson (eds), *Borders, Nations and States*, Aldershot: Avebury Press.

—— (1998), 'An Anthropology of the European Union, From Above and Below', in S. Parman (ed.), *Europe in the Anthropological Imagination*, Upper Saddle River, NJ: Prentice Hall.

Wolf, E.R. (1974), 'American Anthropologists and American Society', in D. Hymes (ed.), *Reinventing Anthropology*, New York: Vintage.

—— (1982), *Europe and the People Without History*, Berkeley: University of California Press.

Zabusky, S. (1995), *Launching Europe: An Ethnography of European Cooperation in Space Science*, Princeton: Princeton University Press.

Part I
Institutions, Politics and Society at the Core of the European Union

–2–

Virtual Europe
Marc Abélès

For an anthropologist Europe-building within the European Union (EU) presents at least two original features. First of all, the recent history of post-war European institutions shows an alternating of acceleration and regression. One cannot describe it as a linear process, nor as something which might be considered a priority by the majority of Europeans. Secondly, the process of building Europe is never complete. The vision that 'one day Europe will be a united political entity' was shared by the first generation of the EU's pioneers, but the assertion that 'later the "esprit européen" will triumph' has given room to a more sceptical vision of the future (Abélès 1996). The most salient characteristic of EU officials' discourses and practices is the link between the immediate present and an indeterminate future. In some circles it does not seem possible to be European without projecting oneself into a world which does not yet exist, and which cannot be adequately understood using the classical notions of political science. This chapter focuses on two points. The first part deals with the openness and the structural uncertainty of the European Union's future. The second part examines the difficulty in constructing the common notions which orientate the quest for this future.

Virtual Europe: An 'Unidentified Political Object'

One anthropological approach to the EU is less interested in describing European institutions and their functions than it is in analyzing the imbrication between present and future in a political project which seems unable to exploit the resources of the past. Studying two Directorates General (DGs) in the Commission (Abélès et al. 1993), I was struck by the way in which events were digested, without people being too much involved in their diverse implications. An anecdote illustrates this point.

At the beginning of my fieldwork I spent part of my time in a building where the Forward Studies Unit, a think tank working for President Delors, was located. Everyday in the elevator I met people who seemed to worry. I did not understand this attitude, which contrasted with that of other officials working in the building. Some time later, I learnt that they were the agents of a Directorate General which had been abolished a month before. They were directly affected by the fate of that unit. But for their colleagues of the other DGs, it was as if DG XXII never existed. The abolition of the entire DG was already part of the past. Most of the Commission people considered that they do not have to deal with the past even if it directly affects their neighbours in the office. Doing this job means, above all, facing the future.

In the European Commission people like working with a sense of urgency. This organization seems to perform a better job when short-term objectives are targeted. The verb 'to finalize' is often in the official repertoire. Whether it be a file, a meeting, or a negotiation, what really matters is to finish in due time. Action must be taken. Going forward without looking behind is how the European Community has been built. In quiet times, the atmosphere becomes darker. In such times one can observe the flow of uncertainty and anxiety, due in part to the absence of the strong supports and referents, such as the state's rules and structures of government, which bolster national civil servants.

The Commission seems unable to look back on itself, and a large number of its officials have difficulty locating themselves historically. As one official said, 'in the Commission, everything is quicker than in an ordinary administration. One goes ahead without looking back, as if one were driving without a rear-view mirror.' The goal seems to be to digest events without considering all of their consequences. This process tends to occult reality. It is as if efficiency and effectiveness would be impaired if there was much self-reflection. As one official concluded, 'one must move forward, the rhythm of work is accelerated by the demands of the current situation'. In other words, returning to the past is a luxury more than it is a necessity. Everything happens as if the Commission was not able to think about its own relation to history, as if it was propelled by two opposing forces. It must exhibit the past, putting forward an image of 'the glorious time of the pioneers' in a sort of apologetic discourse, while at the same time it represses memories of conflict, however recent they might be.

However, 'driving without a rear-view mirror' is both inconvenient and difficult to achieve in an institution which is continually requested to question itself. The member states and their citizens are always calling upon the Commission to clarify the meanings of Community action. My relations with Euro civil servants allowed me to apprehend the impact of this quest for reflexivity. Practically it meant their inclination for many long and repeated interviews. The recalling of past events, and discussions of evolutions in the Commission, preoccupied us in these interviews, even though such topics were not all related to official agendas. A Euro civil servant, Philippe Burghelles-Vernet, head of division, General Secretariat of the European Commission, used an expression which captures very well the experience of time in the Commission universe. He speaks of 'a culture of uncertain urgency'. Everything goes very fast, and is exciting and stimulating. The risk is that the linking between the events does not always result from an order which can be controlled by the actors. The situation can induce a sort of schizophrenia, in which individuals watch themselves acting frenetically without having the capacity to internalize the global rationality of their acts.

One of the many questions which often comes to the mind of the Commission's practitioners is about the meanings of their actions. This question can be raised in various ways, for it concerns, among others, the meaning of the project of the Community, as well as the meaning of their daily work. Such questioning does not in general betray a sense of pessimism. Those who enunciate this kind of interrogation are normally committed to their activities, and are truly involved in the collective activities of the Commission. But they also seem to lack the will to exert control over time and duration. When the civil servants I met in my fieldwork spoke of themselves, they did not privilege a narrative of a journey, with the ongoing process of building Europe in the background. In their context, the demand for reflexivity corresponds to a deeper quest for references, to a process where memory can play an essential part.

However, in the culture of the European Commission, archives do not seem to be highly regarded. One may think that this lack of attention corresponds to some sort of eternal youth, or to some unconscious anguish related to the idea of recording and measuring time and the evolutions it induces. Whatever the reason, the institution seems little concerned with managing its relations to time and this troubles its more lucid members. Everything happens as if Europe will be inventing itself every day, thereby reconfirming its permanence. One seems to ignore the specific work of memory in such a way that each crisis is immediately enveloped by a cloak of forgetfulness. Reference to the past is usually limited to a brief remembrance of the founding fathers. Any reference to tradition seems to be completely incongruous in the context of the European institutions.

The deficit of tradition as well as the difficulty to grasp its own past contribute to the originality of Europe as compared to other kinds of communities, especially those which are classically studied by the anthropologists. The European institutions permanently work under the pressure of the calendar. To understand the omni-presence of the agenda, one should remember that most of the work done in the Commission requires the face-to-face interaction of several partners. Deadlines are compulsory in order to reach a conclusion on subjects which are always very complex. Thus constraints become both stimulating and stressful for European civil servants.

The Commission gave itself a calendar when it proposed the Single European Act. The most spectacular aspect of this initiative was to establish a deadline for realizing the Single European Market. More recently, the Treaty of Maastricht programmed Economic and Monetary Union on the basis of a very precise schedule. What was essential in these moves was to avoid at all costs remaining stationary. Each step in European integration is a preparation for the next one. This is true for all the domains of competence of the Commission (agriculture, environment, etc.), for each step forward means a full series of measures in the name of harmonization, and these measures call for yet others in order to achieve a better running of the European market, and so forth. Political scientists call this mechanism 'the spillover effect' (Haas 1958; Keohane and Hoffmann 1991).

The spillover dynamics accounted for the implementation of directives and rules which could never have been imposed separately by the member states' governments. For the European process to go ahead it seems necessary to banish dead time and introduce new priorities, even if some of the latter are completely artificial. This process explains the ambiguous relations the institutions have with history, wherein the obsession for the future and for concluding the European project leaves no space to the past and memory.

The question I have framed in this chapter is this. Without a rear-view mirror how can the Commission actors escape the spillover logic and locate themselves and the institution in a cumulative historical perspective? Without a sophisticated sense of history and memory the Europe of the EU seems trapped in a cycle of successive take-offs and the recultivation of its roots. The Community purposely denies history. For the practitioners of European integration in the Commission, history is no more than a suspicious form of introspection. They prefer the delights of a future whose contours they choose not to draw precisely. The care which is taken for erasing any sign of a political form yet to come (one can simply refer to the sad fate of those who have proffered a notion of a future 'federal' Europe), allows us to understand that the New Europe, tomorrow's Europe, looks more like an ethereal dream than a utopia which could stir people into action.

This very peculiar relation to time supports the impression that the Community is disconnected from reality. Divided between the urgencies of the present time and the ideal of a better future, the actors themselves have the impression that they are very far away from the European society for which they are working. 'We are angels with no body,' said one of them, completely disillusioned. 'Disincarnation' must be understood here in the context of 'Community time' and the necessity of re-appropriating history and duration. Otherwise, the actors seem to be either hung up on an abstract ideal or swallowed up by the contingencies of the present, putting them in a perilous situation which targets them for criticism by diverse social groups. Europe is, more than a hideout for technocrats, an ideal device, a project whose end term is always postponed. At the moment that the Europe implied in some notions of integration becomes concrete, the EU will produce its own derealization.

This situation accounts for some of the difficulty faced by Europeans who seek to appropriate a project which has always been kept distant, as if it was lurking far beyond history. The Monnet method which was supposed to be anchored on a solid realism had the paradoxical consequence to project Europeans towards a political object of a completely new kind, a dehistoricized Europe (which extends in a time without memory) and a deterritorialized Community (which is located in a space with no territory). The idea of the founders of Europe (Jean Monnet, Robert Schuman, Konrad Adenauer, Paul Henri Spaak, etc.) was that a transnational unity be created to focus on specific areas, beginning with an open market for the European Coal and Steel Community (ECSC). They imagined that once the European member states co-operated in these areas, the interdependence of the policy logics would promote the 'spillover effect' into others. The aim of the Monnet method was to initiate 'engrenage', an 'action trap' in which once the agents are set in a specific course of action, they find themselves obliged to take further actions which point them in a direction which they did not necessarily intend to go. As a result, the 'engrenage' functioned in such a way that now it would be impossible for the member states to step back. They are more and more involved in the whole process, even though no great formal proclamation on federalism has been announced.

As a descriptive neofunctionalist device, 'engrenage' has its limits. It is symptomatic of British attitudes to such integration that when the British government refused in 1950 to be part of the ECSC, the memo explaining its position underlined that the UK refused any 'commitment'. It is true that to be effective 'spillover' involves the 'commitment' of the member states. The UK always resisted this kind of involvement. In the 1980s, the British government generated the notion of 'opting out' as an alternative to the 'engrenage'.

Irrespective of its success in advancing European unification, upon further reflection one notices that the Monnet method had one unexpected consequence. The political aim of the European project has never been clarified. But what is most interesting for the anthropologist is that it *must not* be clarified. Jean Monnet had a vision of a federation of member states with a substantial component of supranationality on the model of the nation state, i.e., the United States of Europe. This vision has not been realized. On the contrary, the word 'federation' may indeed be repulsive to some member states. For example, the word 'federalism' was not used in the text of the Maastricht Treaty. Such reaction against federalism is meaningful, for it demonstrates that the European political leaders do not wish to give a name or a definition to the European political system as it is constructed.

Delors' expression ('un objet politique non identifié') to qualify Europe has been echoed among political elites. It reflects the tension which occurs when the reality of a political process leading towards more integration meets the impossibility for the architects of Europe to promote any representation of a possible completion of the European project. The most notable attempt to propose a global pattern for the European Union was a report entitled 'Reform of Treaties and Achievement of European Union' (1982), elaborated by Altiero Spinelli for the

Committee of Institutional Affairs of the European Parliament. This report exposes an explicit federalist orientation along with the reinforcement of the power of the European Parliament, but the Draft Treaty has never been ratified by the member states. So, maybe the European Community is 'unique' in the sense that the integration has never been achieved. Although some authors analyze the Community as a 'part-formed political system' (Wallace 1990), the lack of a constitution is but one symptom of the non-achievement of Europe as a new political entity. The Maastricht Treaty did not give precise shape to the future of Europe either. With the negotiation of the Treaty of Amsterdam, national politicians often referred to a 'Europe of variable geometries', defining the possibility of different associations of the member states according to their needs, and taking into account the perspective of an enlargement to more than twenty different nations.

The absence of identification of what could appear as a 'political Europe' (a new sort of nation state? a federation? a postnational government?) can be interpreted in two different ways. For many politicians and political scientists such a situation reflects only conjectural difficulties which can be overcome. The anthropologist considers not only the difficulty to find an adequate word to designate the future shaping of Europe, but also the denial concerning the opportunity to adopt a clear position on this point. In all the speeches, reports, and literature produced by the EU political actors, the indeterminacy has become commonplace. This can be illustrated in the field of communication.

Many attempts have been made to create an image of a united Europe and to communicate this image to the people (Shore and Black 1994). Directorate General X of the European Commission is in charge of promoting the idea of a united Europe, making the people feel like European citizens. Its action has been concretized by initiatives such as the adoption of the Community flag and anthem, the implementation of ' European years' on several themes (like road security, movies, etc.), the use of a European passport and driving licence. The Community sponsors sporting events. It promoted a European Youth Orchestra. European participation in regional projects is marked on the ground by the erection of billboards. These actions demonstrate a constantly reaffirmed will not only to make Europe better known, but to allow citizens to appropriate fully their European identity. A 'European public opinion' has also emerged through polls on big issues of politics and society. This has led to the organization of the Eurobarometer whose methods and criteria are better defined every year. In fact, nothing is discounted by the Community authorities in order to bring closer the public and the Europe they are building. The Treaty of Maastricht confirmed the goal of a European citizenship. It stipulates that citizenship is for the protection of the rights and interests of the member states' citizens.

Two meaningful examples illustrate the permanent wish to inform and associate a large audience. The first one is given by the European Parliament which opens its doors to all kind of visitors. Every year, some 120,000 people visit one of the three seats. Strasbourg is the main attraction but some 10,000 visitors visit Brussels too. Some of the plenary sessions are so full that the building is nearly saturated. In certain weeks 120 groups of visitors have been counted. Many young people are invited. Through contract with the Parliament, educational establishments are urged to deliver one year of training and information on Europe and they get rewarded by an invitation for a session. A European programme, EUROSCOLA, has been designed for receiving in Strasbourg, outside of parliamentary sessions, several hundred young people from the fifteen member states to attend a one-day session of exchange and dialogue. At the end of the session, they receive a certificate signed by the president of the European Parliament. These manifestations of openness do not only reflect the pedagogical interest of the European Parliament. They are a concrete sign of EU transparency.

The European desire for openness became clear during the preparation of the referendum on the Maastricht Treaty whose text had been sent to millions of electors. A wealth of information was also made available through a wide number of other publications, produced with the support of the EU. There is no other example of a Treaty being so widely publicized. But, in another example of the European paradox, the quest for transparency did not produce the desired outcomes. The large majority of readers proved so sensitive to the opacity of the text that more explanation was required. It had to be explained that the Treaty was as much the fruit of a compromise between languages as an agreement between politically divergent orientations.

This operation shows the existence of a basic problem. Europe is part of our daily life in that it is a regular topic for national political debates, but the internal working processes of the EU, the Community's political practices, remain distant and opaque for its citizens. Although European citizens are the intended public, European practices do not create a strong public opinion. One may think that some collective points of reference exist as guidelines for those involved in Community affairs. It does not seem so, as Europe looks like being deprived of rituals or symbols which could exert a real attraction. If such a thing as a community exists, it is some 'disenchanted' community. After fifty years, the symbolic production is disconcertingly poor, as found in one flag, one anthem, and some material signs like passports, stamps, and border posters. In fact, the European emblem was adopted with great difficulties, after twenty years of work, meetings, trials and errors. In 1950, the Council of Europe proposed the creation of a flag to 'disseminate the European idea' (Bichet 1985; Lager 1994). Two years passed before a first project, a blue flag with fifteen golden stars, emerged. The stars represented the fourteen members of the Council of Europe, and an associate member, the Saarland. But the Federal Republic of Germany was opposed to the choice of fifteen stars. After the German veto, in December 1956, the Council of Europe adopted a blue flag with twelve golden stars. Thirty more years were necessary before an official ceremony celebrated the adoption of this flag by the European Community on 29 May 1986. Most people think that the twelve stars corresponded to the twelve member states at that time, but the symbol was chosen for more negative reasons. Fourteen or fifteen stars raised the problem of the status of the Saarland, and thirteen was a bad omen. From the aesthetic point of view, a circle of twelve stars presented harmony and left enough space for introducing in its centre the particular emblem of the various European organizations.

Discussions about such an emblem did not stir the governmental authorities, or the public. Moreover the need to adopt a single symbol has never been perceived as an urgency of any kind. The European flag has been the object of a prosaic negotiation which ended with an acceptable compromise for everyone. The same kind of negotiation was organized in 1964 when the Europeans were about to choose a European anthem, after the Council of Europe made a formal resolution. Seven years were necessary to agree Beethoven's 'Ode to Joy'. No memorable debates have been recorded and the time to conclude the project reflects only a relative indifference. The European anthem is a silent music, or better to say a music with no words. The lack of text is meaningful. Like the empty space in the twelve-starred circle, it reflects and illuminates the symbolic deficit of the European Community. Similarly, though many institutions secrete specific rituals, neither the Parliament nor the Commission attest such an activity. I had the opportunity to attend the fortieth anniversary of the Parliament in 1992. The ceremony was the occasion of very brief speeches from most of the officials. There was no particular splendour, and none of the gestures and signs which give to rituals their power of evocation. The imagery of the instituted Europe is desperately poor. In contrast to the French Republic, which found in Marianne a substantial incarnation (Agulhon 1989), the European Community seems to be satisfied only with the flag and the anthem. Are there no other identity markers and references? It seems that one does exist, the 'European idea', which the practitioners of Europe refer to as a powerful guide for their actions. In fact, in the day-to-day work of the Commission, the material constraints, the discipline, the weight of everyday routine seem to be articulated by a non-material investment which takes its origin in this 'idea of Europe' which is as regulatory as it is disincarnated. No one waits for Europe to exist, one builds it up every day. Under these conditions, it appears that Europe functions in large part as an 'ideal', a concept under which Godelier (1984) subsumes the products of thought in its activities of representation, interpretation, organisation and legitimation.

As a project Europe combines humanist and rationalist connotations. It corresponds to the affirmation of the ideas of Enlightenment and Reason. It means the emancipation of particularisms in the name of a triumphant universalism. It is also about the primacy of Human Rights. The idea of Europe wants to be synonymous or coterminous with modernism. The priority given to economics is constantly operating in the discourses which celebrate the ideal of a community. For most of the civil servants I met, Europe is less a territory than a method. More than a system of value, properly said, it corresponds to a philosophy of action based on the realization of a project which directs the individual's ideals. In such a philosophy the symbolic dimension has no place. The emblem and the few rituals may be simple operational artefacts which express, more or less effectively, a rational will. What has been called a 'symbolic deficit' in fact seems to correspond to the absence of a coherent set of political concepts and discourses. Everything is working as if Europe was destined to remain a virtual object.

European Politics: A Permanent Negotiation

Does this situation correspond to the lack of a common political project? The opposition of the UK and the division between the big and small countries in Europe do not facilitate the realization of a politically identifiable Europe. However it seems that the problem remains located elsewhere. It lies in the permanent confrontation among the different cultural and political identities in the European arena (Bellier 1995). Any sort of political unification would imply an agreement on the basic political concept of the state. Currently the meaning of this notion varies from one culture to the next. For example, there is a huge difference between the Jacobin tradition of France and the federalist tradition of Germany, just as there is between Britain's parliamentarianism and France's presidentialism. The differences have introduced many misunderstandings and disagreements. Therefore the crucial issue raised by the EU's construction is cultural. In the building of Europe can we discern something like a European identity which would transcend national borders? The concept of a European Community would be meaningful then. As Europeanist anthropologists have demonstrated, a community is not just a group of people involved in practices of production and exchange in the same territory (see for example, Goddard, Llobera and Shore 1994). Communities also share language, values, symbols and rituals. The notion of community connotes identity construction. Can this dimension be distinguished at the European level?

The Europe of the EU constitutes a community in a number of ways. From the spatial point of view, it is a large-scale community incorporating multiple populations and diverse traditions; from the temporal viewpoint, it is a community in the making which defines itself as perpetually in the form of a project, focusing on an ideal whose realization is always postponed. These original characteristics have important consequences regarding the representations the individuals can formulate about belonging or the definition of a common identity. Different from the existing nation states which manage a well-delineated territory, Europe defines itself like an open space. It is impossible to foretell its future limits. It started with six member states, then enlarged to nine, then ten, then twelve and now fifteen. A new enlargement of the Community is already in design.

So Europe means a change of scale which as a consequence leads to the de-territorialization of Community practices. The best expression of such a de-territorialization is the nomadism of the members of the European Parliament, who are always transhuming between Strasbourg and Brussels, when they are not at a meeting somewhere else in Europe. The lack of a centre and blurred boundaries make difficult the identification of landmarks or of any sign of identity for those who desperately seek some anchorage. In the case of civil servants, living together in Brussels means sharing the common negative point of residing abroad (with the exception of the Belgians of course) and being a foreigner in a city where Eurocrats are often criticized. The problems of multiple languages further contribute to a feeling of lost points of reference experienced by European officials.

The example of the European Parliament is enlightening (cf. Abélès 1992). It is a real tower of Babel where shifting from one language to another neutralizes debate. The plenary sessions often look like a succession of monologues. From time to time, when two MEPs (Members of the European Parliament) from the same country take the floor one after the other, one may foresee the beginning of a more spontaneous discussion. The shared community of language allows more direct exchanges and favours some liberty of tone. The speakers draw on the same vocabulary and same frames of reference. They displace themselves in the same discursive universe. On other occasions, the lack of linguistic unity depersonalizes debate. Pluralism then becomes an important factor contributing to opacity. Because each country's political language mobilizes a different rhetoric, certain subtleties are almost impossible to translate across linguistic and political cultural divides. The speakers who do not simplify their discourses must expect some distortion of their words. This is not because the translators are incompetent, but simply because some terms are difficult to be found in another language, in the time allotted to the translators. Some MEPs who speak several languages are often surprised by certain liberties taken by the translators. In fact, translators and interpreters face severe difficulties in their quest for the utopian objective of doing justice to both the words and the message of each speaker in the Parliament.

One day, when a Greek MEP was talking, the interpreter in charge of the translation suddenly declared that the speaker was making a good joke that was impossible to properly translate, and he called for the courtesy of the other MEPs. The whole assembly laughed at this remark, while the Hellenic MEP was delighted to be so well understood. In general terms, when the humour of MEPs is well translated it elicits adequate reactions, but the laughs can often be heard slightly after the humorous point is made. This is because of the gap between the enunciated and the interpreted word. Sometimes the speaker is surprised to hear his colleagues laugh after the content of his discourse had become more serious.

Plurilingualism corresponds to a well-regulated timing of the sessions but it does not stimulate the political debate. The risk of misinterpretation is less problematic than the irreducibility of the linguistic differences which disrupt the communicative process and make impossible a direct exchange. The plenary sessions are a sort of limping compromise between a political debate and the transmission of information and reports. Arguments are juxtaposed and dialectic forms of expression or opposition are rarely observed. A Portuguese socialist MEP, Maria Belo, who is a psychoanalyst by training, commented on the situation: 'one speaks without hearing; it is organised in such a way that one does not listen nor hear the other'. For Mrs Belo, true communication is even less possible in the context of the plenary session: 'we speak for the minutes of the session'. Simultaneously one notices that the deputies speak from their seat and never address anyone but the President of the Assembly. 'All the discourses begin with an address to "Mr President"; it is symptomatic that nobody ever addresses the European citizens.' While such forms of address are standard parliamentary procedure, they underline the characteristic opacity of European parliamentary practices, which transform the agora into a new Tower of Babel.

Should one fear the deepening of the gap which separates the citizen at the grassroots and an assembly which wants to be democratic? For the debates to concern the public a little more, it would be required that a real discussion start among the MEPs. While it looks as if multiple languages are an obstacle to communication, one must suppose that Europeans from different nationalities really want to communicate. Shifting from one political language to another means simultaneously remembering the diversity of traditions and histories which have so heavily weighed upon our countries. While national political parties, drawn together by their programmes and objectives, constitute common political groups in the Parliament, they also confirm the existence of transnational ideologies and diverse families of thought. Convergence of political programme and practice, however, do not erase the differences of political methods and political culture.

The former French President, Valéry Giscard d'Estaing, when he was newly elected an MEP, learned this lesson when he tried to convince the liberal members of his group to affiliate to the Christian-Democrat group. He had to face strong opposition, essentially from the Dutch, Germans, Belgians and Portuguese who considered 'liberalism' as synonymous to the separation of church and state when the French considered it mainly as an economic project. Between partners differences may occur, more often in the field of international relationships where national parties from the same political family have sometimes adopted different positions over time. Similar tensions were observed in the Socialist group during the Gulf War. They reflected the transformations undergone by socialist parties over the last half century. The majority of the French and German members of the Socialist group in the European Parliament supported American moves, while the

Greek socialists kept denouncing US imperialism. This shows how it is difficult to harmonize political strategies in spite of belonging to the same parliamentary group and speaking a common political language. These observations also suggest that the process of deterritorialization does not necessarily facilitate the creation of a public space of debate in the EU. As in the Commission, intercultural contact may actually reinforce national barriers instead of generating a common identity. Commission civil servants, perhaps even more than elected officials, suffer from the loss of references and the lack of elaboration of a new universe of representations.

It seems clear that the prefiguration of a Community culture is not well established in the Commission or in the Parliament. To be modest, what is generated inside the European institutions is a universe of compromise where the conjugation of multiple identities is done essentially in a pragmatic fashion. In the frame of the permanent process of negotiation which characterizes Community political practice, the most common notion which everyone refers to as emerging from the European project is the idea of a 'common good' (Abélès, Bellier and McDonald 1993).

This notion, which is omnipresent in Commission discourse, sustains the process of differentiation between the EU and the other economic powers, most notably the USA and Japan. The notion of a common good is also used in the dialogue between the Community and the member states. I observed how the notion of a 'Community interest' was advocated during the negotiation with the member states to define the level of the European subsidies given to each country under the regional policy. In this particular context, what was required was to satisfy the different needs of the member states, but to implement a fair distribution it was necessary to take into account the notion of a superior interest. To take a decision from the point of view of the Community interest meant also following up a policy orientation in order to reduce regional disparities and achieve the necessary transfers for regions to adapt to the Single Market. It meant the simultaneous identification and prioritization of real needs in the countries, at both the regional and national levels. From their side, the member states put forward the principle of subsidiarity which, as a consequence, introduced more flexibility for the Community to deal with regional and national problems. During the preparation and the conduct of the negotiation, the opposition between the Community interest and subsidiarity was observed in operation.

The Community is, to a certain extent and quoting Claude Levi-Strauss (1950), a 'floating significant'. He uses this concept to designate notions which are both essential and vague, allowing for their evocation alone to be of great significance. It is similar to the case of the '*mana*' which somehow stitches together indigenous discourses (Lévi-Strauss 1950: xlix). In this sense *mana* has an excess of meaning which gives value to the word used in a political context, as well as in its invocation in magic and rituals. From *mana* to Community interest the distance is huge, but the essential point is the marking function and the power of acknowledgement which are attributed to this concept. The usefulness of this concept may be seen in the debate about the Structural Funds, which highlights the growing importance of subsidiarity against the background of the danger of the renationalization of Community policies.

The consciousness of a common belonging therefore finds in the invocation of a Community interest, and in the reference to the European idea, the possibility of affirming itself against what is established as alterity (that of nation states as opposed to Community) and as particularisms (the national histories as opposed to modernity). We cannot assert here and now that what is happening is the production of a European identity. On the contrary the practice of the European institutions dramatically demonstrates the effects of deterritorialization which are created in part by Europe-building. From an anthropological viewpoint, one may consider deterritorialization as an enriching and stimulating factor (Appadurai 1991).

Cultural pluralism does not produce only centrifugal effects. Learning relativism, as can be observed in Community institutions, is one of the most interesting aspects of the process of pluralization. It implies a continuous questioning about methods, ways of thinking, and management which in a national context are supposed to be 'natural' and legitimate, all but preventing any form of questioning. The situation in Community institutions induces the need to compromise between different ways of facing problems, on different grounds (such as economic, environmental, audio-visual, etc.). At the Community level, dossiers acquire a higher complexity because they must account for different national regulatory arrangements. The material interests of the social categories affected (like fishermen, farmers, miners, or bankers) also vary from one country to another. At the same time, national analysis and perspectives may diverge because of the weight of cultural traditions (for instance the Northern and Southern member states of Europe do not share the same viewpoint regarding ecology) and the political dividing lines do not necessarily coincide from one state to another (see for instance the case of the media).

MEPs learn practically the meaning of cultural complexity, and they are sometimes confronted with a very difficult choice between what is best for Europe and what is dictated by their national affiliation. In political debates, the fact that European parliamentary groups exist does not necessarily produce common positions. These positions can be the outcome of very laborious compromises which may reflect the differences between national political traditions and the apparent similarity of parliamentary party orientation. It is quite striking that political practices at the European level imply the primacy of compromise and negotiation. In parliamentary committees or in the plenary sessions, there is less of an air of confrontation and more a sense of perpetual negotiation between rival powers. Similarly, within each political group what is primarily sought is compromise between national delegations.

Thus, bargaining is an essential component of European political and administrative activity. As Keohane and Hoffmann (1991: 17) have pointed out, interstate bargains are the necessary conditions for European integration. When one underlines the role of lobbies in Brussels and in the corridors of the Parliament, one refers to the exponential growth of the firms and consultants working for the interest groups of the different member states. But one may simultaneously indicate that lobbyism, as a typical operation of influence, as a pragmatic way of solving problems, and as the embodiment of the primacy of informal relationships, has progressively become the main feature of the European political practice. MEPs become experts in lobbying, bargaining and compromising, or else they cannot leave their mark in this arena. Rather than observing real political debate in the Parliament, one can see a small group of specialists in a permanent quest for compromise. The generalized bargaining leads to a progressive loss of political content, thereby obscuring the traditional oppositions which demarcate the political domain.

Community practices look like a large 'do-it-yourself', where one tries to fashion new conceptions of language, politics and administration. The written production (notes, rules, official documents) which comes out of the never-ending mixing of cultures is often considered esoteric, because for many it is simply not comprehensible. However it is precisely because European writers take into account the difference of languages and the need to compensate for the difficulties of translation that such a jargon has come into being (Bellier 1995). Eurospeak is the emblem of the multicultural job demanded in European institutions. Some observers notice a movement towards homogenization which would be characterized by a global impoverishment of meaning. 'In the Commission grey is the dominant tone' said one of my interlocutors. If there is any sense to a Community culture, it is that of the lowest common denominator.

The Community which is incarnated in the European institutions does not look like the communities which have fascinated anthropologists for so long (Bellier 1997). It has been shaped by law and economics and remains principally a coalition of interests. The body politic of the Community is every year better articulated, and now possesses the necessary regulations for the maintenance of its vital functions. But this body has multiple heads. The community is one body with multiple souls. Neither the embedding of the national cultures in a homogeneous whole, nor an overtaking of particularisms in a larger identity, the European Community remains constrained by the economics which have made it successful. The machinery is more and more efficient in certain domains, but it generates frustrations because the feeling of belonging remains diffuse.

The changing of scale which characterizes the political culture of the European Community cannot be interpreted as truly encompassing the national in a whole which would be more important than the constituent parts. The definition of a global policy, for instance regional policies, is the fruit of an agreement, and to a certain extent of a true bargaining between Europe and its member states. Bargaining is never ending, since building Europe means continuously renegotiating the conditions which make possible a global approach. Community practice can be described as the whole system of actions which contribute to the quest for compromise. The double constraints resulting from sharing sovereignties and displacing scales determines a style of work completely oriented to negotiation. But the requirement of 'transparency', often invoked in Brussels, is not only the outcome of the 'langue de bois' used to communicate with outsiders. It must be interpreted as the permanent necessity to be accountable to European partners. The flourishing number of notes and memos, and the multiplicity of types of information gathering and dissemination which have originated in the Commission's services are the manifestation of this preoccupation.

Circulating and exchanging ideas are essential to the culture of compromise (Abélès 1992). Working on European dossiers and problems implies, to play the role of 'the specialist' correctly, a kind of competence which may induce some compartmentalization. One result of this compartmentalization is the growing gap between European officials, caught in this 'competence trap', and the reality of the problems which confront the very real societies which make up the Community. The agents of the Commission, caught in a continuous round of negotiation, organizers of an entity deprived of territory, appear to national officials and other interlocutors as a kind of disconnected mutant, with no roots, whose actions nevertheless are influential regarding the political evolution of the member states. The culture of compromise generates a 'bizarre' universe. No claim to power is made here but the wish to harmonize and rationalize is pursued to the extreme.

Imagination seldom has a place in this cultural universe. The founding fathers could see in it the lasting mark of excess and passion. They associated imagination with political rhetoric. Jean Monnet was never more irritated by anyone than by General de Gaulle, whose uncontrolled imagination allowed him to develop visionary flights of oratory in Asia, South America or Quebec. However, can we say that Community culture is unable to invent? On the contrary this is were a real paradox lies. Below the proclamation of rationality new concepts are generated which are the pure outcome of compromise, defined by negotiation. The couplet of Community interest and subsidiarity is one way to read the actions of the Community from the perspective of invention and imagination.

A 'Bizarre' Europe

The semantic elasticity of the notion of Community interest makes it an incantatory significant, similar to the Polynesian *mana*. It is largely used to advocate a political Europe (Abélès 1996), as well as being at the heart of very concrete policies. In the latter sense, the European interest encompasses two possible interpretations.

For some, it is first of all 'a disinterested' interest, fully achieved through the implementation of the Single Market. This is the philosophy presented in the Commission's service by those agents who are in charge of the Internal Market. However, and in contradiction with the first interpretation, structural policies are put forward on behalf of an 'interested' interest. The Community must affirm itself, pushing forward development policies (and perhaps a social policy over the long term), in the name of the principle of cohesion. As we can see, the Community interest which is overwhelmingly present in the mysteries of Europe is a hybrid. Under the apparent clarity of the words 'Community interest' hides a real ambivalence which reflects the complexity of the Community building process.

In the 1980s another notion appeared in the Community vocabulary – subsidiarity. The principle was first found in the project of Treaty for the European Union, which had been drafted by Altiero Spinelli in 1982, but was never ratified by the member states' governments. It addressed the relationship between Europe and local, regional and national collectivities, in a non-hierarchical perspective. It has been necessary to wait for almost a decade for the notion to be advocated in the course of the European debate. It is now written in the Treaty of Maastricht, which states that in accordance with the principle of subsidiarity the Community acts only and when the objectives of the intended action cannot be achieved satisfactorily by the member states.

Subsidiarity has become a Community agenda and trope. It is supported by opponents to the deepening of political Europe as much as it is appealed to by the partisans of an integrative federalism. During the renegotiation of the structural policies, subsidiarity was used by the member states who attempted to insist upon their prerogatives in the domains which, according to them, belong strictly to their field of competence. But the Commission itself used the concept of subsidiarity to draw attention to the role of the regions and their representatives as natural interlocutors and partners of the Community. Synonymous with a decentralized approach to problems, subsidiarity can be used as an argument to support the renationalization of structural policies. It might also serve to justify the 'Europe of the Regions', which most member state governments dislike.

The complexity of the coupling of the two concepts of common interest and subsidiarity is highlighted by a consideration of the political and philosophical character of subsidiarity, which cannot be separated from the doctrines of Social Catholicism (see Holmes's contribution to this volume). The principle of subsidiarity is essentially relevant when it is associated to the principle of solidarity. The human being cannot open up without help (*subsidium*). This requires multiple communities structured at the appropriate levels. This philosophy influenced Christian-Democrat thought in Germany, Italy and Benelux, but it was not so well echoed in France or in the UK. It represents the ideological foundation for thinking of the Community as an agglomeration of solidarity groupings in a decentralized federation. This principle is very far from Rousseau's concept of a 'general interest', which supports the idea of a Community interest which has been explicitly defined by Jean Monnet as the merging of the member states' particular interests. From this viewpoint, what is necessary is for the Community centre progressively to capture the control levers, specifically mastering the common policies which it organizes. The interventions and ideology cultivated by Monnet at the French Commissariat Général au Plan strongly influenced the Commission.

It is interesting to note that the key concepts of Community interest and subsidiarity come from two very different cultural and ideological traditions. Making them work together introduces a symmetry which corresponds to a homogeneous opposition between centralization and decentralization (as seen in the case of the structural policies). However, such an approach undervalues the gap between the two categories and introduces the risk of entertaining a real misunderstanding of the political and theoretical content of the concepts in use. Hence, the Community discourses may become a factor of opacity for the Commission's partners. This is not a circumstantial issue which could be dealt with in communicational terms ('Europe is badly explained') but a structural characteristic ('Europe produces concepts of compromise'). Complexity, ambiguity and ambivalence are constitutive features of the European political culture whatever its slogans for openness are. Anthropologists must approach the Community on the terms of the words it uses, identifying the implicit meanings and evaluating the national impact of the conceptual outcomes of compromise. Under these circumstances, observers also should accept the idea of a 'bizarre' Europe, which generates strange notions, such as the 'êtres de raison', the 'chimeras' that Spinoza proposed when he was referring to square circles and other creations of the human understanding. The Community is the melting pot of national cultures which are sometimes very contrasting. The consequences of the permanent mixing undertaken by European institutions merit more detailed analysis.

A good example is the case of the Public Services which have been the object of Brussels preoccupations and the work of the Commission these last years. The sectors of energy, transportation, communications and municipal services are all distributed through networks. More than other services they concern the collectivity as a whole. But the regulation and management of their infrastructure, services and networks vary widely from one European country to another. In the French case, the concept of 'service public' is highly codified. It implies simultaneously the consideration of the general interest and the reference to a public authority (cf. Thiry 1994). The British use the notion of 'public utility' to qualify the activities which provide services which are considered essential. Their specificity depends on the importance of the infrastructure and the existence of a network. As with French public services, British public utilities play an essential role in economic development. The need for regulation and public controls is also well acknowledged. The deregulation and privatization programme which has been implemented in the United Kingdom, in the sectors ruled until then by public monopolies such as British Telecom and British Gas, accentuated the contrasts between the French orientation and what is usually qualified as the 'Anglo-Saxon' one, in reference to the American and British models. In the domain of public services, France and the United Kingdom are situated on the opposite ends of a large spectrum. In Germany, the local authorities are given a real power of definition and control of the public services and the nation state stays in the background. In Southern Europe, however, central authorities are in the foreground. Obviously, diversity reigns across Europe in the area of public services, reflecting the range of cultural and institutional traditions.

Is it possible to harmonize these national systems which, until now, operated according to their own logic and efficiency? Instead of looking for harmonization, the EU wanted to promote the adaptation of this economic sector to market rules, particularly after the adoption of the Single European Act. The implementation of the principle of free competition could not be compatible with the existence in some countries of public monopolies over large portions of the economy. Article 90 of the Treaty of Rome is especially interesting here. On the one hand, it is written that the rules of competition are applicable in this domain as much as in other areas of the economy. On the other hand, some limits to the enforcement of the principle of competition have been accepted in order to consider the 'particular mission' imparted to firms in these sectors. It belongs to the Commission to enforce the dispositions with no need for a Council of Ministers' decision. Article 90 is a clear example of one of these typical constructions of compromise, with a key concept emerging, that of the 'general interest economic service'. It is a mixed-up concept which combines an orientation towards deregulation with a philosophy which privileges social cohesion. Effectively, the characteristics of an 'economic service' make 'public utilities' into commodities, slightly different from others but which can be accommodated to the deregulation called for by liberal economists.

But if one emphasizes the importance of the general interest as an irreducible correlation of such an economic service, one reaches the French classical definition, in which the general interest cannot be separated from a doctrine of the general will. Such a will cannot exist apart from the state which is the sole bearer of a legitimacy truly recognized by the citizens as a whole. Therefore any service to the collectivity should be under the supervision of the central state. Opening public services to competition fundamentally threatens the French approach. Community law has further developed the ambivalence which is contained in the concept of 'general interest economic service'. In the five years 1988–93, decisions were taken and directives issued which made liberalization inescapable, giving it a very precise agenda in such areas as telecommunications, postal services, and gas and electricity. All these measures lead to the opening up of the market, paving the way to a more competitive use of 'public utilities'. But simultaneously, the invocation of the general interest draws attention to the specificity of the public service. Two decisions of the European Court of Justice are significant here. The Corbeau decision (19/5/93), which deals with a post service related dispute, considers that the 'necessity to ensure a general interest service' may justify the limitation of competition. The Commune d'Almelo decision (27/4/94), referring to the distribution of electricity, underlines the importance of the 'general interest mission' and considers the related obligations of providing the equality, continuity and distribution of the service. In a similar perspective, the Green paper on telecommunications (1987) introduces the notion of a 'universal service' which has been borrowed from American law. The 'universal service' is defined as a 'basic service provided to all, in the whole of the Community, with affordable tariff conditions and with a standard quality level'.

Now one can notice in Community discourse alternative references to notions of a universal service and of a general interest economic service. The Council of Ministers' decision (December 1993) on telecommunications refers to the universal service. The Commission's directive proposals for energy refer to the obligation of public service, and the Council resolution (November 1994) appeals to the notion of 'general economic interest'. The two notions have different meanings. Universal service is correlated to the necessary services which should be provided to ensure the cohesion of the collectivity. The general interest economic service corresponds to assuming responsibility for the collective interest of users in the provision of services which could be subject to a purely commercial logic.

The European political culture which is elaborated in the Commission entertains some vagueness, but in accepting the coexistence of the two concepts, it progressively achieves a compromise which is best translated by the predominance of the Anglo-Saxon tradition. The notion of 'French-like public service' sometimes invoked by the French authorities underlines the exceptionality of this country as regards the European norm. Under these conditions, the French firms which are concerned by this sector of activity are urged to adapt. A recent report from the Commissariat Général au Plan calls for 'network actors' to change their culture, to modernize these concepts, and to reach a common vocabulary with their partners in order to better negotiate within the Community.

This order corresponds to the consciousness that the national framework is every day more closely integrated into a larger global framework. We are observing here a true process of acculturation. But European political culture cannot impose itself by a flat projection over national approaches which are based on their own history and a specific social reality. This is why, in France, any policy which seems to suggest the dismantling of public services creates very strong opposition in civil society (as witnessed in the many strikes of November-December 1995). The question posed is that of the pertinence in the national context of the concepts and values which are negotiated in the Community framework, as there may be a complete discrepancy between the two. There is no mechanical adaptation to artefacts which are produced in a different scale and concentrate on often incompatible approaches. Hence taking seriously the notion of the 'political culture of compromise' (Abélès and Bellier 1996) can allow a better understanding of the specific working of organizations like the Commission and the Parliament, as well as of the complex relations they entertain with the member states. Such a position means admitting that the construction of the 'Community reason' which has been conceived in order to harmonize domains which may be treated in very different ways in the member states, can also itself be disharmonious. Merging potentially contradictory approaches, such as liberalism or deregulation with the exaltation of the general interest, the culture of compromise could become a chimerical reason and produce square circles if a dominant orientation were not introduced.

The European culture of compromise is above all a political culture. It reflects very real relations of power. Evidently, the Community conceptualization of public service is inscribed in a logic which is more familiar to some states than to others. The difficulty regarding the implementation of the Community orientation, which is felt by French officials and civil society, for instance, cannot be reduced to a problem of translation. With the adoption of the Community lexicon one takes note of a substantial reorientation of the concept of public service. Indeed, this concept is sufficiently foreign that one now speaks in the national sphere of the notion of 'French-like public service'. This kind of gap leads to the reinforcement of the idea that the European norm is produced by a group of anonymous and far-away Eurocrats with which the Commission is identified.

Conclusion

The pursuit of a European common good only makes sense in reference to the future. This is the underlying paradigm of the European political process. Here, the notion of unification has no meaning. Instead, we should talk of a harmonization, conceived as an indefinite quest whose accomplishment is forever postponed. Working towards harmonization rather than unification means accepting difference and the necessity of compromise. Can an atmosphere of compromise strengthen an already feeble European identity? In other words, do these compromises produce notions and norms that permit Europe to overcome the cultural limitations which are tied to national differences? These are the questions which derive from the various areas of European policy making and which may generate new attention by anthropologists and other ethnographers.

Politics at the European level implies that decisions made in any domain must encompass numerous interests and national traditions. It is at times very difficult to come to a compromise in matters that pertain specifically to the economic development of sectors that are perhaps central to one nation and only peripheral to another. In this way, Europe is seen by the public as a veritable 'mise en scène' of negotiation. European publications are opaque. It seems as if Europe was built by an ensemble of technocrats who tinker around with various arrangements without citizens being able to discern the general political orientation of their work. It seems as if, moving from a national level to the European level, everything becomes more complicated and loses its general sense. Consequently Europe appears to dissolve into a multiplicity of partial compromises. The European Parliament which, in principle, should publicize the construction of Europe instead reflects a disconcerting image characterized by a multitude of different subjects and the lack of debate on fundamental European issues (Abélès 1992). Even the institutional question is addressed in technical terms. The permanent need for relevant compromises sometimes gives birth to a legislation which is very difficult to apply to all the member states.

To sum up, several issues raised by European Community politics are closely linked. First, there is the difficulty to communicate a homogeneous vision of Europe and to develop a European citizenship. Second, there is a deficit of European ritual and symbolism. Third, there is a permanent quest for harmony which could be concretized in the production of common notions and concepts. All these issues deal with the very nature of what is called Europe-building and its structural failures and incompleteness. Europe has to be studied as a process, not as a product. It cannot be reified under the categories of community and of identity. Community in the EU is a dream or a metaphor rather than a concrete reality.

The impact of Europe in terms of harmonization, the way European political practice begins to influence the national approaches to politics, reveals that, as an emerging unidentified political object, Europe affects deeply a very old and maybe obsolete perception of identity rooted in territorial grounds. It would mean that deterritorialized Europe, virtual Europe, does not change people's identity but brings them to a completely new perspective on their own traditions. Even if there is no word in the political vocabulary to qualify Europe (as postnational, supra-national, postetatic, or multigovernmental), it appears that Europe as an emerging form creates significant changes in our conception of politics and of identity.

References

Abélès, M. (1992), *La vie quotidienne au Parlement européen*, Paris: Hachette.
—— (1996), *En attente d'Europe*, Paris: Hachette.

Abélès, M. and Bellier, I. (1996), 'Du compromis culturel à la culture politique du compromis', *Revue Francaise de Science Politique* 46 (3): 431-56.

Abélès, M., Bellier, I. and McDonald M. (1993*)*, *An anthropological approach to the European Commission*, Brussels: European Commission.

Agulhon, M. (1989), *Marianne au pouvoir*, Paris: Flammarion.

Appadurai, A. (1991), 'Global Ethnoscapes. Notes and Queries for a Transnational Anthropology', in R.G. Fox (ed.), *Recapturing Anthropology*, Santa Fe: School of American Research.

Bellier, I. (1995), 'Moralité, langue et pouvoirs dans les institutions européennes', *Social Anthropology,* 3 (3): 235–50.

—— (1997), 'De la Communauté à l'Union Européenne', *Socio-Anthropologie* 2, Paris.

Bichet, R. (1985), *Le Drapeau de l'Europe*, Besançon : Jacques et Demontrond.

Goddard, V.A., Llobera, J.R., and Shore, C. (1994), 'Introduction: The Anthropology of Europe' in Goddard, V.A., Llobera, J.R., and Shore, C. (eds), *The Anthropology of Europe. Identities and Boundaries in Conflict*, London: Berg Press.

Godelier, M. (1984), *L'idéel et le matériel. Pensée, économies, sociétés*, Paris: Fayard.

Haas, E. (1958), *The Uniting of Europe: Political, Economic and Social Forces*, Stanford: Stanford University Press.

Keohane, R. and Hoffmann, S. (eds) (1991), *The New European Community*, Boulder: Westview Press.

Lager, C. (1994), 'Europe d'azur et d'or. Histoire et interprétation symbolique du drapeau européen', *Historiens de l'Europe contemporaine*, 9 (1–2): 61–86.

Lévi-Strauss, C. (1950), 'Introduction à l'oeuvre de Marcel Mauss', in Mauss, M. *Sociologie et anthropologie*, Paris: PUF.

Shore, C. and Black, A. (1994), 'Citizen's Europe and the construction of European Identity', in Goddard, V.A., Llobera, J.R., and Shore, C. (eds), *The Anthropology of Europe. Identities and Boundaries in Conflict*, Oxford: Berg Press.

Thiry, B. (1994), 'Rapport introductif', in *Actes du Forum européen des acteurs sociaux sur les Services d'intérêt général*, Bruxelles 25–26 Novembre 1994.

Wallace, W. (ed.) (1990), *The Dynamics of European Integration*, London: Pinter.

The European Union, Identity Politics and the Logic of Interests' Representation

Irène Bellier

With the Treaty of Maastricht, the European Community, initially based on the economic integration of the member states, is leading towards a more politically integrated Union. The endeavour started in 1957 with the setting of specific organizations, among which the European Commission was given the unique role of 'guardian of the Treaties' and the initial source of rules and directives. These European institutions, however, have been alternatively and variously seen either as the source of progress towards a 'better world', a stage which brings together ideas of peace, security and cohesion, or as menacing traditional patterns and national futures, bringing back ideas of disruption and crisis. This is because the Europe-building process is controversial as it evolves in response to different interests. European institutions are the main agents in this change, and for the anthropologist, they represent a real political field in which to analyze the effects induced by institutional discourses and agents' practices on the formation of collective identities.[1]

Anthropological perspectives on Europe-building which are derived from within the European institutions allow us to problematize the ways in which 'cultures' and 'identities' are essentialized by the nationalist movements who assigned fixed categories to the dynamic process of identification. Such essentialism feeds stereotypes which in a multinational environment can be manipulated positively or negatively, according to the context (see also Zabusky's contribution to this volume). Inside the European institutions, the overlapping of professional and national stereotypes paves the way for the enunciation of value statements pointing out different attitudes regarding administrative or managerial efficiency (Bellier 1994). But the fact is that, with the process of unification, the use of national stereotypes does not reflect the ways in which collective action is now structured in EU institutions. The centre of power has been progressively displaced from the nation states' capitals to Brussels, enlarging the space of action for political and administrative leaders and introducing multicultural perspectives in their national frames of references. As a consequence, the diversification of actors and interest groups challenges the states' representation in the policy-making process.

This evolution concerns the mode of communication between nation states, which are incorporated in an institutional system of dialogue through which they assess their conversion into the wider EU. However, these member states, as well as their citizens, are differentially interested in the construction of this coherent global entity. The 'politics of interests' which result from the political dynamic of making unity out of diversities is of anthropological concern. This chapter, while contributing to this line of investigation, focuses on the cultural meanings embedded in this institutional process of widening and deepening the EU, especially as it relates to the definition and articulation of interests. To analyze the multiplication of interest groups in Brussels, we have to go beyond a political economy explanation and attempt to capture the contradictions they bring into the European project.

Different perceptions, meanings and interpretations are attached to the notion of 'interest' as it is exposed in Kaufman (1996 : 445–8). The etymology of the word 'interest' (*intérêt*) is rooted in the Latin word *interesse,* literally 'to be between' (*être entre*). It means 'to be at a distance' (*être à distance*) from which derives the impersonal Latin *interest,* meaning 'it matters' (*il importe*). The meaning has evolved, from the notion of 'damage' (*dommage*) to that of 'compensation' (*dédommagement*) which, since the sixteenth century, implies the economic acceptance of profit as value realized on a loan. At the same time, the initial meaning 'it matters' still exists, thus imbuing some ambiguity into the word 'interest'. The anthropological concern with the concept of interest, on the one hand, and with groups of interests on the other, is related to the desire for both understanding what matters in Europe as well understanding those organizations which seek to defend what matters for their members. In this vein it may be useful to consider a psychological approach to an individual's formation of interests, which often entails an imaginary identification with distant objects. This could well help to explain the formation of new expressions in the EU, such as 'community interest', and the consolidation in Brussels of a large number of groups which propose to their members that they identify with a place where they cannot themselves be. The growth of professional, social and economic organizations which base themselves on corporate forms of representation to defend their members' interests is changing the political dimension of the EU. Now the initial meaning of interest, 'it matters', also concerns social scientists in other fields for these groups of interests are alternatively called 'pressure groups', an expression which specifies their functions in influencing political power and sources of decision. The overlapping of the two categories makes the issue of social and economic 'inclusion' and 'exclusion' problematic, as the rhetoric over the latter reverberates across the political arena of the EU. Four points are discussed in this chapter. The first considers the ways that the 'logic of interest' has been introduced in the Europe-building process. The second deals with the description of 'who represents what'. The third point considers the 'formation and manipulation of interests', and the fourth reviews the impact of new interests' representation.

The Logic of Interests in the European Union

The incorporation of European nation states in a regional organization is one of the circumstances which, following Appadurai's analysis of modernity and globalization (1997), allows us to question the hyphenated link between nation and state to imagine what sort of post-national government is emerging. In the case of the European Union (EU), the question addresses the developing formation of an imagined community (Anderson 1991) beyond the nation; a European Community (EC) which includes cultural and political forms, normally associated with the nation state, which are in a process of transformation. A critical analysis of the hyphenated link between state and nation must consider who are the 'actors' of this reconfiguration of the EU, how they enter into the process, and how they make their 'voices' heard.

The notion of 'voice' is accurate in the context of European institutions for two reasons. One is that it constitutes a political category within the construction of democracy, linked to the recognition of rights to vote and participate in the political system, *ad personam* or on behalf of a collective. The other is that it is a demonstration of what has been suggested by Clifford (1986: 15): 'Once dialogism and polyphony are recognized as modes of textual production, monophonic authority is questioned.' Field research in EU institutions supports this notion. The member states' permanent representatives in Brussels, or officials in charge of European matters in central administrations, regularly mention in the course of interviews the 'voice of the country' they represent. The following citation is an example: 'it is more difficult for us to make them [the lobbies] understand that *we speak with one voice* to defend the national interest in the COREPER. If different sounds are heard how can we defend a position?'[2] For each national interest at stake there are multiple bodies, a great deal of interaction, and a real difficulty to know who is doing what at which moment. The issue is that there is only one national voice in any one political moment, while the overall European voice is being formed. When the United Kingdom assumed the Presidency of the Community, the British Foreign Minister declared that 'Finally, *we want to see Europe speaking with a clear and loud voice* on the world stage, which means an efficient co-ordination of the external action of each of us.' (*Liberation*, 5/1/98, my emphasis).

It is a challenge for the political anthropologist to analyze the mechanisms of 'voicing' within the organization of inter-governmental dialogue. There are multiple sources of voice, multiple representations, and multiple channels through which influences related to specific categories make their way to the European policy-making system. What makes the system different from the national policy-making system is not simply the 'lobbying' which leads us to analyze the formation of interest groups at the European level. It is the fact that lobbies are challenging states' representations in a multicultural platform with rules in which national officials are not necessarily well trained.

I had the opportunity to observe the day-to-day lives and professional interactions in the European Commission (Abélès et al. 1993). The agents of this institution are committed to an ideal, which helps them to support the difficulties of a multicultural environment. As one official said: 'we are making history, building the European future'. But they are not only concerned with idealistic views, their conviction is that if interest groups are not officially recognized they will go underground and subvert the organization. In this context the notion of interest, linked to the definition of interest groups to be registered, operates like a category which is used to classify people and to define their rights to participate in the policy-making process.

A 'New Europe' proceeds from the idea of bringing peace to a continent characterized by a previous state of wars. It results from the commitment of 'big men' like Jean Monnet, Robert Schuman, Konrad Adenauer or Altiero Spinelli who are considered the 'founding fathers of the European unity'. That ideal – 'Europe is peaceful' – is a perception widely diffused among the agents of the European Commission (Abélès et al. 1993). The inability to stop the war in Bosnia was shameful for a number of faithful Europeans, thus making it urgent for them to have the EU achieve the political integration of member states. Now, although a political consensus led to NATO's operations in Kosovo and Yugoslavia, the solution to war in Europe remains controversial.

The New Europe is based on the best way of solving conflicts of interests at different levels. Jean Monnet refused to assess negotiation as a principle between member states, which were supposed to genuinely share a common will. But right from the beginning of the EC the logic of negotiation concretized the need to recognize the many interests that were confronted by change. Today 'bargaining' is the main word to refer to a system where everything is counted from the population of representatives to the number of votes given to the national delegations for taking European decisions. From the common will expressed by the founding fathers derives the notion of a 'common European interest' (see also Abélès' contribution to this volume), which has functioned to legitimize the implementation of European integration over the years. The national politicians, submitted to the democratic sanction of their electorate, were not the best placed to further this unpopular notion. Hence they delegated to the administration of the Commission the task to construct the common interest upon which were based European proposals for rules and directives. It is still the Commission's role to identify the common basis, the shared interests and the pockets of resistance in the different sectors of its responsibility.

The common European interest represents simultaneously something of an indefinite materiality shared by distinct communities and political organizations and a premonition that all together there is a global interest. Thinking of the accepted form of its expression rather than about its contents, one may consider that the European common interest is to the national interest what the general interest is to the private interest. This rhetoric, familiar to French political and anthropological cultures, requires some explanation, for the notion of general interest does not operate alike in Anglo-Saxon political cultures.

In the French context, the state is the guarantor of the 'general interest' and it controls the political system for keeping 'a subtle dose of stability and flexibility to maintain the social cohesion and foresee the future, being responsible for the tensions that appear in the social body' (Ladrière 1996). The state apparatus, including bureaucracy and judicial system, cannot be openly mobilized to obey the mandate of the peculiar interests which at any one moment can access power in the electoral system (through such means as financing political campaigns and parties, bribing, or demonstrating in the streets). Besides the regulation of tensions which occurs at the level of the interest groups themselves, the 'general interest' is what assures each individual of the possibilities of achievement within the material and cultural environment at the time. The question is for the state to reach the level of equilibrium between the different sources of tension introduced by interest groups, and to define common values. Universality, secularism and respect for the republican model constitute such values for the French people. The French state and its servants are committed to the defence of the 'general interest', to a degree that senior officials see themselves as its guardians (Bellier 1993), but this notion is often in conflict with the affirmation of one or other private interests.

In the EU there is no common view on such things. Different perceptions raise a number of theoretical and political discussions of European 'transparency', 'accountability' and 'good governance', which are key concepts in the politics of interests within European institutions. These concepts, however, have different meanings in national languages and administrative cultures. The whole notion of 'accountability' which drives a British ministry within the British Parliament is, when it concerns a French minister, converted to its equivalent 'responsibility', which does not require him to justify the measures taken in front of the elected body but rather to assume them through government responsibility. Beyond these differences of political culture between the United Kingdom and France, the concepts of lobby and the level of acceptance of the pressures exerted over the draft-makers vary widely. In France, the lobby system was perceived until recent years as an unclear practice developed in the USA. It is perceived as contrary to the French representation of Republic (*res publica*) and to universalism. Lobbies are not supposed to occur in France where political institutions are dedicated to the public good and do not open their doors to private demands. Contacts between political and economic decision-makers take place in distinct circumstances: officially in the consultative groups which are associated with the administrative system, and unofficially in the private sphere, through old boys' networks and in the clubs and select places which are supposed to be separated from the public sphere of responsibilities. In the EU, such oppositions as 'general' versus 'peculiar', 'public' versus 'private', are not as central to the emergent political culture as is the case in France. Against this diversity of practices and the uncertainty created by the integration process, the formation and defence of the common interest in Europe must be further interrogated, and its content clarified. Some scholars have raised the question of whether the multiplication of lobbies in Brussels allows the political community to develop or if it adds to the opaqueness of decision-making (Mazey and Richardson 1993; Sidjanski 1995).

Forty years after the birth of the Community, its procedures are better known, institutions have been confirmed, people have become aware of a new reality, and legal and technical experts have risen as powerful resources for clearing and feeding the different pieces of the European machinery. Today's European Union integrates political aspects in at least two sectors: the Common Foreign and Security Policy and Justice and Home Affairs. One after the other the institutions have been built, their agencies localized in member states, power has been redistributed, and the system, in a permanent quest for rationality, has grown in complexity. The Treaties in Europe establish common procedures and the basis for Community law whose application is compulsory. The member states are obliged to transpose European law into the national apparatus of law or be sanctioned by the Commission or the European Court of Justice. As the texts must be equally valid in all member states, they are continually evaluated by the Commission's Legal Service. Legal services in the member states also review the applicability of the law. Many conflictual interpretations occur, but according to legal advisers whom I consulted during the fieldwork, they are also due to the difficulties in translation from the main working languages (English or French) to the eleven official languages as to the definition of the law itself.[3] Indeed, European law after it is adopted seems to uncover problems of political cultures and legal discrepancy.

The expression of the tensions which used to take place within nation-state institutions now occurs in European institutions where national governments in the Council of Ministers and elected representatives in the European Parliament make decisions on the basis of proposals drafted by the European Commission. But the European Parliament does not play the same role vis-à-vis the Council of Ministers and the Commission as the national parliaments do vis-à-vis state executives. There is no strict territoriality to European actions, which are implemented through member states' channels. The ways negotiations develop in Brussels are not similar to what happens in the capitals of the member states despite the fact that state bureaucracies are more and more involved in European matters.

In fact, the displacement of the locus of power introduces a distance between European representatives and citizens while legal implementation introduces new rules. As a result, the people in their localized context have to adapt to techniques, practices, codes and standards which have not been negotiated at their level. But awareness both of this negotiation process, as well as of its impact, are not immediate, being mediated by governments, the media, and grass-roots and professional organizations. Together these factors are responsible for the popular impression of being ruled from the top and for the perception, among professional organizations, that to influence the project one must be represented in Brussels.

Over the years, 'Brussels' has become a common name for institutional Europe, where the feeling of a European Union seems real and palpable. The 'Europe' of the EU is also referred to by the name of the places where treaties and compromises have been signed and where the institutions sit. For example, Rome, Maastricht, and Amsterdam identify Europe at the moments when the Union advanced. These namings correspond to the political extension of the European project but they do not localize it properly. One may think of the Europe of the Six, of the Nine, of the Twelve, of the Fifteen, but there is no memory of localities which are associated with these stages. There is now a single market and perceptions of where and when New Europe starts and stops, but the cultural definition of Europe runs second to its institutional definition. While the capitals of the member states assume by half-year rotation the presidency of the EU, two cities are fighting for recognition as its permanent capital: Strasbourg in France is the seat of the European Parliament, Brussels in Belgium is the seat of most of the institutions. They are where the action takes place and where the anthropologists of the EU institutions do most of their fieldwork. All sorts of people travel there to deal with the institutions, and the diversity of languages, attitudes, and culinary arts there demonstrates that Europe is a multicultural place.

As mentioned above, building the EU converts the nation-state with its legal, cultural, political and territorial definition into a member state involved in new sets of obligations. The process does not obscure the fact that cultural and linguistic diversity are constitutive of Europe, but delocalizing the place for policy making creates a space of dialogue between a larger number of actors. It opens up the arena for defining new strategies between allies to design different aspects of Europe-building. This explains the popularity of media perceptions of France and Germany as 'the motor of Europe', of 'the small countries as always being more pro-European', or of the 'Europe of the lobbies', 'Europe of the elite', and 'Europe of the Regions'.

Seen for a long time as a conglomeration of foreign affairs handled by diplomats, the EU has become a domestic affair, handled by experts. Across fifteen member states there are thousands of actors who are considered as normal interlocutors with the institutions. Among them, one counts 20,000 European civil servants, more than 10,000 registered lobbyists, and the national civil servants posted to the Permanent Representations. The Union-building process is linked to the emergence of European specialists. *Europeans by destiny* are those who are committed to the idea or, like the Commissioners, pledge an oath to serve Europe. *Europeans by obligation* are those who, like member states' representatives or officials who are posted to Brussels, interpret the European process for national understandings. Between them, there are *Europeans by interest,* such as the representatives of social and professional groups, who adapt their actions to the best level of efficacy, meaning that they influence the political power where the rules are taken. Of course there are also administrators, politicians, and interest group representatives, who are not European-minded but who also try to make their voices heard in Europe.

Who Represents What? Voices and Representatives

In deconstructing the political process which takes place in the triangle of the main institutions, the Commission, Parliament and Council of Ministers, it is necessary to analyze the issues of interest representation and meaning. Among the interests represented are those of nations, regions, and professional organizations whose spokespeople must be identified and analyzed. Do their acts represent peoples' diversity, political constituencies, ideologies, corporate and financial interests, or national traditions? Anthropologists must observe carefully the dialectics of 'representation', for the complex society which is in the making in a United Europe is simultaneously generating a number of interest groups and categories of the included and the excluded.

Animated by officials who develop practices which affect the respective positions of individuals in their own societies, European institutions can be seen as microcosms. This statement gives rise to controversial issues about the nature of the relationships between professional practices and cultural identifications, or the analysis of what takes place in the microcosm as representative of what is happening in the global world. But it is a good image for describing the density of the relations generated by these organizations. The political institutions are 'small worlds' because they incorporate their agents in a cultural form which specifies their position in institutional, social and political context (Bellier 1997a). Because institutional life cannot be reduced to the procedures adopted to fulfil its goals, it is better understood through the analysis of the discourses of agents who introduce 'culture' in a way which cannot be separated from their practices. It is especially relevant in European institutions where the people's practices are always related to their cultural background, through identification to what is called 'their national culture', or through the demonstration of what could be 'European culture'.

To cite an example of the latter, the fact that the agents of the European institutions demonstrate a singular capacity to adjust to a multicultural environment full of a disorder and uncertainty (Abélès et al. 1993) can be related to their present concern for 'flexibility'. Although European societies are being incorporated into a larger identity, a kind of European identity is in fact mostly demonstrated in the EU institutions, and often in reaction against the agents' national backgrounds or world competitors, like the USA and Japan. Such an identity is not easy to pinpoint, especially when in Europe or in the USA emphasis is put on difference while continuing the debate on universalism (Taylor 1997; Wieworka 1997). Moreover, the spread of cultural relativism in EU institutions prepares the ground for adopting a consensual concept: like 'flexibility' whose range of application extends from labour organizations, to EU definition of the self, of the tools, intentions, and political means of integration.[4] Rather than defining a concrete European identity, institutional discourses promote the idea that a European has to be flexible as part of the new freedoms of Europe. So 'flexibility', which is in fact an attitude and not a marker of identity, is a response to the multicultural context. It is also a response to market needs, along with other common ideas associated with globalization such as deregulation, competition, and adaptability.

In the European process, the main participants represent something more than themselves, and this can best be observed in the ways they sit together. It is exemplified by the denomination system. At one level of the European debate the member states are identified by their capital names, which are also associated with national policies. Thus the media refer to Bonn, Paris, Madrid, or London's position on, say, single currency, mad cows, or institutional equilibrium. Whoever is speaking, president, prime minister, minister or private secretary, their voice is identified as if it speaks from an unambiguous national centre, as when, for instance, 'Paris declares'.

In EU institutional meetings the situation is different. The national delegations are called by the name of the country they represent, while their EU official interlocutors are called by the institution from which they come and which entitles them to speak. In the Council of Ministers' sessions the dialogue and the negotiations develop between three main characters: the 'Presidency' (the position is assumed by the representative of the member state in charge of the six months Union's presidency), the member states' delegations (ideally) arranged by the alphabetical order of their country's names in each language, and the Commission. Delegates address the 'President', a specific minister in charge of sectoral affairs in his own country (or an official representative). This one gives the floor to 'France', 'Germany', 'Portugal', or 'Italy' represented by the corresponding ministers, or the permanent representatives, and to the 'Commission', represented by a commissioner, a general director, or a director. They speak in French and English in most cases, the use of the eleven languages being restricted to the discussions in Parliament and among ministers.

The rigidity of the official denominations corresponds to the protocol ordering diplomatic relations. It relates to the management of political distance and administrative hierarchies. However, the centrality exposed by the European denomination system is not referring to governments, as is the case when speaking of a capital in a national context, but to nations newly incorporated in moving boundaries. To go further, official denominations put forward global identities, like national ones, but they are played by individuals who can be identified by other characteristics. Not all representatives are alike, or equally accepted by their partners. An official position is always shaded by the personality of acting individuals who are acknowledged as having singular aptitudes, which affect the margins of the negotiations they handle. Though predominately known for their official roles and official voices, the public and private dimensions of the negotiators have to be considered simultaneously, because the personal conditions of their alter egos are relevant to the eyes of the main actors.

Despite their commitment to defending the national interest, member states' representatives often suggested to me that a European position cannot be achieved by people held to a strict national line, to a selfish interest, or simply following orders. The matter is therefore to understand the articulation of public and private lives in such contexts. The display of official and private identities is especially important in Brussels, where the non-official world is very much involved with the institutional arena. Receptions, clubs, or meeting over cocktails are considered by the actors as key elements in their insertion into Europe as well as for the circulation of professional information.

The opposition between 'public' and 'private' finds its origin in the Latin; the notion of public is that 'which concerns the people', while that which is private is 'not allowed to be public'. Differently constructed from north to south Europe these meanings have evolved but the opposition remains, as does its impact on individual practices in the European Commission. Scandinavian officials leave the office on schedule to attend the children at home and, like the Germans, eat early. The Italian or the Spanish come late, eat late, and are not reluctant to stay the whole night if necessary, but take the next day off. The French take more time for lunch than the British, and follow different rules regarding office hours according to their position in the professional hierarchy. Though it affects the use of a common space, the cultural variation of what is 'public' or 'private' cannot be harmonized by the institution.

However, the European actors move in a multicultural space, which progress-ively transforms their practices often to their own astonishment. This evolution results from the private involvement of the person inside a public sphere whose boundaries shift. 'Public' does not only consist of the places defined by the offices, the institutions, or the official labels. It reaches everything which is not domestic, and is linked to the professional world but not necessarily within its physical boundaries. Ironically, the 'private' invades the offices in the form of decorating walls and desk (children's pictures) or in the propensity to call the Commission's directorate generals, in the vernacular language, 'houses' (Bellier 1997 a, b). This provides a symmetry of public and private practices.

European officials and national administrators participate in Europe-building from opposite positions. The former, representing 'Brussels' in the collective imaginary, defend what is called the 'European interest', the latter, incarnating the member states, defend the 'national interest'. What these categories mean and how they function is a matter of considerable anthropological interest. The institutional partners build official positions through their own procedures of clearance, in the government structures on the one hand, in the institutions' services on the other hand. The process is defined as a game with rules, enacted to solve the problems. A European position is fixed in the Commission and voiced by its agents. A national position is fixed by the central governments and voiced by administrators and ministers. At the end, a European directive or a regulation is adopted, which is no longer just the offspring of the Commission but also now that of the Council of Ministers and the Parliament.

For the member states the question is to discuss the position taken by the European Commission which has been given the exclusive right to propose directives and rules. For the Commission the matter is to resolve national resistance against various types of change, and to work out the limits posed by the national delegations in what has been termed a bargaining system. There are very few agreements reached without any discussion, unless they are highly technical. The elaboration of a common position takes place in a paraphernalia of consultative or management committees and Council of Ministers' working groups. The member states take the decisions at different levels of officials and ministers by a qualified or simple majority, or unanimously, according to the policy sector.[5]

The Formation and Manipulation of Interests

The European interest as articulated in EU institutions seems to be above any and all national interests, but it cannot be opposed to them. It results from the aptitude of the European Commission for anticipating national issues and reducing incongruities. Jurists demonstrate that the notion of 'general interest' which supports the republican model of polity does not correspond to the sum total of private interests. In fact, the concept of 'European interest' proceeds from another philosophy than a simple aggregation of parts. Each member state develops its corpus of interpretation. One can see the 'European interest' as a merger between the French notion of 'general will' and the British notion of 'liberalism'. A good example of this might be the ways the European wish for social cohesion goes along with the strategy of 'deregulation', which seems to be in the French mind a contradiction, especially regarding the role of the state. This is partially expressed through the use of two translations, *déréglementation* and *dérégulation*, that a former director in the Forward Studies Unit intended to clarify (in French). To his eyes, *déréglementation* is an acceptable positive attitude to demolish the internal (national) borders for uniting the Single European Market, whereas *dérégulation* cannot be implemented since Europe is constantly evolving through a rule-based mechanism (Vignon 1997). Evidently, two French words for one Anglo-Saxon concept do not reduce the semantic space for European misunderstandings.

There are among the actors involved in Europe-building two ways of perceiving the notion of European interest according to their position in the system. Within national institutions the notion results from what has been agreed by the Ministers in Council. Within the European institutions the notion is framed by the officials and representatives who put themselves above national particularisms and think of a common future on the basis of actual diversity. For example, the European Commission, whom Monnet (1975: 551) considered 'a new breed of people', develop common notions (an 'esprit européen') and introduce European community law by 'working together'. While agents from fifteen different nationalities, languages and cultures constitute a common organization to build Europe, their efforts do not create the homogeneous culture that was once thought would proceed from the establishment of a European collectivity. The Commission's collegiality is confronted by political tensions and management problems. Some are due to the bureaucratic propensity to create divisions among the services, others derive from the national interests which are put forward in the organization through the acceptance that national governments control appointments at the highest level.[6] In contradiction to their necessary independence which is written into the legislation governing the European civil service, this practice generates 'problems' of circulating information and of clarity. In that respect, building a European will to define a common policy requires solving contradictions at the international level, at the political European level, and inside the Commission.

The example of 'the case of the banana' will illustrate these issues. The management of the apparently anodyne fruit was responsible for a delay to the Treaty of Rome, has been the occasion of a recent crisis when the Single Market came into being, and is still dividing the north and the south of Europe. According to their origin, there are three sorts of bananas in the world, colloquially called: 'dollar-bananas' which are produced in Latin America and controlled by the American multinational companies; 'ACP bananas' produced in the countries of Africa, the Caribbean and the Pacific isles, associated with Europe through the Lomé Convention; and 'Community bananas' produced in the peripheral regions of the member states. Correspondingly, there are three services caring for bananas in the European Commission, one in the Directorate General (DG) in charge of Economic External Relations, one in the DG in charge of Development and

Cooperation, and one in the DG in charge of Agriculture. Each service defends its 'constituency', its nexus of regulations, and its style of working.

When the Single Market was implemented, the Commission pushed forward the Common Organization of the Banana Market, in the frame of the World Trade Organization. It built a European strategy to resist the pressures exerted by multinational companies and by the German and Benelux lobbies. These lobbies invoke the large number of consumers interested in the low price of the dollar-banana in order to make governments receptive to the proposals of multinational companies, producers and shipowners, who have invested a lot of money on port infrastructures in Northern Europe. They have powerful lobbies at the Commission and they use the national governments to pressure the Commissioners, the Director Generals and the heads of units. Their influence works in two ways: through the expectation of concrete help from the agents of their nationality in the DGs; and through the ability to convince any administrator of the rightness of their expert advice, thereby creating division among the services. European officials experience a high level of pressures because the overall European interest is supposed to take precedence over the interests of their own countries.

The strategy used by the multinational companies to capture the European market subverts the argument of satisfying the European 'consumer' at best price and cost. The offensive is countered by EU officials by negotiating reciprocity in the American market, in the same sectors or in others, or by attempting to preserve European concerns on Third World interests through different sets of bilateral or multilateral agreements. But the most important issue is to preserve the Community interest (the European producers) and push forward a European model of development based on priorities such as the respect of human rights and labour rights. Banana production, the 'green gold' of the Caribbean Islands, is often presented as the counterweight to drug production in Colombia or Costa Rica, but the labour conditions are regularly denounced by the Community and ACPs' producers who require the application of fair trade and respect of labour and environment conditions.

The banana case illustrates the multiplicity of the interests and the kind of contradictions with which the institutions are confronted. The virtual opposition between the services in the Commission is solved through co-ordination. The contradictions between the 'producers' and the 'consumers' may be regulated through the market system and some European funds. But building a 'European model of development' while celebrating the 'global world' remains controversial. And the problem of governance linked to the political manipulation of lobbies and to lobby manipulation of politicians continues.

EU officials are thus caught in the contradiction of demonstrating 'independence' and 'competence'. As one official said to me: 'I am at the service of the Community, not in favour of my home state or against the member states.' This statement reveals the antagonism between cultural and political identities in the European context, opposing on the one hand national culture and an emergent European culture, and on the other hand the set of cultural definitions embodied in political institutions. Officials must adopt an independent policy. This role apparently isolates them from the grass-roots realities for they express the feeling of being 'cut off from their roots', 'living in a golden cage', or even 'flying like angels in a world with no territory' (Abélès et al. 1993). Their perception of being apart is due not only to their status as expatriates and the high level of their wages, but also to their role in constructing an expert discourse as a means to overcome political divergence (Bellier 1999b).

Although there is a general feeling expressed by officials of 'living in a very rich multicultural environment', multi-linguistic practices and the perception that fifteen cultural systems cannot make simply one Europe also introduce a need for uniformity and harmonization. Europe provokes the meeting of different cultural systems whose incongruity may be noticed in attitudes regarding the roles of money, state regulation, the divide between private and public sphere or the use of time and space. On these different topics, one notices some lines of opposition between Protestant and Catholic cultures, Northern and Southern Europe, Western and Eastern Europe. At the day-to-day level, local mismatching (McDonald 1996) explains some of the disillusionment of Euro civil servants confronted with the resurgence of national stereotypes, and part of the tensions which take place within the Commission.

But in the New Europe, the notion of meeting takes precedence over the notion of incongruity. The fact of working in daily multicultural practices explains the emergence among this people of a common language. Be it called jargon, eurospeak or franglais, it goes with the use of common notions (Bellier 1995b, 1999a). However, whereas what is experienced in the European Commission is worth being considered as something special, genuine, or unique, the process of cultural convergence cannot be restricted to within its walls. Linguistic Europeanization diffuses through the member states with the active participation of national officials and representatives associated with the European policy-making system. Bathing in a European environment causes multiples and long-lasting changes, as most of the people I interviewed said. British officials in the UK say it too, in a pejorative form, in reference to some British nationals in the Commission who are considered to have 'gone native'. The process can be seen as an alchemy, in reference to the initiation which makes it possible for an individual to be 'converted' to Europe (Bellier 1997b: 95).

The expert European, technical, multi-lingual discourse does not replace national or regional political interpretations. The divide between European and national discourses, in fact, allows both European and national officials to localize their responsibilities, or escape them altogether. For instance, 'Europe' is often used locally in member states' societies to explain current social and economic difficulties. These actions assign to the European Commission the role of a scapegoat, a traditional character in European mythologies, which is usually attributed to someone alien. The fact that European dialogue is rooted in a compromise (Abélès and Bellier 1996) creates a gap of meaning, a lack of understanding about the European policies which are implemented through new concepts, new rules, and new displacement of sovereignties. Moreover, the cultural meaning of compromise may explain different commitments to European decisions. For a Spanish speaker, a compromise has to be respected because of the positive meaning of this word in her language and for the political importance of being European. For a French national a compromise with social and economic partners remains a matter of discussion, because of the negatives attached to the concept in a country ruled by the procedure of arbitration in which the executive must solve the conflict and decide the line to be followed. For a British official, a compromise formulated in the terms of law is compulsory because 'Parliament is supreme' in political life. The implementation of a European law depends on its translation in national terms, and on its interpretation by administrators and lawyers. EU interests should not be seen to be in open contradiction with national interests. This allows national officials to interpret European policy impact at their convenience, within their cultural and political environment. Anyone who controls the discourse of the directive is therefore winning the game. Thus the multicultural components of a common EU rule reveals much about Europe-building and its experience.

If the 'European interest' results from a compromise drafted by officials and decided by ministers, what is a national interest? Primarily, the national interest is defined by the representatives of a nation state, generally in front of other nation states' representatives. When a nation state becomes a member state, it participates equally in a political game whose rules are defined by the interplay of the political cultures. This mechanism changes the boundaries which were previously given to the formulation of a national position within the administrative departments and the political structures. It makes more relevant the question of representation and visibility. Secondly, the national interest encapsulates the conflicting demands between the private, sectoral, and regional interests. In the open space of European institutions it appears that the 'national interest' is not only what state representatives have officially voiced. These representatives have to incorporate within the national position views expressed by other actors, in other instances. They work under pressure to sort out what they will consider as part of the national interest or representative of a particular interest.

In Brussels, the member states maintain a Permanent Representation, whose main role is that of a mediator to explain to the national government what is happening in Brussels, and defend in Brussels what has been decided in the capitals. Also present are the lobbyists representing large or middle-range firms, NGOs, or the regions of Europe, which open offices, sometimes as big as the national representation, sometimes sharing the space with private business. Each of these actors, recently incorporated in the policy system, is there to know what happens in the institutions and to push some group's own interests. National delegations, which are the first line to defend the national interests, must be aware of the lobbies' multiple demands and contacts, which generally have the means to by-pass the official national structures. Many conflicts of interest are solved by the Commission who, on the basis of European interests, arbitrate in favour of local and sectoral interests. The European Commission seems to find in lobbies and in interlocutors other than national delegates the resources needed for arbitrating the positions formulated by the member states.

The procedures to introduce national positions regarding European negotiations are highly codified, but the fact is that every member state has its own way of doing policy in Europe. There is a sort of conflict between the countries which have a political culture of coalition and those which are ruled by a culture of *arbitrage*. The first ones solve the problems, at the government level, before taking a European decision, by associating the different partners in advance. They are better prepared to build alliances, which makes compromise in the EU favourable to their interest. The second ones are often facing problems of communication with subordinate levels in the member states, and difficulties of internal co-ordination for the implementation of the Community law. Defining a national position before a European decision is taken results from internal and external negotiation within the central and local administrations (Bellier 1995c). These organizations are identified by their area of competence, and are sometimes in conflict with the government machinery. A decision in Agriculture might be contradictory to the enactment of new standards in Environmental policy. Industrial adjustments (downsizing, reduction of labour costs) often oppose social perspectives (full employment, reduction of labour time). As the discussion within government is now oriented by the negotiation at the supra-national level, a double co-ordination is required, and this obliges administrations to change, to become more conceptual and less executive. This evolution of executive bodies in charge of policy-making raises the problem of accountability, especially if one considers the new importance of lobbies, the potential for corruption, and the lasting problem of allegiances and loyalties.

Civil society is also a force in Europe-building. But the concept of civil society is too vague as compared to the notion of political society. It allows multiple individuals and bodies like mayors, youth, women, firms, trade unions, and non-governmental organizations to call themselves 'representative' or 'expert' for consultation by state and EU organizations. Hence, the question is to know which are the different sections of civil society which are consulted and how they reach the level of decision-making? One reason for them to access the decision-makers is that the Commission does not only rule on already existing policies, leading towards simplification and harmonization, but it also opens new fields for policy such as 'equal opportunities' or 'sustainable development'. Building a European position independent of the national governments makes the Commission sensitive to the social demands which come to it. This is one reason for the development of the lobbies, and for the regulation of their activities.

The Impact of New Interests' Representation

Private lobbies seek to influence European decisions. The problem raised by these people in the EU political landscape is linked to the debate regarding the notion of 'general interest' versus 'private and vested interests'. Interest groups are encouraged by European institutions to register and declare their intentions, to build 'transparency', a vernacular concept linked to 'good governance'. In Brussels, lobbying has become a normal practice, which nevertheless has to be regulated. Registration has been the only way for the European institutions to counter-balance the strongest lobbies which sometimes are better trained and better informed about the institutions and their agents than are national administrations.

National governments have responded too. The first adaptation by some governments has been to encourage national firms to lobby institutions, thinking that this would reinforce national influence in global terms. This was especially the case for France when the authorities started to compare its performance to the UK or Germany, and for Spain for whom a senior official in 1994 considered that 'the country suffered from the lack of powerful lobbies in Brussels'.[7] The regions of the member states, firmly encouraged by the European Commission, have also learned how to lobby. The Committee of the Regions has been created to discuss all issues of regional policy. The Committee now seeks to make the regions, instead of the member states and capitals, the leaders in this field. In part through these efforts the EU has stimulated direct investment, trans-border programs, and decentralized co-operation. It has given to local elites more power to represent their interests as collectives, contributing therefore to the consolidation of EU citizenship through regional anchorages. Such an evolution raises several issues. One concerns the aptitude of the local levels to represent the whole (nation or state) which is what the Länder in Germany and the regions in Belgium can do, and which is a power still coveted by the Autonomous Communities in Spain. Another regards the state's faculty to compensate for internal disequilibrium and to produce social cohesion.

The recognition of the locality for implementing policies at a level closer to the citizens reinforces local powers and democracy. But contesting central politics also stimulates the resurgence of ethnic identities, or the pursuit of regional linguistic policy. This move may induce the formation of new political boundaries within states. Such an evolution in Alsace has reinforced the extreme right. In Italy it has fed a separatist League in Lombardy. In the UK or Spain, nations make an explicit use of 'Brussels' to change the terms of their relationship with the capital. For these and others throughout Europe the EU is a means to reaffirm political, economic and cultural identities.

The second adaptation by European institutions and state authorities has been to consider the autonomy of the lobbying sector. Enormous efforts are now produced by national administrators in Brussels to be informed of what the lobbies do and to co-ordinate their own positions of negotiation. As a consequence, private, sectoral and regional interests make their best efforts to develop their own position in Europe. On one hand, deregulation tends to limit state controls and introduce a fair competition. On the other hand, the Union helps to provide new forms of political organization for the regions of Europe, which are sometimes as big as small member states, and for the multiple categories concerned by European policies. As a result, building a New Europe divides the traditional political forces and suggests new realignments.

In Brussels and elsewhere, not least in academic circles, these new forces and alignments focus on the concept of 'exclusion' which opposes the idea of a state in charge of the 'general interest'. The redefinition of the participants in policy making is related to the question of the democratic deficit of Europe, in terms of the role played by the Commission, which is not an elected body, and in relation to the discrediting of the classic political class. However, this issue must be interpreted in a broader sense to consider the relations between politics, administration and economics, among elected representatives, government executives and interest groups. There are claims by people other than national civil servants and politicians to represent civil society. Behind the issue of political representation, cultural, ethnic, religious and professional identities are at stake. Their affirmation as identity groups claiming recognition and rights feeds the debates on differentialism or universalism. Though building Europe induces many changes in its economic and social bases, such changes do not always operate symmetrically with political integration in the larger space of the Union. Being 'in', not obviously alike but sharing with others, or being 'out', not necessarily foreigners but outside the mainstream, are issues for the political anthropologist, and the European stage represents a special field of observation in this regard.

Conclusion

The New Europe is changing the political game by changing the conditions of policy making, by reshaping the territory of nations and regions, by redistributing economic resources and by redefining identities, cultures and citizenship. The final form of the construction is not yet clear. The consciousness and official defence of the 'European interest' challenges the definition of national interests, which are in turn in conflict with regional and local interests. Behind each interest lies a group of people, affirming identities, claiming recognition, acting upon the political process. But most of these conflicting views are kept silent, as they are channelled by the organization of a political dialogue at the upper levels within the state organization and at the supra-national level.

Sometimes they manifest themselves, and the media reports local resistances and rhetorical oppositions. More often, a state of anomie is observed, which results from the growing gap between the people's lives and those of the institutionalized world. Europe is not in the forefront of peoples' minds, as can be noticed in the national campaigns for the 1999 elections to the European Parliament. Nevertheless, social and professional groups, confronted by changing rules and norms, try to preserve or improve their relative position.

Most of the interest groups act silently through the development of lobbying, which is definitely changing the means of policy making. But one notices other evolutions such as regular demonstrations in the streets, in the different member states, as well as new initiatives taken by the European federation of working unions. These demonstrations take place in multiple sites: in Brussels when Agricultural Policy is reformed; at borders when farmers and fishermen defend their sources of income; in Paris when the people take to the streets to defend the French notion of public service (1995); in Belgium when workers oppose the Renault delocalization. These movements show the interest of people who are not part of the decision-making process to assume their rights as full members in national and EU society. These events are the practical outcomes of what has been characterized as the European democratic deficit. They represent a real challenge to European institutions and to all the partners who, by and large, are building a European political space.

Notes

1. This chapter is based on my fieldwork in the European Commission, in collaboration with M. Abélès and M. McDonald (1993), and in the national administrations 'who make Europe from their capitals' in Madrid (Spain), in London (UK), and in Brussels (several Permanent Representations). The research has been financed by the European Commission (in 1993) and the French Ministry for Civil Service (in 1994–95).

2. To complete my anthropological approach to the European Commission, I spent several months researching national administrations in Spain, the UK and

Belgium. This research included observations, interviews with senior officials, informal discussions with the staff and clerks, and archival research.

3. Danish, Dutch, English, Finish, French, German, Greek, Italian, Portuguese, Spanish, Swedish.

4. Flexibility as a political means is exemplified in the Green Paper drafted by the European Commission: '*how programming could be adapted for giving more flexibility to the politics of co-operation?*' (1997: 50).

5. With the Treaty on the European Union (TEU, Maastricht), three pillars have been established for the future construction of the EU: (1) Internal Common Policies; (2) Foreign and Security Common Policy; (3) Justice and Home Affairs. In each sector, the respective powers of the European institutions and the member states are specified. Unanimity and right of veto are operating in the so-called intergovernmental sector, the second and third pillars of the TEU. Qualified majority voting is applied in the community sector (designed in the previous treaties) involving agricultural policy, structural funds, social policy, trade and commerce, development and co-operation.

6. The top levels of the European administration, graded A1 to A5, are distributed to senior officials, coming from the fifteen member states, and appointed according to the government interests: they are called 'Flag posts' (Bellier 1995a, 1997b; Abélès and Bellier 1996).

7. Interview in the State Secretary for European Affairs, *La Trinidad*, Madrid 1994.

References

Abélès, M. Bellier, I. and McDonald M. (1993), *An anthropological approach to the European Commission*, European Commission, Brussels.

Abélès, M. and Bellier, I. (1996), 'La Commission Européenne: du compromis culturel à la culture politique du compromis', *Revue Française de Science Politique*, 46 (3): 431–55.

Anderson, B. (1991 (1983)), *Imagined Communities: Reflections on the Origin and Spread of Nationalism*, London: Verso.

Appadurai, A. (1997), *Modernity at Large, Cultural Dimension of Globalization*, New Delhi: Oxford University Press.

Bellier, I. (1993), *L'ENA comme si vous y étiez*, Paris: Editions du Seuil.

—— (1994), 'La Commission Européenne: hauts fonctionnaires et "culture du management"', *Revue Française d'Administration Publique*, 70: 253–62.

—— (1995a), 'Une culture de la Commission Européenne? De la rencontre des cultures et du multilinguisme des fonctionnaires', in Y. Meny, P. Muller, and J.-L Quermonne (eds), *Politiques Publiques en Europe*, Paris: L'Harmattan.

—— (1995b), 'Moralité, langue et pouvoirs dans les institutions européennes', *Social Anthropology* 3 (3): 235–50.

—— (1995c), 'Questions locales entre administrations nationales et institutions européennes', *Pôle Sud* 3: 147–65.

—— (1997a) 'Une approche anthropologique de la culture des institutions', in M. Abélès and H.-P. Jeudy (eds), *Anthropologie du Politique,* Paris: Armand Colin.

—— (1997b) 'The Commission as an Actor', in H. Wallace and A. Young (eds), *Participation and Policy Making in the European Union*, Oxford: Clarendon Press.

——(1999a) 'European Institutions and Linguistic Diversity: a Problematic Unity', in H.S. Chopra, R. Frank and J. Schröder, *National Identities and Regional Cooperation: Experiences of European Integration and South Asia Perceptions*, New Delhi: Manohar.

—— (1999b) 'Le lieu du politique, l'usage du technocrate: hybridation à la Commission Européenne', in V. Dubois and D. Dulong (eds), *La question technocratique. De l'invention d'une figure aux transformations de l'action publique.* Strasbourg: PUS.

Clifford, J. (1986), 'Introduction: Partial Truths', in J.Clifford (ed.) *The Poetics and Politics of Ethnography*, Berkeley: University of California Press.

European Commission (1997), *Green Paper on the Relations between the European Union and the ACP Countries at the Dawn of 21st century*, Luxembourg: Office des Publications Officielles des Communautés Européennes.

Kaufman, P. (1996), 'Intérêt (philosophy and human sciences)', *Encyclopedia Universalis*, volume 12: 445–8, Paris.

Ladrière, J. (1996), 'Groupes de pression', *Encyclopedia Universalis*, volume 10: 1007–10, Paris.

Mazey, S. and Richardson, J. (1993), 'Interest Groups in the European Community', in J. Richardson (ed.), *Pressure Groups*, Oxford: Oxford University Press.

McDonald, M. (1996), '"Unity in Diversity". Some Tensions in the Construction of Europe.', *Social Anthropology*, 4 (1): 47–60.

Monnet, J. (1975), *Mémoires*, Paris: Fayard.

Sidjanski, D. (1995), 'Nouvelles tendances des groupes de pression dans l'Union Européenne', in Y. Meny, P. Muller and J.L. Quermonne (eds), *Politiques Publiques en Europe*, Paris: L'Harmattan.

Taylor, C. (1997), *Multiculturalisme: différence et démocratie,* Paris: Flammarion.

Vignon, J. (1997), interview by D. David, *Le Courrier ACP-UE*, 164: 58–60.

Wieworka, M. (1997), *Une société fragmentée?; le multiculturalisme en débat,* Paris: La Découverte.

—4—

Debating Europe: Globalization Rhetoric and European Union Employment Policies

Gilbert Weiss and Ruth Wodak

In his book *La concurrence et la mort* the French social scientist Ph. Thureau-Dangin examines the 'economism' of the present day and describes a society that appears to be completely preoccupied with the principles of competition and competitiveness. At one place in his book the author draws attention to the etymological relationship between *agon* (competition) and *agonia* (fear of death). A society that gives itself over completely to the idea of permanent competition and forgets co-operation and solidarity would accordingly be a 'society in fear of death' (Thureau-Dangin 1995; see also Jeismann 1997). We will leave this assumption aside for the moment and will return to it in the conclusion to this chapter.

In this chapter we wish to present an extract from ethnographic and linguistic analyses of the discourses and decision-making processes of the European Union (EU) on employment and unemployment. Since the Treaty of Maastricht (1993) the EU has defined itself explicitly as a *political* union. And as a political union it must be able to solve political problems. If mass unemployment is one of the major political problems in Europe – which it definitely is from the perspective of the bulk of the population – then the legitimacy of the EU as a political entity will crucially depend on how this problem is solved or not solved. In other words, supra-national co-ordination in EU employment policy will contribute significantly to determining the institutional future of the whole union. It is not only one area of politics among many, but also one that is immediately bound up with the identity and legitimacy of a common Europe. Not least it is concerned with a transformation of the welfare state – as a genuinely European achievement – from the national to the supra-national level (Michie 1994; Eatwell 1994; Schubert 1998).

The central concern of this chapter is the decision-making process in an advisory committee of the European Commission, a group of experts, the so-called *Competitiveness Advisory Group* (CAG). We shall limit ourselves to one aspect that we characterize as the 'globalization rhetoric' of employment policy discourses. The CAG constitutes one example of those 'epistemic communities' or 'trans-national knowledge and expertise communities' which 'process, possess and provide common definitions of problems, assumptions of causes and policy recommendations' (Beck 1998: 39). International organizations depend increasingly on this kind of 'transnational expert-rationality' which, from the opposite viewpoint, is forcing itself upon an increasing number of areas of social practice. It is also characteristic of such communities that the border between reflective-objective expertise and political action is becoming blurred. It can no longer be determined without ambiguity who is a politician and who is an expert. As Bach (1999: 95) points out, a sociological analysis of EU institutions has to systematically elaborate on the specific rationality criteria of 'expertises' that pretend to be unpolitical but nevertheless have become an integral part of the policy-making process. The particular policy paper of the CAG that we wish to present here was produced by this group for a European Council summit of November 1997 that was exclusively concerned with employment. It represents that dimension of EU decision-making that takes place, so to speak, 'behind closed doors'.

After some general and introductory remarks on globalization rhetoric and its function in discourse, we shall then present, against this background, the concrete results of a sociolinguistic analysis of the CAG paper and its genesis in the discussions of the working party. Our analysis of the ethnographic data will primarily rely on the methodological tools of systemic-functional linguistics as developed by M.A.K. Halliday (1994; see also Thompson 1996).

Globalization Rhetoric and its Function

First of all, what do we mean by 'globalization rhetoric'? We use this to refer to the discursive construction of a state of affairs known as 'globalization' that exists in a very close argument-relationship with other constitutive elements of EU employment discourse, e.g. competitiveness, location, liberalization and flexibility. The 'need' for competitiveness and liberalization, as a precondition for employment growth, is substantiated by globalization rhetoric – and this is true for both macro-economic and structural measures. Moreover such rhetoric is invoked to proclaim a European identity distinct from other 'global players', particularly the USA and Japan.

Here we should insert a few words on the concept of globalization. This notion has undoubtedly achieved great prominence, in political speeches as well as in zeitgeist magazines and scientific publications. In the social sciences a range of positions on globalization is to be found. Some think it is almost a 'myth' that has no evidence in economic and political reality (for example, see Hirst and Thompson 1996). Some think it does exist and has to be strongly criticised for it ultimately leads to the domination of international capital, financial markets and global players (for example, see Bourdieu 1997, 1998) on the one hand, or to the domination of the 'McWorld' of mass consumption and mass infotainment on the other (for example, see Barber 1995). Some are quite enthusiastic about it because they see the chances for realizing the *Weltbürger* and a new/old form of 'cosmopolitical democracy' (Beck 1998). Some just soberly describe the emerging tensions between globalization on the one hand and fragmentation/regionalization on the other (Clark 1997; Luhmann 1996).

The battle between these different positions cannot be resolved here. What makes it more difficult to define the concept precisely is that it is invoked in different processes: economic, political, cultural, media-related and so on. We are interested, in the present context, primarily in its application in economic processes. We cannot go more deeply into the situation on the product, consumer, labour and financial markets (see Huffschmid 1997; Hirst and Thompson 1996). It must suffice to point out that, for example, in the eleven member states of the EU that have adopted a common currency still significantly less than 15 per cent of their total foreign trade is conducted outside their borders. What we are concerned with in present-day economic processes is something that could at most be characterised as 'intraregional internationalization' (Huffschmid 1997).

Globalization rhetoric is marked by two constitutive discourses: (1) the de-politicization of socio-economic fields of activity (here the role of the financial markets is important); and (2) the passing of the nation state, which is also a passing of the welfare state (sometimes presented as the 'impotence' of the nation state in the face of 'new economic constraints'). Financial markets take on a very special position in these discourses, especially in the first. Financial markets have experienced truly incredible pressure to internationalize. Whether one can speak of globalization, however, is questionable even here, if one considers that only a handful of economies or trading blocks (EU, US, Japan, G7) are dominant. The real fact that we are concerned with is not the 'global' nature of capital but deficient political control of capital. Be that as it may, in political discourse the financial markets have the essential function of supporting globalization rhetoric. The development of the financial markets is presented as an immutable constraint, as an almost supernatural phenomenon, to which one must simply adjust. Usually, however, this reference is less direct. The financial markets remain concealed behind 'new economic constraints' and behind 'criteria', in other words behind the criteria of price and monetary stability as necessary preconditions for the so-called 'confidence of the financial markets' in politics.

What is happening here, in simple terms, is the following: a particular sector of the economy, the financial market, is being made into a universal horizon for the whole of the economy. Simultaneously it is being depoliticized, since it is explained as an inevitable destiny. It is no longer an area of control in the field of political activity, but rather the inalienable framework for this field of activity. Political action then no longer questions this framework but is content to fulfil it adequately, i.e. by guaranteeing competition and flexibility. It is not the case, however, that the development of financial markets can be traced back to divine influence. It is rather a result of political decisions taken in the 1980s to deregulate the financial markets (Thurow 1996).

The construction of economic constraints by the 'global' financial markets leads directly to the second discourse, namely to the deconstruction of the nation state as an effective and above all responsible political entity. It thereby leads simultaneously to the invocation of new supra-national units of action. Confronted by these economic constraints, the nation state is said to be overburdened, or powerless, and supra-national entities such as the EU must take its place. Now even if the nation state is by no means as powerless as it is said to be, this type of argument does have a degree of plausibility. The snag with this is that an effective and integrated supra-national entity of this sort does not yet exist, particularly in the area of social policy and welfare. In this area the EU is still a 'project in a state of uncertainty' (Müller 1997: 817), in the uncertainty between intergovernmental co-operation and supra-national institutionalization. This uncertainty between the end of the old model (nation state) and the development of a new model (supra-national institutions) opens up a political vacuum that permits the financial players in particular to play their game without too much interference from political regulations. In particular they are liberated from the uncomfortable corset of the welfare principle. If one ignores the intentions hidden behind this, it is a great paradox that political discourse itself – through the rhetoric of global economic constraints, competitive pressure and impotence of the nation state – promotes an anti- or at least apolitical liberalism.

The core of globalization rhetoric can be summarized as follows: proceeding from a particular sector of the economy (the financial markets) a total economic development is established. If one overlooks the fact that the true state of affairs is already somewhat distorted by this manoeuvre, the next two steps in the argument are decisive: this contingent development is declared to be a necessity determined by destiny, and in a further step this necessity becomes a virtue. We are dealing, therefore, with a two-step argumentative transformation in which contingency is transformed into necessity, and necessity into virtue.

The central function of this globalization rhetoric is disciplining by economic arguments. It is not enough to restrict this to the disciplining of employees or trades unions. It is rather a disciplining "beyond left and right" (Giddens 1997). It does not only affect one class, it is all-embracing. Its goal is ultimately what Sennett (1998) called "flexible man".

The process of disciplining works essentially on fear. In this, unemployment undoubtedly plays a major role. Here a certain degree of distinction must be made between the primary experience of unemployment (i.e. immediate experience affecting oneself, or a partner, or a family member), and secondary experience (i.e. indirect or acquired experience that there are more and more unemployed, that society is running out of work, and that it could affect me at any time). This uncertainty and fear of losing one's job is spreading everywhere, it is undermining self-respect and disturbing social relationships even in the most private domains. To put it slightly more cynically, the fundamental problem that undermines a society is not an unemployment rate of 10 per cent but the *fear of unemployment* in the other 90 per cent. Instability and uncertainty are becoming a norm. Again, in the words of Sennett: 'personal fears are intimately connected to new capitalism' (1998: 128). It seems that the *flexible man* is not (yet) a self-confident man.

Economic disciplining and the flexibility that it demands have far-reaching consequences as far as the welfare state is concerned. They cause it to be undermined. In this context, it is not necessary to develop any emotionally loaded scenario of collapse (Martin and Schumann 1996); it will suffice to describe matters factually: falling wages, decline in real income from gainful employment, reduction of social support and social security in general – everything, therefore, included under the label of *Abbau* (reduction) policies. This may be shown to be a particularly pervasive development in the USA. But in Europe, too, there are already sufficient indicators of this development (Thurow 1996; Koch 1997; Radermacher 1997).

EU Employment Discourse: The Competitiveness Advisory Group (CAG)

We will now turn our attention to the analysis of an EU policy paper on employment strategies which originated in a kind of 'think tank' of the European Commission, the CAG. The CAG is a very specific interaction system within the complex organization of the EU. Like every organizational system, the EU reproduces itself through decision-making processes within interactional systems that are connected to one another in many ways (Luhmann 1996). Decisions are made at various points within an organization: in meetings, during conversations in corridors, on the telephone, or at social and informal events. Individual cases are very difficult to reconstruct. Every organization, however, *stages* its decision-making processes, dramatically, so to speak, in meetings and in the production of reports, directives and other written bureaucratic genres (Wodak 1996). Such dramatic scenes are hierarchically ordered. Not everyone has access to everything, and in this way power and status are produced and reproduced. The linguist Dennis Mumby (1988: 68) characterizes the value of meetings within organizations as follows:

> meetings are perceived as a necessary and pervasive characteristic of organizational life – they are events that people are required to engage in if decisions are to be made and goals to be accomplished. While this is the most ostensible rationale for meetings, they also function as the most important and visible sites of organizational power, and of the reification of organizational hierarchy.

Meetings are thus one of the major sites where decisions are taken and where conflicts evolve and are resolved through discursive practices; it is through these discursive practices that meanings are produced and transmitted, that institutional roles are constructed and power relations developed and maintained. The socio-linguistic analysis of meetings is therefore an important contribution to the research on institutions since it can help render visible and intelligible apparently coded, opaque and mythical phenomena.

We will now turn to the concrete example and the context. The CAG is a committee that was set up by Commission President Jacques Santer to prepare particular drafts and proposals directly for the European Council. It consists of 12 people, 2 women and 10 men. High-ranking representatives of industry, politics and trade unions, together with one representative of the Commission, discuss sensitive subjects and draw up a report every six months. The group is chaired by Jean-Claude Paye, who was formerly Secretary-General of the OECD and whom we interviewed in Paris. Meetings are recorded on tape and reports (both hand-written minutes and resolution drafts) are produced. In the autumn of 1997 the committee was given the task of preparing an employment policy paper for the European Council summit in Luxembourg in November. The recordings of these meetings and all the written materials (reports, letters, faxes, etc.) were available to us for the analysis. There were six documents, all in all: a topic list, an outline, and then three drafts (D1, D2, D3) and the final version. We also analyzed the handwritten minutes of the meetings. In this way it was possible to reconstruct very precisely the entire discussion process and the mode of text production in the CAG, from the first step of listing the themes down to the finished paper. The meetings themselves were conducted in three languages, Italian, English and French, and the document was repeatedly edited by the Chair, in English, even though he is himself a native speaker of French (for analyses of language policies in the EU, see Wodak and De Cillia 1995; Wodak and Corson 1998; Born 1999).

The document, in genre a policy paper, consists of four sections. The first is an introduction on the implications and consequences of globalization. Here globaliza-tion is presented as an uncontested and naturally occurring phenomenon. It is also argued that globalization is a positive phenomenon, and that Europe must take measures to recognize the signs of the times and adjust to this process (note the transformation of contingency into necessity, and necessity into virtue). As competitors the document names the USA and Japan. The second section deals with the mistakes that Europe has made hitherto, and here they use as a starting point, and in a generalizing and over-rhetorical fashion, common-sense opinions that can then be refuted. Accordingly, unemployment is not the consequence of globalization but rather a result of over-strict and inflexible employment laws and excessive taxation. The third section deals with the construction of a European identity, wherein the European location is acclaimed as in a promotional brochure.

It is claimed that the positive arguments for investment in Europe, in spite of high levels of taxation, are above all education, know-how, culture, justice, and the traditions of even-handedness, equality and democracy. In the fourth section concrete proposals for combating unemployment are finally made. In the meetings themselves the different drafts of the document were discussed and suggestions for changes were made. The entire process of text genesis, and with it the decision-making process, was characterized by a conflict between the trade union representatives, who insisted on the status quo, not wishing to question the welfare state, and demanded social cohesion, and the employers' representatives, who proposed a liberalization of labour market policies.

On the basis of the first two drafts of the document the following chain of argument can be shown:

1. Globalization is accepted without question as a natural phenomenon
2. Globalization is related to unemployment
3. This relationship is contested
4. The positive aspects of globalization are pointed out and arguments are formulated against 'common-sense' opinions and 'popular beliefs'
5. Previous European mistakes are enumerated
6. An assurance is given that the specific European ideals will remain untouched and that a specifically European way will be sought
7. This European way, which will be an innovation, will guarantee Europe a leading role in worldwide competition
8. Migration and change are therefore inevitable
9. Otherwise Europe will fail in competitiveness

Competitiveness is therefore the overall instrument to combat unemployment. Simultaneously the necessary changes in Europe, unlike the USA and Japan, will serve as the building blocks of a new European identity – a 'social identity'. Changes are needed; on this all members of the CAG were in agreement. But the concrete appearance of such changes must first be negotiated, and is a source of conflict.

The 'Life' of Arguments

In order to follow the 'life' of arguments and the semiosis of the text genesis we refer to the linguistic concept of 'recontextualization' (Bernstein 1990). The latter is particularly useful as it can be applied to chart shifts of meaning from one context to another, either within one genre – as in different versions of a specific written text – or across semiotic dimensions in organizational discourse, for example, from discussion to monologic text to actions which may even belong to a different semiotic mode. Thus interaction during a meeting, for instance, may not only be recontextualized in a written text, but meaning shifts are also observable from dialogue to monologue (monologizing), from dynamic to static, from process to entity, from negotiable to fixed. Many 'voices' (in the Bakhtinian sense) coalesce to form one continuous strand, where violations of text coherence in the document in question indicate the different stances, views and interests voiced by those who took part in the meetings.

We will present the first two paragraphs of the document in two versions that give a definition of globalization and its consequences. Between these two versions a meeting took place which was characterised by heated discussions between trade unions and employers. After this the second version was greatly moderated and shortened. Globalization rhetoric here dominates the course of the argument:

1st Version:

> Topic list:
> The globalization process
> a) is natural: it is the continuation and spread of the process of economic development and social progress on which the prosperity of our countries is based
> b) is a good thing since it
> c) helps to satisfy consumer needs,
> d) enables an increasing number of countries throughout the world to take part in the economic development process, thereby raising their living standards and thus giving us increasingly attractive trading partners;
> e) is therefore inevitable and irreversible.

2nd Version:

> Outline:
> The so-called globalization is the result of interaction between two main factors: liberalization of trade and technological progress in all its forms (innovation in product services management). This makes competition even fiercer.

The chain of argument in the first draft is turned into a single sentence and transformed, so that instead of nature metaphors it now contains moderated euphemisms. Particular attention should be paid to the expression 'so-called' globalization, which now suggests that it is not at all clear what this means and that it has distanced itself from the dogmatism of the first draft. The summary given in this single sentence in no way corresponds to the preceding document.

Let us now look at the third paragraph, where we would like to use only the two versions of 14 October 1997 (D2) and 28 October 1997 (D3). Between these a meeting took place, on 17 October 1997, where there was renewed conflict between trade unions and employers.

1 But it (globalization) is also a demanding one, and often a painful one.
2 Economic progress has always been accompanied with destruction of obsolete activities and creation of new ones.
3 The pace has become swifter and the game has taken on planetary dimensions.
4 It imposes on all countries – including European countries, where industrial civilization was born – deep and rapid adjustments.
5 The breadth and urgency of the needed adaptations are indistinctly perceived by public opinion, which explains widespread sense of unease.
6 The duty which falls on governments, trade-unions and employers is to work together

   – to describe the stakes and refute a number of mistaken ideas
   – to stress that our countries have the means to sustain high ambitions; and
   – to implement, without delay and with consistency, the necessary reforms.

This paragraph changes and is recontextualized in the following version:

1 But it is also a demanding process, and often a painful one.
2 Economic progress has always been accompanied by destruction of obsolete activities and creation of new ones.
3 The pace has become swifter and the game has taken on planetary dimensions.
4 It imposes deep and rapid adjustments on all countries – including European countries, where industrial civilization was born.
5 Social cohesion is threatened.
6 There is a risk of a disjuncture between the hopes and aspirations of people and the demands of a global economy.
7 And yet social cohesion is not only a worthwhile political and social goal; it is also a source of efficiency and adaptability in a knowledge-based economy that increasingly depends on human quality and the ability to work as a team.
8 It has been difficult for people to grasp the breadth and urgency of necessary adaptations.
9 This explains a widespread sense of unease, inequality and polarization.
10 It is more than ever the duty of governments, trade-unions and employers to work together
   – to describe the stakes and refute a number of mistakes;
   – to stress that our countries should have high ambitions and that they can be realised; and
   – to implement the necessary reforms consistently and without delay.
11 Failure to move quickly and decisively will result in loss of resources, both human and capital, which will leave for more promising parts of the world if Europe provides less attractive opportunities.

What, then, are the recontextualizations, which can be grouped under four transformation types: the addition of elements, the deletion of elements, the rearrangement of elements and the substitution of elements? For showing this, concepts from Halliday's Functional Grammar are of particular importance, namely the distinctions between 'Theme', 'Rheme' and 'Transitivity'. For Halliday, the Theme is the given of a message; it is the starting point for the message or 'the ground from which the clause is taking off' (Halliday 1994: 38), whereas the Rheme is the new information introduced in the clause. The Theme constitutes the beginning of the clause and is often identical with the Subject (see Thompson 1996: 119f). The changes in the structure of Theme and Rheme can be interpreted as a change in focus on given or new information – what is understood as presupposition and not questionable on the one hand, and what is emphasized and contains the new information which should be focused upon on the other. Going on to Transitivity, we turn from the textual function of grammar to the ideational function because the latter shows how the 'world' is represented in language in a text, and ultimately in the clause; from this perspective, 'language comprises a set of resources for referring to entities in the world and the ways in which those entities act on or relate to each other' (Thompson 1996: 76). Different 'process types' illustrate how certain agents act and what kind of semantic constructions are used to relate actions to agents. In our case, this is of great importance: who are the actors and what do they do? What kind of actions are ascribed to which agents? As will be shown, experts act rationally, whereas the non-experts, i.e. the citizens, act irrationally which is manifested in different verb processes.

Returning to the above-quoted paragraph, in the fourth sentence changes in word order are to be seen, affecting the Rheme, i.e. the new information. The intonational focus falls in 'European countries' in the final version, rather than on 'adjustments'. This admits of at least two readings, where, on the basis of the overall context, the reader can decide between the two interpretations. Firstly it may be a matter of a purely stylistic change, or of a tendency towards intelligibility and efficiency of 'plain English' – and efficiency characterizes the entire document, in terms of both content and form ('business-speak'). It could also be a question, however, of placing Europe and its traditions at the centre and of constructing in this way the new identity.

The fifth sentence does not appear at all in the first document. At this point the voice of the trade unions is clearly heard. The sentence is therefore a concession to the trade unions. Social cohesion is promoted here, and it is established that the welfare state is threatened. After that, in the next two sentences (6 and 7), this danger is again aired and justified. The trade unions' line of argument is directed towards presenting the welfare state as an efficient entity and not only as a burden. Investment in human capital, according to this view, has proved to be important for competitiveness. Consider the following short sequence of the discussions in the group for illustrating the conflicts between trade unions and employers in negotiating the text:

Speaker A (representative of trade unions):

> If we talk about competitiveness we also have to talk about social cohesion. And you said it now, [. . .] Mister Chairman, but I' m thinking in the paper I can't see it in, in a, in the same words as you have now [. . .]. So as the report is now, it is too much that is not acceptable in my point of view. But I don't think it's acceptable either if you look at the Commission's guidelines for the job summit or if you listen to, for example, prime minister Junker when, he, Junker, when he talks about what [. . .] the job summit will talk about.

Speaker B (representative of employers):

> Mais ce qu'on vous dit la première fois, je parle très franchement, parce que ça c'est utile pour discuter les choses. J/je pense alors, je ne veux pas détruire le welfare-state, le modèle social Européen mais je veux accomoder, flexibiliser, ajuster ce modèle! Mais voir commercial, c'est, tout ça c'est bien, on doit continuer et garder ça. Mais, mon opinion c'est, oui, on doit garder le modèle social, mais on doit le discuter et donner un message de flexibilité, d'ajustement, et vous donnez là un message de rigidité. Excusez-moi, mais c'est mon opinion.

> [But, if one speaks with you the first time, I speak up very frankly, because it is necessary to discuss the things. I think thus, that I do not want to destroy the welfare state, the European Social model, but I want to adapt, be flexible, accommodate this model. One has to look from the point of view of the market, one has to continue and preserve the model. But, in my opinion, one has to preserve the social model, but one has to discuss it and to give a message of flexibility, of accommodation; and you give a message of rigidity! I apologize, but this is my opinion].

We would now like to draw attention to two elements that permeate the rest of the document like a motto: the tension between people's hopes and the requirements of globalization (where we need only look at the multiple embedding of the nouns and the anonymization of people as well as their characterization as irrational); and secondly, the 'knowledge-based economy' that is construed as the trademark of Europe.

The next sentence in the first document is complex, and is transformed in the new version into two sentences and rearranged:

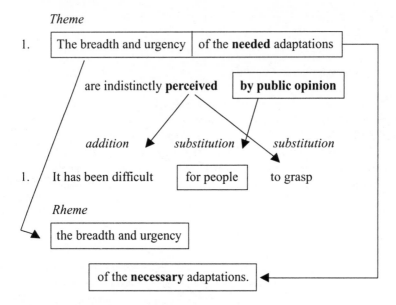

Theme

1. The breadth and urgency | of the **needed** adaptations

are indistinctly **perceived** **by public opinion**

addition   *substitution*   *substitution*

1. It has been difficult | for people | to grasp

Rheme

the breadth and urgency

of the **necessary** adaptations.

2. **which** explains a widespread sense of unease.
2. **This** explains a widespread sense of unease,
   inequality and polarization.

Simultaneously there is also a shift of Theme – given information – and Rheme – new information. On the one hand we are again dealing with 'business-speak', with a simplification, while on the other hand the focus of the information is changed. There are, moreover, additions in the description of the atmosphere and of human feelings. The transformation of 'public opinion', a noun phrase, to 'people', an agent, is relevant. All through the document the 'people' are characterized as having hopes and beliefs, while the experts argue rationally on the basis of knowledge. The distancing which the group of experts establishes from the lay people is diminished, but the designated group still remains anonymous, and we do not know who is included or excluded.

The final sentence in the new version has also been added: the slogan of danger is here clearly displayed, and a rhetorical technique is used to convince the politicians that they must act quickly. The slogan of speed and urgency also permeates the document in the same way as the semantic field of *urgent, rapid, quickly* and so on: efficient and swift action is required. The fundamental message of the document amounts to a need to act and no longer simply *think*. Otherwise Europe would be in danger of no longer participating in, or of losing out to, global competition.

The last example which is of importance for illustrating the recontextualizations and changes in the drafting process is the one paragraph in the section 'Explaining the stakes and refuting the mistakes' where no consensus could be achieved. A footnote in the final version states that 'the three trade union leaders in the CAG are not convinced of the evidence of this assertion on the effects of the labour laws. Future work of the CAG could assess these effects.' Consider the two draft versions D2 and D3 and the final document – D2:

> Contrary to what many people believe, laws protecting existing jobs do not serve job creation. They deter entrepreneurs from hiring, out of fear of not being allowed, in case of need, to reduce their staff. This is in particular the case with SMEs, while they are the main potential source for job creation. Such laws, as they are now in force in many member states, undermine the innovation and adaptation capacity of firms and eventually trap in doomed companies the workers they intend to protect.

After the October meeting and due to the debate there, this paragraph changed to the following in D3:

> Contrary to popular belief, laws to protect jobs do not serve job creation. They deter entrepreneurs from hiring, out of fear of not being allowed to reduce their staff if necessary. This is particularly true of smaller enterprises, even though they are the main potential for job creation. The laws in force in many Member States undermine innovation and the capacity of firms to adapt. They eventually trap the workers they intend to protect in doomed countries.

Finally, the version presented to the European Council contains the following paragraph:

> Contrary to the belief of many people, laws to protect existing jobs do not enhance job creation. They serve worthwhile purposes of human dignity and increase the motivation for investing in human capital. But they often deter entrepreneurs from hiring, out of fear of not being allowed to reduce their staff if necessary. This is particularly true of smaller enterprises, even though they are the main potential for job creation. When laws hamper firms' capacity to innovate and adapt, they eventually trap the workers they intend to protect in doomed companies.

The whole section about 'Explaining the stakes and refuting the mistakes' first contains six points and then seven in the final version. They are all constructed in a similar way, introduced by the same clause or nominal group which is a rhetorical device. In the first draft, we find 'contrary to what many people believe' which is then changed to 'contrary to popular belief' and finally expressed as 'contrary to the belief of many people'. A verbal process of sensing is first recontextualized to a more static noun and relates to the more material language of administration (see Iedema 1999). Through this introductory remark, a distinction is made between *us* and *them*, the experts and the lay-persons. Throughout the whole paper, the laypersons are constructed as believers and irrational, while the experts are the thinkers and rational. As the whole policy paper is formulated as argumentative text, this section is of great importance in the argumentative chain: by refuting 'mistakes' which are all due to state intervention and the existing labour laws, the we-group presents itself as knowledgeable, willing to change structural aspects of European economy and above common-sense arguments and lays the ground for the following section of recommendations which do not have to be justified anymore. Their legitimation is given through the juxtaposition to the enumerated mistakes. The quoted paragraph is the only one where no consensus could be achieved; in all the other issues even the leaders of the trade unions agreed that structural changes at labour markets are necessary.

Who are the 'many people'? They stay anonymous and could mean European citizens, non-experts or also experts of different opinion. 'Popular belief' is even stronger, and clearly labels the non-experts, the public opinion which is not informed or misinformed. The compromise of recontextualization in the final version mitigates 'popular belief'; 'many' indicates that not *all people* are meant. Already this recontextualization of the they-group illustrates the discussion in the meeting and the debates which occurred. The mitigation in the final version demonstrates that administrative language is not the aim and that the strategy of positive self-presentation and negative other-presentation is formulated in a more indirect way.

As mentioned above, this paragraph is one of the most interesting ones of the whole policy paper. It symbolizes the conflict between the unions and the employers explicitly because the delegates of the unions insisted that a footnote be added to the final version expressing their opposing position. Thus the paper does manifest a consensus in the CAG, but only after numerous faxes were exchanged to compromise on this paragraph and the footnote. The conflict underlying the whole paper between welfare state and market economy, between the believers in social cohesion and those in favour of efficiency and globalization, is symbolically manifested in this one paragraph where no consensus in the wording could be achieved. When we interviewed Paye he expressed the opinion that the footnote was a symbolic gesture. The trade unions gave in on many points to save their face. But there had to be at least some opposing opinion in the paper. In his words 'a sacred cow had to be slaughtered'.

Conclusion

In this outline analysis we have only been able to draw attention to a few features of a linguistic nature that characterize decision-making processes in an EU committee on economic and employment policy. Business-speak, location-publicity, globalization rhetoric and efficiency determine the entire procedure. In total, detailed analysis of the discourse shows four contradictory tendencies in the recontextualization that accompanies the process of text creation. These may be explained with reference to the interaction and to the negotiations and compromises that took place during the meetings:

Statics versus dynamics
Simplicity versus complexity
Preciseness versus vagueness
Argumentation versus declaration and generalizing assertions.

This means that recontextualization depends to a significant extent on the semiosis of the meetings (Wodak 1999; Iedema 1999). In the transformation from oral to written, and from dialogue to monologue, contradictions and violations occur that are the linguistic manifestation of the interaction. Every document therefore ultimately represents an interactional structure that may be made transparent by means of precise linguistic analysis. The analysis that was conducted illuminates the decision-making process which we, as outsiders, never witness. We are more usually confronted with decisions imposed 'from above'. It was not by chance that we chose our particular examples from the wealth of available material. They provide the key to the theoretical considerations behind the notions of globalization, competitiveness and liberalization. Globalization rhetoric, with its priorities of competition and flexibility, provides the framework within which a new European political system and identity should be constructed. The questioning of this framework – by the trade unions – is stopped with reference to economic 'necessities', or else it is reduced to the level of a footnote. Simultaneously the hopes and fears of the 'people' are consigned to the realm of the irrational that must be kept in check by the sober rationality of experts. The conflict between different social groups and needs (i.e. the basic alignment of social partnership or consensus politics) is detached from what it really is – a conflict of power and interests – and concealed behind the distinction between economic sense and nonsense. What is totally lost from view is that politics, even 'new' European politics, is about power and distribution, and that a common *political* union can only become a social union capable of survival if it provides democratic and representative tools to regulate these conflicts. Economism may be appropriate as a way of formulating the law of supply and demand. But it conceals the socio-political 'laws' of power and dominance to the extent to which it applies them to separate winners from losers. No democratic society can survive if it empowers an army of losers.

All of this should not be taken to mean that at the end of the twentieth century new economic demands cannot be overpowered, but that these demands are more than ever also social demands. The task of politics is to ensure that the latter are not pushed out by the former, and particularly in times of economic and social change. Politics is the more responsible in that the contemporary economic situation did not come about in some metaphysically inexplicable way but is to a considerable extent the result of earlier political decisions. Undoubtedly the social state must redefine itself and it must do this against the background of the shift of sovereignty from the nation state to supra-national institutions. And undoubtedly this redefinition will become the cornerstone of a 'new' European identity. At the same time it is clear a new identity in a unified Europe will find no acceptance among its citizens if it sacrifices its 'social appeal' in favour of competition and flexibility. The 'Europe for Citizens' proclaimed by the EU would then be finally exposed as a hypocritical slogan. Then the EU would indeed remain in a 'state of uncertainty', resembling more and more a political fear of death (agony). Against this prospect there is the possibility of a politically competent union in which neither particular national interests nor (certainly necessary) structural renewal of markets can cripple the common project. From a linguistic point of view, however, the 'social appeal' would then have to move back from the footnote into the main text.

References

Bach, M. (1999), *Die Bürokratisierung Europas. Verwaltungseliten, Experten und politische Legitimation in Europa*, Frankfurt a. M./New York: Campus.

Barber, B.R. (1995), *Jihad versus McWorld. How Globalism and Tribalism Are Reshaping the World*, New York: Ballantine.

Beck, U. (1998), 'Wie wird Demokratie im Zeitalter der Globalisierung möglich? Eine Einleitung', in U. Beck (ed.), *Politik der Globalisierung*, Frankfurt a. M.: Suhrkamp.

Bernstein, B. (1990), *The Structure of Pedagogic Discourse: Class, Codes and Control*, Vol VI, London: Routledge.

Born, J. (1999), 'Multilingualism and Power: Vagueness as a Strategy. Text-Constituting Principles in Supra-national Organizations', in R. Wodak and Ch. Ludwig (eds), *Challenges in a Changing World. Issues in Critical Discourse Analysis*, Wien: Passagen Verlag.

Bourdieu, P. (1997), *Der Tote packt den Lebenden*. Schriften zu Politik & Kultur 2, Hamburg: VSA.

—— (1998), *Gegenfeuer. Wortmeldungen im Dienste des Widerstands gegen die neoliberale Invasion*, Konstanz: Universitätsverlag.

Clark, I. (1997), *Globalization and Fragmentarization. International Relations in the Twentieth Century*, New York: Oxford University Press.

Eatwell, J. (1994), 'The Coordination of Macroeconomic Policy in the European Community', in J. Michie and J. Grieve Smith (eds), *Unemployment in Europe*, London: Academic Press.

Giddens, A. (1997), *Jenseits von Links und Rechts. Die Zukunft radikaler Demokratie*, Frankfurt a. M.: Suhrkamp.

Halliday, M.A.K. (1994), *An Introduction to Functional Grammar* (2nd ed). London: Edward Arnold.

Hirst, P. and Thompson, G. (1996), *Globalization in Question. The International Economy and the Possibilities of Governance*, Cambridge: Polity Press.

Huffschmid, J. (1997) 'Globalisierung – das Ende von Wirtschaftspolitik', in BEIGEWUM (ed.), *Wege zu einem anderen Europa*, Köln: Papyrossa.

Iedema, R. (1999), 'Formalizing Organisational Meaning', in *Discourse and Society*, Vol 10, No.1, 49–66.

Jeismann, M. (1997), 'Tischlein deck dich. Neue politische Gesellschaftsliteratur in Frankreich', *Merkur. Deutsche Zeitschrift für europäisches Denken*, Sept/Oct: 929–35.

Koch, C. (1997), 'Im Diesseits des Kapitalismus', *Merkur. Deutsche Zeitschrift für europäisches Denken*, Sept/Oct 1997: 763–77.

Krugman, P. (1994); *Peddling Prosperity. Economic Sense and Nonsense in the Age of Diminished Expectations*, New York: Norton.

Luhmann, N. (1996), *Organisation und Entscheidung*. Bielefeld: Unpublished Manuscript.

Martin, H.-P. and Schuman, H. (1996*), Die Globalisierungsfalle. Der Angriff auf Demokratie und Wohlstand*, Reinbeck: Rowohlt.

Michie, J. (1994), 'Introduction', in J. Michie and J. Grieve Smith (eds), *Unemployment in Europe*, London: Academic Press.

Müller, H.-P. (1997), 'Spiel ohne Grenzen?', *Merkur. Deutsche Zeitschrift für europäisches Denken*, Sept/Oct: 805–20.

Mumby, D.K. (1988), *Communication and Power in Organizations: Discourse, Ideology and Domination*, Norwood: Ablex.

Radermacher, F.J. (1997), 'Zukunft der Arbeit', *Merkur. Zeitschrift für europäisches Denken*, Sept/Oct, 829–43.

Schubert, A. (1998), *Der Euro. Die Krise einer Chance*, Frankfurt a. M.: Suhrkamp.

Sennett, R. (1998), *Der flexible Mensch. Die Kultur des neuen Kapitalismus*, Berlin: Berlin Verlag.

Thompson, G. (1996), *Introducing Functional Grammar*, London: Edward Arnold.

Thureau-Dangin, Ph. (1995), *La Concurrence et la Mort*, Paris: Syros.

Thurow, L. (1996), *The Future of Capitalism. How Today's Economic Forces Shape Tomorrow's World*, New York: Penguin.

Wodak, R. (1996), *Disorders of Discourse*, London and New York: Longman.

Wodak, R. (1999), *Decisionmaking in Organizations: Recontextualization as Transformation of Meanings* (forthcoming).

Wodak, R. and De Cillia, R. (eds) (1995), *Sprachenpolitik in Europe*, Vienna: Passagen Verlag.

Wodak, R. and Corson, D. (eds) (1998), *Language Policy and Political Issues in Education*, Den Haag: Kluwer.

–5–

Surrogate Discourses of Power: The European Union and the Problem of Society
Douglas R. Holmes

If one reads the major treaties that have served as the constitutional instruments guiding European integration a very challenging picture emerges.[1] The Schuman Plan, the Treaty of Rome, the Single European Act, and the Maastricht Treaty each address the issue of an 'ever closer union' in highly pragmatic, though often circumspect, terms. Indeed, the scholarship by political scientists, international relations theorists, and political economists that addresses the structural and developmental character of European integration provides a convincing framing of this process. The 'uniting of Europe' has been defined by the classic work of David Mitrany, Ernst Haas, Leon Lindberg, Joseph Nye, Paul Taylor, Robert Keohane and Stanley Hoffman, who elegantly theorize the internal dynamics, the 'invisible' hand, of integration, and the intricate 'prerequisites' and 'spillovers' that punctuate each stage of the process. They have also shaped the debate on the specific outcomes of the transference of governmental competencies and powers from member states to the institutions of the European Union (EU) in terms of 'inter-governmental' versus 'supranational' processes.[2] What these approaches have in common is their emphasis on evolving economic interests that have emerged in the last half of the twentieth century as the driving force for integration (Moravcsik 1998: 18–85). What they tend to overlook is the abiding social character of the European project, its deep preoccupation with society. It is this dimension of the project that lends itself to wide-ranging ethnographic analysis. Put simply, an ethnographic perspective on advanced European integration can and must link the study of the EU to a wider consideration of European society.

The approach I developed to begin to address this ethnographic imperative focused not on the abstract modelling of the structural forces that impel European integration, but on two distinct questions: first, how is the EU, as an embryonic polity, spliced to European society? And second, what kind of social order does the project of advanced European integration engender? Pursuing these questions led me to examine what I call 'surrogate discourses of power', which are neither official doctrines nor policies of the EU, that have, nonetheless, defined its organizational makeup and its technocratic practice and, most centrally, its wider societal premises. These two discourses – French Social Modernism and Catholic Social Doctrine – defined a science, political economy, and metaphysics of solidarity that have established a very specific social architecture for the European project.

I first developed this approach while doing fieldwork at the European Parliament in the early and mid-1990s, during the period when the Maastricht Treaty was being drafted and implemented. I interviewed scores of elected Members of the European Parliament (MEPs) including the leaders of all the political groups represented in the Parliament. I sought to capture the ways in which they, as *participants*, endowed European integration with political meaning. The Parliament represented a context from which one can pursue a variety of ethnographic questions including the daily routines of its personnel, the organization and activities of its political parties, the operation of its committees and delegations, and the nature of the relationships between the Parliament and other institutions of the EU. However, from the outset I was interested in different issues. In many respects this task was made easier by the publication by Marc Abélès of *La vie quotidienne au Parlement Européen* (1992). His ethnographic study covers precisely those domains of the Parliament's internal organization and activity that allowed me to pursue alternative issues. The questions I focused on could be studied from within the Parliament, but were, in fact, largely independent of it. In other words, I was far more interested in how transformations unfolding across Europe were expressed within the European Parliament, than in the Parliament per se. Again, this raised fundamental questions of how the European project was spliced to European society.

Broaching these issues revealed a striking contradiction; the EU project is predicated on a broad-based societal theory blending a complex moral vision and technocratic practice, yet lacks virtually any formal constitutional theory of its own. François Duchêne is emphatic about this haphazard historical character, whereby the power of the EU appears to operate through fragmented and partial arrangements:

> [T]he European Communities were steps to a federation that might have to operate indefinitely in intermediate zones. It was federal minimalism confined to certain economic areas. New instruments and ideas had to be devised for dealing with such a partial condition of life. The creators of the Community were surprisingly ignorant of, and indifferent to, historical precedent. The system corresponds closely to no previous constitutional norm. (Duchêne 1995: 407)

Tony Judt is more forceful, positing a vacuous fanaticism at the heart of the project.

[T]he history of the formation of an 'ever-closer union' has followed a consistent pattern: the real or apparent logic of mutual economic advantage not sufficing to account for the complexity of its formal arrangements, there has been invoked a sort of ontological ethic of political community; projected backward, the latter is then adduced to account for the gains made thus far and to justify further unificatory efforts. It is hard to resist recalling George Santayana's definition of fanaticism: redoubling your efforts when you have forgotten your aim. (1996: 23–4)

My interviews with senior political leaders began to demonstrate how this apparent discrepancy between theory and practice is resolved. As suggested above, there are in fact two surrogate discourses of power, that are entirely independent of the EU, yet have imparted a moral framework, organizational theory, and technocratic practice to the construction of this federal polity. Catholic social doctrine and French social modernism serve as the symbolic frameworks that have sustained this wide-ranging political development. Both permit the conceptualization of a highly contingent political program based on the pursuit of a comprehensive agenda of solidarity. Again, they are both conceptual approaches which are intimately involved in the development of European federalism and yet are independent of it.

Paul Rabinow has examined the remarkable lineage of the type of administrative engineering at the heart of French social modernism as it developed between 1832 and 1939. Since the 1950s, what Rabinow terms 'middling modernism' has been superimposed on Europe. '[T]he . . . focus is not on "high culture" nor the practices of everyday life, but on a middle ground where social technicians were articulating a normative, or middling modernism. In their discourses, society became its own referent, to be worked on by means of technical procedures which were becoming the authoritative arbiters of what counted as socially real' (Rabinow 1989: 13). Jean Monnet and, more recently, Jacque Delors were the pre-eminent carriers of the tradition of French modernist planning and practice from Paris to Brussels (Duchêne 1995; Ross 1995).

The project of French social modernism, as it took form in the last two decades of the nineteenth century, was centrally about conceptualizing society as a field of human interdependence susceptible to planning and administration through the application of 'scientific' norms and principles. With roots in de Tocqueville, Le Play, Proudhon, and Durkheim a highly pragmatic socialism coalesced in France as a 'school of solidarity' (Rabinow 1989: 182). This peculiar configuration of 'socialism' was impelled not by a revolutionary elite, but by a cadre of social technicians — middling modernists — who through their administrative interventions sought to arbitrate a distinctive social order. The subject of their interventions encompassed infrastructures of industry, public services, and social welfare. What these theorists and planners devised was a comprehensive technocratic politics of a modern industrial society which circumvented what they saw as disabling clashes between the ideologies of left and right. In other words, they sought a degree of independence from the give and take of parliamentary politics, and thereby from democratic accountabilities. The elite technocratic practice of the EU draws directly on the legacy of middling modernism for its method of 'convergent action,' which has come to serve as the paradigm for institutional decision-making. [3]

Social Catholicism, with its roots also in the emergence of industrial societies of the late nineteenth century, has imparted to the EU not just a metaphysics of solidarity but a model of federalism. The ecology of power is difficult to schematize in an evolving polity like the EU. It spreads over institutional competencies, the boundaries of which are ill-defined; it resides in executive bureaus which translate abstract legislative formulas into administrative practice; and it adheres to the informal agreements and understandings that co-ordinate political contests. 'Subsidiarity', a pivotal concept in Catholic social doctrine, serves as a central axis in the struggle over the definition and the disposition of power. The effort to define subsidiarity discloses not merely a single concept but a range of concepts and formulations that constitute a comprehensive societal theory.[4] Subsidiarity denotes a means for circumscribing domains of action for public authorities, establishing formulas for allocating governmental powers, defining norms of societal stewardship, and the conditions of individual freedom.

Virtually all my interlocutors deferred to Jacques Delors, then President of the European Commission (1985–94), when it came to the philosophical and practical tasks of synthesizing these two traditions. There is no doubt that he was the person most responsible for guiding the actual construction of the EU. It was Delors and a close cadre of associates working at the Commission who played a direct role translating basic tenets of Catholic social doctrine and French social modernism into the text of the Maastricht Treaty on European Union (Bellier 1994). Delors is generally portrayed as the transcendent 'Eurocrat'. Like Jean Monnet he carries the technocratic tradition of French socialist modernism from Paris to Brussels (Ross 1995). But he is more. In the early 1990s there was no one within the European Community (EC) who had a more subtle and far-reaching understanding of Catholic social teaching than Delors (see Delors 1989, 1991). I asked Leo Tindemans, a highly respected Christian Democrat, why Delors, a French Socialist, was such a passionate champion of 'subsidiarity,' the key principle of the Catholic discourse on political power and social justice. Tindemans pointed out the crucial importance of Delors' formative experience in the 1950s and 1960s when he had been deeply involved in the modernization of the Catholic labour movement in France.

Delors played a central role within the 'reconstruction group' of the *Confédération Française des Travailleurs Chrétiens* which became *Confédération Française et Démocratique du Travail* (Ross 1995: 17). While engaged in that endeavour

Delors developed a thorough understanding of Social Catholicism, particularly the theory of 'personalism' as interpreted by Emmanuel Mounier. From Mounier, Delors derived a distinctive sociological perspective:

> Society according to Mounier, could not be reduced to a market writ large or a utilitarian agglutination of isolated individuals . . . Society grew from delicate interdependence in which different social groups owed one another active solidarity . . . The state and politics had a role, but in facilitating, rather than substituting for, the active agency of groups and moralized individuals working together. Delors was thus not immersed in, and did not emerge from France's secular Left tradition, whether socialist or communist. (Ross 1995: 17)

Delors, in fact, only became a member of the *Parti Socialiste* in 1974 during the party's reconstruction under François Mitterrand, when he served as Mitterrand's Minister of Finance before his appointment to the European Commission (Ross 1995: 253 n. 9). Thus, in the person of Jacques Delors, the two traditions of Social Catholicism and French social modernism intersected, and through his leadership both were brought to bear fundamentally on the construction of the EU.

In the following sections I briefly summarize the traditions of French social modernism and Social Catholicism in terms of the distinctive social and cultural dynamics they have conferred on the EU. These two traditions are consummate discourses on society that can open the political project of the EU to various forms of ethnographic analysis and critical scrutiny.

Middling Modernists

The project of French social modernism was centrally concerned with the conceptualization of society as a field of human interdependence susceptible to planning and administration through the application of 'scientific' principles. Paul Rabinow has examined the remarkable history of this type of administrative engineering as it took shape in France between 1832 and 1939. For the very foreshortened summary that follows, however, I have selected three figures as distinctively illustrative of this technocratic tradition: Henri Sellier (1883–1943), Etienne Clémentel (1864–1932), and Jean Monnet (1888–1979).

Rabinow locates the basic conceptual innovation that opened the way for this modern political engagement with society in the activity of a group of reformers who sought to reorient the project of the French state around 'the social question'. They viewed the fundamental problem of societal integration in the face of widening material inequalities between classes as the pivotal challenge for the state. To address this social question the leaders of the movement formulated a broad-based project of interdependency that spanned the centre of the political spectrum. Their interventions initiated a major shift in the regulatory regimes of French society. 'Just as these groups were arguing that society, and not the individual, constituted the *real*, so too the state (along with new social sciences) was beginning to replace both the church and industry as regulator of social relations' (1989: 169–70).

This ambitious political movement was led by social theorists and planners who devised the comprehensive technocratic politics of a modern industrial society. The subject of their interventions encompassed a broad field covering infra-structures of industry, transportation, public works and social welfare. Rabinow sees major elements of this development personified by Henri Sellier, socialist politician, Minister of Public Health, and a major figure in French urban planning.

> The norms guiding Sellier's emerging socialist modernism were the welfare of the population, the maximizing of individual potential, and the linkage of these two engineered by an efficient administration manned by committed specialists dedicated to the public good . . . [He] conceived of the problem in terms of mobilizing political support for this flexible, new administrative structure – based on statistical projections and abstract social unities – while retaining traditional political accountabilities and social bonds. While explicitly concerned with social justice, Sellier sought to move beyond right/left political distinctions as well as traditional class divisions. (1989: 320)

Out of the work of a group of highly pragmatic socialists like Sellier, a move-ment emerged with cadres of social technicians – middling modernists – at its centre, who, through their analyses and administrative interventions, sought to arbitrate a distinctive social order, through a 'science of solidarity'. What gave the movement vibrancy was a spirit of 'experimentation', its legitimacy derived from a thorough engagement with the nuance of the contemporary political and cultural 'milieu'.

A crucial change began to ensue at the turn of the nineteenth century as the field of administrative planning shifted from the highly differentiated 'historico-natural milieu' to an 'anonymous space of regulation and rationalization'. In other words, the laboratory of social intervention for middling modernists was no longer *la cité* – a public space of politics – but increasingly an administrative abstraction, a 'socio-technical' *agglomération*.

> While Sellier clung to history and locale as sources of legitimacy and solidarity, his younger assistants and successors were more relentless, gradually stripping away such architectural, historical, and social references in the name of efficiency, science, progress, and welfare: middling modernism. (Rabinow 1989: 322)

This move disenthralled socialist modernism from an engagement with the social and cultural specificity of the small towns, the urban districts, and the regions of France and allowed its principles and practices to be universalized.

Etienne Clémentel (1864–1932), as Minister of Commerce (1915–20), established a program of state-directed management of the French economy by a small group of what Rabinow calls 'unbureaucratic bureaucrats' (1989: 326). The First World War was a profound catalyst for this transmutation. Clémentel's power during the War was vast, spanning control of industry, trade, transportation, supply, and postal services. He was the real organizer of the French war effort and Jean Monnet, still in his twenties, became his *directeur de cabinet*.

> Clémentel was an ardent advocate of increasing the role of bureaucratic technicians in order to rationalize the economy. He planned a considerable expansion of the research and information components of the Ministry and enforced compliance on the part of reluctant industrialists through his control over the allocation of resources. Clémentel proposed the annual publication of production statistics, the creation of a prices board to determine normal prices through the expert assessment by bureaucrats of production costs, and the establishment of an industrial council, which was to be a state-supervised alliance of industry and science to ensure that French industry would remain in the vanguard of modern technological advance. (Rabinow 1989: 325–6)

In fact, Clémentel's work went much further in the direction of an international regime of planning and co-ordination broaching a new dimension of the 'science of solidarity'. He and Monnet were confronted at the outbreak of the War with the intrinsic limitations of economic management under the domination of competing nation states. In response they organized an integrated supranational system of co-operation among the Allies that managed with great efficiency wartime allocations of food and transport (Monnet 1978: 53–77). They constructed a remarkable arrangement to handle the distribution of vast resources among France, Italy and Britain under the co-operative control of a tiny coterie of managers.

It is no surprise that with peace Clémentel and Monnet advocated an extension of their planning regime for the reconstruction of Europe. The United States refused to support the Clémentel Plan, insisting on free-market arrangements, and leaving Clémentel to lament: 'That's the end of the solidarity we worked so hard for. Without it, and without the altruistic, disinterested co-operation that we tried to achieve among the Allies and should have extended to our former enemies, one day we'll have to begin all over again' (quoted in Monnet 1978: 75). Monnet, however, continued to struggle for a few more years with the technical operation of another ill-fated supranationalism. As deputy to the Secretary General of the League of Nations, he helped to prevent the partitioning of Austria while witnessing the dismal struggles over Upper Silesia, the Saar, and German reparations. Monnet's experience at the League confirmed the conviction expressed earlier by Clémentel, that peace in Europe based on national sovereignty was impossible (Monnet 1978: 84). He left the Secretariat in 1921 and returned to his family's ailing Cognac business.

By 1938 Monnet was already intimately involved in the preparation for war and for the duration of the Second World War he filled a series of important posts in London and Washington. Much of his work in exile focused, as it had during the First World War, on the management of high-level military supply and co-ordination among the Allies (Nathan 1991). A quote attributed to John Maynard Keynes credits Monnet's labours with shortening the Second World War by a year (Mayne 1991: 114–28). Monnet's logistical activities were punctuated in 1943 with eight months in Algeria during which he participated in the founding of a de facto French government under the *Comité Français de Libération Nationale* (CFLN) that quickly came under the control of Charles de Gaulle (Monnet 1978: 150–211).

A Method

Monnet returned in 1946 to formulate what was to become the penultimate expression of the French social modernist project: the French Plan – also known as the Monnet Plan – for the reconstruction of post-war France (Bloch-Lainé and Bouview 1986; Mioche 1985). Monnet and his close advisors laid out a 'philosophy' and 'method' for the Plan with technical management of the economy at its centre, though its modernist aims went much further: 'To transform France, we must first transform the French Establishment' (Monnet 1978: 245).[5] The Plan reiterated a familiar litany of the science of solidarity, however it also advanced a logic of power increasingly under the sway of a technocratic universalism, that prepared the way for French social modernism to assume a European scope.

Monnet self-consciously laid out what he conceived of as a 'democratic method', one which was intended to subvert ideological differences and promote what he referred to as 'participationism'. The Plan 'is essentially a method of convergent action and a means whereby everyone can relate his own efforts to those of every-one else. It is concerned as much with orientation as with control' (1978: 258). The first French Plan (1947–52) was well suited to bringing to bear the practices of middling modernism on the political economy of post-war France.

Time was propitious for experiments in collective effort: the patriotic impulses released by the Liberation were still powerful, and they had not yet found an adequate outlet. The nationalization of various industries, long awaited and recently achieved, was no longer a goal, but a vehicle for making collective progress in ways that now only had to be defined. Everyone felt that progress was possible, but no one knew precisely what to do. In this situation, the Plan could be a genuinely 'national enterprise' – an expression that could at last take on practical meaning. (Monnet 1978: 239)

This new stage of the social-modernist project was accompanied by a shift in rhetoric substituting contingent notions of 'interdependence', 'participation', and 'convergence' for the monolithic ideal of 'solidarity.' An open-ended 'method' was formalized as modernist planning was superseded by more routinized technocratic practice. The persuasive power of the method would render political pressure or coercion unnecessary. Monnet quotes himself describing to his associates how convergence would take hold: 'When you take people from different backgrounds, put them in front of the same problem, and ask them to solve it, they're no longer the same people. They're no longer there to defend their separate interests, and so they automatically take a common view. You'll see: the Plan will work without imposing anything on anyone'(1978: 248). This 'empirical attitude' and faith in progressivism was unassailable. 'The Plan, like life, is a continuous creation' (1978: 259). 'Once it [the Plan] was set in motion, its own impetus would create the internal and external conditions that were essential to its success' (1978: 254).

Two institutions, the Council and the Commission, were at the centre of the Plan. Both institutions, with only modest changes, were ensconced as the core structures of the EC in 1967. The Planning Council, which was the supreme political body, was headed by the Prime Minister, and composed of twelve government ministers and twelve public figures chosen for their special expertise (Monnet 1978: 240). The role of the Council was to direct and oversee the wide-ranging activities of the Planning Commission. Monnet described the Planning Commissioner's remarkable role – which he both created and filled – and its sweeping administrative powers: 'He was to be the Head of Government's permanent delegate to all Ministerial departments; he was given extensive powers of inquiry, and the Commissariat which he headed was empowered to enlist help from the staff of all Ministries and in particular from the statistical institutes' (1978: 240). In this remarkable manoeuvre Monnet established his newly created position in the Prime Minister's office but independent of the bureaucratic structure of the ministries. His shrewd insistence on ambiguous accountability for the Planning Commissioner created a radical basis of power which he subsequently superimposed on the organizational structure of the European project.

> Traditionalists would have placed the Commissariat under one of the economic Ministries, and the whole weight of civil service tradition tried to drag it back into this state subordination every time there was a Cabinet change . . . No Ministerial post would have offered as much scope as the indefinable position of Planning Commissioner, attached to the Prime Minister's office. I was taking no one's place and becoming no one's superior. I was moving into territory that had hitherto had neither occupant nor name. (Monnet 1978: 240–1)

As Commissioner, he defined the role of the paramount *technocrat* with enormous latitude for intervention, wide-ranging spheres of authority, and an overriding set of political aims and goals. He 'invented' a tightly designed institutional structure, independent of direct ministerial jurisdiction and bureaucratic scrutiny, yet capable of influencing, if not compelling, change focused directly on the power elite of France. Above all, his institutional innovations recast the full domain of political economy as a field of 'convergent action' under sway of technocratic surveillance. It was a deceptively simple and profoundly subversive formula.

Key to the method that Monnet established as first Planning Commissioner was a broad definition of societal problems that brought together what might otherwise be considered opposed parties and incompatible interests. It was implacably anti-bureaucratic, an approach supremely adroit at circumventing conventional divisions of power and patterns of authority. In a sense this is what made the approach pre-eminently middling modernist, since it could circumvent the traditional apparatus of French power and decision-making. Monnet had created in the spirit of French social modernism, an entirely new framework for the conceptualization of issues, the formation of broad and unlikely alliances, and the delineation of unprecedented possibilities for intervention.

> We had to ensure that everything – the most pressing needs and the most distant ambitions – obeyed the rule we had set ourselves: always start with an overall view. The experts who brought us their statistics, the industrialists with their dossiers, the trade unionists with their programs – all went away with extracts from our 'Treatise on Method.' We wanted them to digest it first and come back later, when we had established the framework within which we could all confer. Nor did it merely have to be established: it had to be invented. (Monnet 1978: 236–7)

He proudly notes: 'there were never more than thirty senior officials on the Planning Commissariat, and the whole staff, including secretaries and doormen, was no more than a hundred or so' (1978: 241). This spirit of economy and circumspection was reflected even in the style of communication favoured by his associates in the Planning Commissariat: 'short sentences, numbered paragraphs marking the transition from one idea to the next without clumsy bridging passages, a limited number of concrete words, and few adjectives' (1978: 243).

In the wake of the Schuman Plan and subsequent treaties, Monnet and his associates transplanted virtually all the major traditions of French socialist modernism, with a few refinements from the *agglomération* of the French nation state, to evolving *l'espace* of a federal Europe. The European Commission and the European Council, counterparts to the Planning Commission and Planning Council under the French Plan, became the dominant executive and legislative institutions respectively of the Community, and now of the Union. The European

Parliament's role was minor, as a consultative body that conferred democratic legitimacy on the project's actions. Only after the adoption of the Maastricht and Amsterdam Treaties has the Parliament assumed significant powers of its own and, more importantly, forced public debate on what is euphemistically called 'the democratic deficit'. Over the last half century the legacy of middling modernism has become deeply ingrained in the fabric of the very lean institutional structures and practices of Europe. By the late 1990s there were fewer than 20,000 Eurocrats practicing the method and 'austere art' of convergent action to deal with the daunting complexities of an expanding polity stretching over fifteen member states. And, in the waning days of the century, these European middling modernists ponder a daring enlargement of their project deep into East Central Europe to include perhaps ten or more new member states under the jurisdiction of their technocratic universalism.

Sacred Modern

The founders of the EU shared a common political philosophy and personal experience. 'Robert Schuman, Konrad Adenauer, and Alcide de Gaspari, were three exemplary Catholics, three men who had lived near foreign borders and were themselves of divided nationality'(Bromberger and Bromberger 1969: 84). They drew on Christian Democratic principles to delineate a federal architecture for the Community, referred to in its early history wryly as 'Vatican Europe'. Social Catholicism influenced by 'neo-Thomist' writers, most notably Jacques Maritain and Emmanuel Mounier, became a dominant force in the European Movement (see Amato 1975; Hellman 1981; Maritain 1950; Power 1992). Their philosophy and political economy promoted a durable and wide-ranging politics oriented towards discriminating a 'common good' upon which a broad societal consensus could be built.[6] This politics, in turn, fostered a style of political analysis, a tempo for institution building, and an ethical grounding for EU action.

Social Catholicism, like French social modernism, has its roots in the emergence of industrial societies in the late nineteenth century. It addressed, however, the 'social question' in a radically different way. Rather than pursuing technocratic interventionism, the Catholic approach seeks to foster an intricate moral discourse through which conditions of individual autonomy and ties of social interdependence are subject to ongoing analysis and facilitation. Catholic political economy starts from a distinctive conception of the relationship between society and the individual:

> Man is a social person, who achieves his perfection only in society. The state exists to help the persons who live within the society. This is the meaning of the Latin word, subsidium, aid, help. Normally, this aid is indirect by the care of the complex conditions that enable the subordinate [groups] . . . and the individuals to care for their own needs.

This complex of conditions is what has been traditionally called the 'common good'. (Mulcahy 1967: 762)

The Catholic discourse is preoccupied with shifting patterns of interdependence encompassing virtually all groups in society. Its interventions are oriented towards sustaining dynamic bases of solidarity expressed in reciprocating ties of aid and stewardship. The peculiar power of Catholic social doctrine derives, however, as much from its activist outlook as its principled forbearance.

The activist dimension of the Catholic engagement with society is counter-balanced with a notable commitment to restraint. The autonomy and the 'active agency of groups' are to be preserved and protected thus requiring explicit limitations on governmental intervention, particularly as exercised by the state. This endows the Catholic discourse with what appears to be a conservative dynamic that fundamentally distinguishes it from the interventionist premises of French social modernism. To read this Catholic commitment to restraint as conservative, however, is misleading since it may in fact constitute the most radical elements of Catholic political economy. Restraint operates in a paradoxical way in this framework, since by preserving the autonomy of various groups Catholic political practice in effect sustains *diversity*. This commitment to pluralism in turn promotes ongoing societal differentiation and advancement of a 'common good.' Jacques Maritain (1950) formulated this philosophical approach to diversity as follows:

[A] sound application of the pluralist principle and the principle of the lesser evil would require from the State a juridical recognition of the moral codes peculiar to those minorities comprised in the body politic whose rules of morality, though defective in some regard with respect to perfect Christian morality, would prove to be a real asset in the heritage of the nation and its common trend toward good human life. (quoted in Sigmund 1988: 175)

This also accounts for a deep suspicion within the Catholic movement of the unbridled operation of capitalist markets and, in the notable case of Emmanuel Mounier, misgivings about the influence of the liberal democratic state.[7] Both were understood to debase 'moral diversity' and 'spiritual autonomy' through the advance of pervasive materialism and insensate rationalism. The Catholic doctrine that has come to encompass this broad-based commitment to diversity and restraint is known as the principle of *subsidiarity*.[8]

The Catholic discourse opens on to a deep substratum of European social philosophy reaching back to the thirteenth century writings of Thomas Aquinas, particularly his appropriation of Aristotelian philosophy to underpin a form of 'Christian rationalism'. For those who embrace the Catholic social doctrine the EU embodies a series of fundamental political and ethical challenges first delineated by Aquinas in *Summa Theologiae*. They engage the European project in terms of what might be understood as a 'sacred modern' epistemology. What they find in Aquinas, the 'Angelic Doctor' as Pius V described him, is an essential sociology, a means to act within and upon the world. They find a conception of 'civil society' that allows them to pursue disciplined political analyses and interventions, a Christian teleology.

Aquinian philosophy was refined into a modern theory of social justice through a series of well-known papal encyclicals beginning with Leo XIII's *Rerum novarum* (1891), which sets out the basic tenets of Catholic social doctrine. Pius XI's encyclical, *Quadregesimo anno* (1931), reviewed the development of Catholic social teaching in the forty years after *Rerum novarum*, and this was further elaborated upon by John XXIII's *Mater et Magistra* (1961) and *Pacem in terris* (1963). What the neo-Thomists – above all Jacques Maritain – added to this tradition of Catholic social teaching is a democratic legitimacy and practice which became the foundation of the Christian Democratic political movement in Europe. Again, the term subsidiarity has come to designate the philosophical and socio-logical architecture of this sacred modern tradition around which many of those who are designing the EU align their intentions and articulate their visions.

By the 1990s subsidiarity had become a central defining concept in the broad-based political debate on European integration; it came to serve as a pivotal idea not just for those preoccupied with the Christian Democratic political economy.[9] The centrality of the concept was based on its suitability to serve as an axis in the struggle over the definition and the disposition of power within an emerging federal polity. The effort to define subsidiarity as a political instrument discloses not merely a single concept but a range of concepts and formulations, centrally concerned with sustaining diversity. Specifically, it serves as a principle for circumscribing domains of action for public authorities, for establishing formulas for allocating governmental powers, for defining norms of societal stewardship, and for setting the conditions of individual freedom. Most crucial, however, is the application of subsidiarity to the basic question of federalism, that is, what powers are to be retained by member states, regions, and localities and what powers shifted to the EU by virtue of integration? In other words, subsidiarity has been employed to mediate a debate on issues of 'sovereignty'. In this section I have very briefly summarized how elements of Catholic social teaching have come to operate as a surrogate grounding of European federalism. I will suggest that the authority of Social Catholicism to serve as the second surrogate discourse of European federalism derives from its potential to sustain simultaneously 'pluralism' and 'solidarity' as principles guiding the creation of a distinctive social order and not just an integrated market or, for that matter, a technocratic polity.

Political Consensus

There are many ways to depict how the foundational principles of Catholic social theory made their way from papal encyclicals to the Maastricht Treaty on European Union. For the purposes of this analysis, I will sketch briefly the manner in which concepts central to Catholic social doctrine have become ingrained in the political discourse of the European Parliament. Leo Tindemans, initially in his role as Christian Democratic Prime Minister of Belgium and more recently in his capacity within the Parliament as President of the European People's Party, and the late Altiero Spinelli, an independent member of the Communist and Allies Group within the Parliament, are the principal figures in this abridged account (see Mayne and Pinder 1990). This discussion is important because it helps explain how and why subsidiarity gained currency among political groups that are not generally seen as sympathetic to Catholic political economy.

In 1974, at a time when European integration seemed stalled, Tindemans was a member of the European Council, the senior governing body of the EC composed of heads of government. He was asked by the Council to define what he meant by the term 'European Union', a concept he had been urging them to consider. Tindemans drafted an ambitious and far-reaching document that formally extended the European idea from that of 'Community' to 'Union'. Known as the Tindemans Report, the document argued for a decisive shift from the mere co-ordination of policy to the creation of common policy over a broad range of competencies including economic and monetary policy, defence, foreign relations, social policy, and citizenship.

Economic turmoil and high rates of inflation and unemployment, provoked by the oil crisis in the early 1970s, served as a backdrop to the report. For Tindemans the crisis revealed the classic contradiction between the powers of the EC and its member states. The inability of Community institutions to formulate unified economic and foreign policies to deal with the oil and related crises, yielded a resurgence of 'purely national preoccupations'. He diagnosed the threat to unity not on the level of the Community, where the weaknesses were expressed, but on the level of the member states. 'The fragile nature of Europe must surely be a reflection of the powerlessness of our States' (Tindemans 1977: 5). The retention of national control – largely devoid of power – exposed the political bankruptcy of the member states and thereby, in his view, doomed the development of the Community. He refers to it as the 'two-fold spiral of powerlessness' (Tindemans 1977: 91).

Tindemans' solution was itself in the classic mode, calling for an acceleration of the construction of Europe. By this means Tindemans sought to recapture the pragmatic foundation of the European project. His central argument was that political, economic, social and, perhaps even, cultural problems that seem to be intractable within or between nation states can be redefined when either raised to the European level or devolved to the level of regions or local authorities. The economies and politics of scale achieved by further integration would provide classic efficiencies that would recast the range and scope of institutional remedies. The less dramatic call for decentralization in his report was intended to improve governmental responsiveness, manageability, and democratic accountability. The simultaneous transfer of powers to the Community, regions, and local authorities held the promise of 'a new type of society, a more democratic Europe with a greater sense of solidarity and humanity' (1977: 9). It also constituted a radical assault on the powers of the nation state from above and below.[10]

Tindemans had pulled together recurring themes drawn from visions of a European Union discussed as early as the League of Nations. What was novel about his report was that it drew together various strands of theorizing about Europe into an integrated plan. The transition from 'Community' to 'Union' was presented as a systematic course; the role of Catholic social doctrine was clear but tacit.

The term 'solidarity' is used throughout Tindemans' text, while 'subsidiarity' he acknowledged was implicit. Tindemans interpreted subsidiarity in an interview as follows:

> Subsidiarity is an old principle. You know people now-a-days refer back to Thomas Aquinas, other people say the principle is much older still. I do not know, I am not an historian. But certainly in Thomas you will find it. In Christian social doctrine . . . there are two principles for the organization of society. The principle of subsidiarity on the one hand and the principle of solidarity on the other. Subsidiarity requires that what can be done in a satisfactory way by a lower authority must not be taken over by a higher one. So in the organization of a country, what a village commune is doing well must not be taken over by a province and what a province is doing well must not be taken over by a region, what a region is doing well must not be taken over by the state.

He explained his reluctance to use the term 'subsidiarity' in the report noting that as a student one of his professors cautioned: 'take care with the principle of subsidiarity . . . because reactionary people very often invoke it to justify doing nothing at the higher level'. There is another 'danger' that the concept might pose in the minds of 'reactionary people'. Subsidiarity establishes a social order in which pluralism is an absolutely fundamental condition. Rather than designing a polity, the Catholic doctrine that Tindemans invoked was concerned with creating a societal milieu – or as he refers to it, 'a new type of society' – within which a polity can be conceived and constructed. While the design of the polity is ambiguous, the nature of the society and political economy advanced by the doctrine is more certain. Centralization is appropriate in this framework only where economies of scale or the nature of a social task make it absolutely essential. In general, however, the principle demands the allocation of authority minimally necessary for groups and associations to fulfil their particular societal roles. The federative authority of subsidiarity also upholds domains of ideological pluralism and thereby the protection of minority positions.

> Different 'spiritual families', in a common French phrase – Catholic, Protestant, Marxists, humanists, or whoever they may be – should . . . be permitted and enabled to follow their own way of life, even when they are in a minority in a nation or group as a whole . . . [Ideological pluralism] reduces conflict since it allows everyone, without discrimination . . . to build up a set of associations which fits his own ideals. (Fogarty 1957: 42)

By maintaining diversity of ideological perspectives, the terms of political engagement are also established. And, though it seems counter intuitive, the doctrine holds that it is precisely in the clash of these diverse orientations and their vigorous expression that solidarity is engendered.

Political discourse, under the terms of Catholic social theory, operates in such a way that issues are contextualized constantly within a wider interplay of interests and remedies. It is this concern for the 'totality' that creates a shifting consensus that can embrace, relativize, and transform a broad spectrum of beliefs and interests. It is an approach which is intended to restrain partisanship and frustrate single-issue agendas. The aim is to achieve a 'common good' in which shifting and unequal societal interests are linked through ties of co-operation and mutual aid to achieve social justice. The powerful sociological consequence of the political practice of subsidiarity is the promotion of a diversely constituted 'civil society' and 'social market.'

The Tindemans Report specified a comprehensive plan for European Union and a program of reform necessary to build a federal polity. He reiterated the historical priorities upon which the European project was founded, and he employed a comprehensive political framework to give his plan theoretical and moral integrity. The report itself, however, did not immediately ignite a program of change. What it did accomplish was to set the terms of debate around which a broad-based political consensus could gradually be formed. It took the skill of Altiero Spinelli (1907-86) to demonstrate how this political consensus could be devised within the European Parliament.

Altiero Spinelli, MEP in the early 1980s, was an independent member of the Communist and Allies Group within the Parliament. Earlier he had served on the European Commission. His commitment to European unification was truly distinguished. Spinelli opposed Mussolini in the 1930s and had been imprisoned by the fascist regime on the island of Ventotene where he composed his famous federalist manifesto for a 'United States of Europe' (see Lipgens 1985: 471–92). Four decades later, as *rapporteur* for the Committee on Institutional Affairs, he drafted a report for the Parliament entitled, 'Reform of Treaties and Achievement of European Union' (1982), which became the basis for the 'Draft Treaty establishing European Union'(1984). Both documents followed closely the agenda set out by Tindemans. Notably, Spinelli employed the principle of subsidiarity specifically as a formula for the reallocation of competencies between the Union and member states. Though the concept of 'subsidiarity' had been applied earlier to questions of Community fiscal policy, this marked the first time that the Catholic nomenclature had been employed as a pivotal formula for conceptualizing European federalism (Spinelli 1983: 210). The Draft Treaty, which was passed by the Parliament but never ratified by the member states, specified revisions of treaties to achieve a political union. Its most distinctive thrust was institutional reform that would have enhanced the democratic legitimacy of the Community by expanding the powers of the European Parliament.

By far Spinelli's greatest contribution, however, was his engineering of a broad and enduring coalition committed to union and embracing virtually all the political groups in the Parliament. Indeed, he established political union as the paramount agenda of the Parliament as a whole. Starting from essentially a left-wing position, he traced a rationale for unification that furthered social justice and democratic accountability. Political union would, he argued, create a powerful new framework to achieve democratic control over the economic forces unleashed by the Economic Community. The federal structure – governed by the principle of subsidiarity – would provide the context within which to revitalize European politics in general and those of the European left in particular. Spinelli demonstrated how one could, from the standpoint of all but the most nationalist political parties in the Parliament, make a compelling case for unification. Spinelli's leadership also established the Committee on Institutional Affairs as the focus for theorizing on constitutional issues within the Parliament. Drawing on senior political leaders and constitutional experts, the committee drafted a series of reports during the 1990s that stated the European Parliament's position on the specific architecture of the European Union, an architecture very much in the spirit of Spinelli.

Thus, Catholic social doctrine took root as a surrogate discourse on federalism, through the deliberations of the European Parliament and the activism of the European Commission under Jacques Delors, and it came to define a critical provision of the Maastricht Treaty:

> The Community shall act within the limits of the powers conferred upon it by this Treaty and of the objectives assigned to it therein ... In areas which do not fall within its exclusive competence, the Community shall take action in accordance with the principle of subsidiarity, only if and in so far as the objectives of the proposed action cannot be sufficiently achieved by Member States and can therefore, by reason of the scale or effects of the proposed action, be better achieved by the Community ... Any action by the Community shall not go beyond what is necessary to achieve the objectives of this Treaty. (1992, Treaty on European Union, Article 3b)

Again, the centrality of this constitutional provision rests on its ability to foster a diversely constituted federal union. It permits the integration of a wide range of member states with different political histories, legal traditions, economic systems, bureaucratic structures, taxation policies, trade practices, education institutions, linguistic conventions, and so on. It means such diverse entities as Sweden and Greece or Luxembourg and Britain can operate within an integrated political framework. The constitutional significance of subsidiarity rests on its ability to serve as a counterweight to the forces of 'convergence' and 'harmonization' promoted by the technocratic operation of the EU; as Nicholas Emiliou puts it, as a barrier against 'the enterprises of ambition'. Subsidiarity is specified as a fundamental constitutional principal: 'This Treaty marks a new stage in the process of creating an ever closer union among the peoples of Europe, where decisions are taken as closely as possible to the citizens' (1992, Treaty on European Union, Article A2 & B). For those who fear that unification will subvert the diversities and distinctions of Europe, 'Article 3b' of the treaty stands as the constitutional bulwark for pluralism.

The reallocations of power orchestrated by European integration under the terms of subsidiarity are both profound and enigmatic. Federalists, like Tindemans, are adamant that European integration is not merely about the reallocation of competencies or sovereignty, but about the *creation* of power. This is a classic federalist argument premised on a forceful acknowledgement of the waning power of the European nation states. It holds that governmental jurisdiction exercised over areas such as trade, defence, or environmental policy are limited or negligible when exercised by small states like Belgium. Yet, when these competencies are pooled among fifteen or twenty member states they can acquire enormous power. Though it is clear that a profound reallocation of sovereignty has taken place among the member states of the EU, the actual consequences of these transactions are very difficult to appraise. The reallocation of competencies cannot be understood in terms of the simple transfer of sovereignty, largely because the nature of sovereignty itself changes as a result of the process of integration. A notion of more or less stable and independent public authority exercised by territorially bounded European nation states is increasingly implausible. What can be said is that the circumspect application of subsidiarity, engineered through a modernist technocratic practice, has over the last half century created entirely new, though deeply ambiguous, bases of political and economic authority. It is authority that does not conform to conventional notions of sovereignty rooted in the history of the nation state.

Conclusion

The technocratic practice of French socialist modernism and the mediatory politics of Social Catholicism arose in response to an era of accelerating capitalist development and at the end of the nineteenth century. They were both challenged at the close of the twentieth century by economic forces channelled through the centre of the European project, though appearing to emanate from beyond its jurisdictions. The creation of the single European market and the advance of European monetary union are aligning the EU, albeit fitfully, with the supranational scope and pacing of a fully globalized capitalism, yet the telos of this economic regime targets precisely those instrumentalities of solidarity and consensus that have endowed the EU's project of political union with its raison d'être.

At the opening of the twenty-first century the rhetoric of global competitiveness has replaced that of European modernization. The premise of statist economic planning is being drawn into question by those who seek to reap what are presumed to be dazzling material possibilities of expanding European and global markets. A neo-liberalism, antagonistic to the social order out of which the European social market and welfare state were wrested, is being untethered in the name, ironically, of 'unification'. Its advance – codified by the single market and monetary union – undermines the possibility of a science, political economy, and metaphysics of solidarity as business and political elites avow a new-found faith in the market as the arbiter of the human condition. While political leaders, particularly on the left, embrace the provisions of the Social Chapter of the Maastricht Treaty as an enduring basis of social justice, the economic provisions of the treaty create a very different set of dynamics. Increasing market liberalization threatens precisely the complex architecture of solidarity that has formed the distinctive substructure of modern European society. It is this contradiction that poses what I think is the core struggle facing the EU: the manifold contestation over the nature of European society. This struggle evokes the classic sociological and anthropological problematic: what are the terms and conditions by which the individual is related to various renderings of collectivity in the new Europe?

I have tried to demonstrate in the above analysis the peculiar way the European Project has drawn on fundamental moral, philosophical, and sociological traditions to bind its political and institutional development with society. I have also traced in very preliminary fashion a perspective on the EU that creates a formidable challenge for anthropologists working in Europe. Indeed, it seems to me that the issues of how we scrutinize the EU as a social phenomenon can serve as a defining problem at the centre of the anthropology of Europe. Put most simply, what kind of social order does advanced European integration engender? This is a question that intersects with virtually every theoretical problem pursued by anthropologists working across the new Europe (Wilson and Smith 1993). It is a question that can reciprocally link the analyses of anthropologists working in the bureaucratic, political, and financial precincts of Brussels, Strasbourg, and Frankfurt to the problems posed by anthropologists working in virtual every other ethnographic setting: from maternity wards in rural Greece to remote fishing villages in Portugal, from high-tech firms in Scotland to decaying urban neighbourhoods in France. By restoring the question of society at the centre of the scholarship on the EU we can begin to formulate analyses that do justice to the stunning transformation unfolding across Europe.

Notes

1. The material in this chapter is adapted from Holmes (2000), and is used with permission.
2. Alternatives to these 'functionalist' approaches have emerged around models of 'flexible integration' as the possibility looms of perhaps twenty-five to thirty very different polities with contingent EU membership. In this view a 'hard core' of European states is surrounded by concentric circles of states which participate in economic and political integration with different rates of convergence.
3. See Jean Monnet's discussion of his method of convergent action (1978: 232–48).
4. In an expression of the difficulty of satisfactorily defining subsidiarity, *The Times* of London goes so far as to claim that the 'principle of subsidiarity is meaningless or even a misleading phrase in English' (*The Times* 18 September 1982 quoted in the OED vol. XVII: 59). Nicholas Emiliou further notes, 'On this there is a general agreement that there is no agreement on the definition of this concept. A narrow approach to the content of the principle of subsidiarity may result in a very limited scope of examination' (1992: 383).
5. In his memoirs he recalls how, at the outset of the planning process, he solicited the views of a 'few exceptional men' who outlined a sombre, though familiar, analysis. 'Their diagnosis was crisp: by modern standards, France was appall-ingly backward' (Monnet 1978: 233).
6. As early as November 1941, in the midst of the Second World War, Maritain proposed a federal Europe to prevent the recurrence of war (Lipgens 1985: 274–5). '[I]n a European federation whose members would all agree to the diminution of sovereignty necessary for the purpose of organic institutional cooperation. No doubt there will be many a profound and terrible upheaval before we reach that goal, but we believe [federalism is] the only hope for Europe and Western civilization' (quoted in Lipgens 1985: 276).
7. For a critical appraisal of Emmanuel Mounier's work in this regard, particularly as editor of *Esprit,* see the chapter entitled 'Spiritualistic Fascism', and the 'Conclusion', in Sternhell (1996).

8. The modern definition of subsidiarity by Pius XI reads as follows:

> It is a fundamental principle of social philosophy, fixed and unchangeable, that one should not withdraw from individuals and commit to the community what they can accomplish by their own enterprise and industry. So, too, it is an injustice and at the same time a grave evil and a disturbance of right order, to transfer to the larger and higher collectivity functions which can be performed and provided for by lesser and subordinate bodies. Inasmuch as every social activity should, by its very nature prove a help to members of the body social, it should never destroy or absorb them. (Pius XI 1931 *Quadragesimo anno* quoted in Mulcahy 1967: 762)

Pius XI's definition of subsidiarity follows immediately upon his assessment of the liberal state and it is clear that he sees the concept serving as the basis of a wide-ranging Catholic political economy.

9. The position taken herein is that subsidiarity refers to a range of concepts and formulations that delineate a political economy. See Millon-Delsol (1992), which provides an excellent introduction to these issues, and Zorgbide (1993). For a basic introduction to Catholic political economy see Rommen (1955). For the application of subsidiarity to constitutional challenges of the EU see Emiliou (1992).

10. Tindemans' first cabinet position required that he plan the transition from a 'unitary' to a 'federal' state. The creation of a 'regionalized Belgium' was an effort to resolve the conflict between Franco-phone and Flemish-speaking communities (Tindemans 1972).

References

Abélès, Marc (1992), *La vie Quotidienne au Parlement Européen*, Paris: Hachette.

Amato, Joseph (1975), *Mounier and Maritain: A French Catholic Understanding of the Modern World*, Birmingham: University of Alabama Press.

Bellier, Irène (1994), 'La Commission européenne: hauts fonctionnaires et "culture du management,"' *Revue française d'administration publique* 70: 253–62.

Bloch-Lainé, François and Bouview, Jean (1986), *La France Restaurée 1944–54*, Paris: Fayard.

Bromberger, Merry and Bromberger, Serge (1969), *Jean Monnet and the United States of Europe*, New York: Coward-McCann.

Delors, Jacques (1989), *Delors Report on the Economic and Monetary Union of the European Community*, Committee for the Study of Economic and

Monetary Union, Luxembourg: Office for Official Publications of the European Communities.

—— (1991), *Subsidiarity: The Challenge of Change*. Proceedings of the Jacques Delors Colloquium, Maastricht: European Institute of Public Administration.

Duchêne, François (1991), 'Jean Monnet's Method,' in Douglas Brinkley and Clifford Hackett (eds), *Jean Monnet: The Path to European Unity*, London: Macmillan.

—— (1995), *Jean Monnet: The First Statesman of Interdependence*, New York: Norton.

Emiliou, Nicholas (1992), 'Subsidiarity: An Effective Barrier Against "The Enterprises of Ambition"?', *European Law Review* 17 (5): 383–405.

Fogarty, Michael P. (1957), *Christian Democracy in Western Europe 1820–1953*, Notre Dame: University of Notre Dame Press.

Hellman, John (1981), *Emmanuel Mounier and the New Catholic Left 1930–1959*, Toronto: University of Toronto Press.

Holmes, Douglas R. (2000), *Integral Europe: Fast-Capitalism, Multiculturalism, Neofascism*, Princeton: Princeton University Press.

Judt, Tony (1996), *A Grand Illusion? An Essay on Europe*, New York: Hill and Wang.

Lipgens, Walter (1985), *Documents on the History of European Integration. Vol. 1. Continental Plans for European Union 1939–1945*, Berlin: Walter de Gruyter.

Maritain, Jacques (1950), *Man and the State*, Chicago: University of Chicago Press.

Mayne, Richard (1991), 'Grey Eminence' in Douglas Brinkley and Clifford Hackett (eds), *Jean Monnet: The Path to European Unity*, London: Macmillan.

Mayne, Richard and John Pinder, with John Roberts (1990), *Federal Union: The Pioneers*, New York: St Martin's Press.

Millon-Delsol, Chantal (1992), *L'État subsidiaire: Ingérence et non-ingérence de l'État: le principe de subsidiarité aux fondements de l'histoire européenne*, Paris: Presses Universitaires de France.

Mioche, Phillipe (1985), *Le Plan Monnet: Genése et Elaboration*, Paris: Publications de la Sorbonne.

Monnet, Jean (1978), *Jean Monnet: Memoirs*, London: Collins.

Moravcsik, Andrew (1998), *The Choice for Europe: Social Purpose and State Power from Messina to Maastricht*, Ithaca: Cornell University Press.

Mulcahy, R.E. (1967), 'Subsidiarity', *The Catholic Encyclopedia. Vol. 13*: 762–3, New York: McGraw Hill.

Nathan, Robert (1991), 'An Unsung Hero of World War II' in Douglas Brinkley and Clifford Hackett (eds), *Jean Monnet: The Path to European Unity*, London: Macmillan.

Power, Susan M. (1992), *Jacques-Maritain 1882-1973: Christian Democrat, and the Quest for a New Commonwealth*, Lewiston NY: Edwin Mellen.

Rabinow, Paul (1989), *French Modern: Norms and Forms of the Social Environment*, Chicago: University of Chicago.

Rommen, Heinrich A. (1955), *The State in Catholic Thought: A Treatise in Political Philosophy*, London: Herder Books.

Ross, George (1995), *Jacques Delors and European Integration*, New York: Oxford University Press.

Sigmund, Paul E. (1988), *St. Thomas Aquinas: On Politics and Ethics*, (Paul Sigmund, trans), New York: Norton.

Simpson, J.A. and Weiner, E.S.C. (1989), *The Oxford English Dictionary*, 2nd edition, Oxford: Oxford University Press.

Spinelli, Altiero (1982), *Reform of Treaties and Achievement of European Union. Resolution adopted by the European Parliament*, Luxembourg: European Parliament.

—— (1983), 'Content of the Draft Treaty Establishing European Union' in Pier Virgilio Dastoli (ed.), *Altiero Spinelli: Speeches in European Parliament, 1976–1986*, Rome: C.S.F.

——, *rapporteur* (1984), *Draft Treaty Establishing European Union. Resolution adopted by the European Parliament*, Luxembourg: European Parliament.

Sternhell, Zeëv (1996), *Neither Right Nor Left: Fascist Ideology in France*, (David Maisel, trans), Princeton: Princeton University Press.

Tindemans, Leo (1972), 'Regionalized Belgium-Transition from Nation-State to Multi-National State', Unpublished manuscript.

—— (1977), 'European Union', in *European Yearbook*, The Hague: Martinus Nijhoff.

Wilson, Thomas M. and M. Estellie Smith (eds) (1993), *Cultural Change and the New Europe: Perspectives on the European Community*, Boulder CO: Westview.

Zorgbibe, Charles (1993), *Histoire de la construction européenne*, Paris: Presses Universitaires de France.

Treaties
(1957), The Treaties Establishing the European Economic Community (EEC) and the European Atomic Energy Community (Euratom), signed 25 March, in Rome.

(1986) The Single European Act, signed 17 and 28 February, in Luxembourg and The Hague.

(1992) Treaty on European Union, signed 7 February, in Maastricht.

(1997) Treaty of Amsterdam, signed 2 October, in Amsterdam.

Part II
Belonging and Identity in the European Union

–6–

European Citizenship, Citizens of Europe and European Citizens
Catherine Neveu

Among the debates concerning the building of a European Union (EU), the issue of European citizenship ranks high. Indeed, attempts to delineate the definition as well as the content of such a citizenship have given birth to a large literature, questioning its actuality, feasibility or even its very desirability. But while jurists, political scientists or sociologists argue heatedly over the hopes or threats such a new (level of) citizenship would entail, much of these discussions tend to stay at a theoretical and/or normative level, and only a few authors refer to actual practices in which citizens would be involved and which would foster new affiliations or sets of references, or to policies and discourses produced by European institutions on the issue.

In this chapter,[1] I will try on the one hand to explore how and why it might prove useful, in attempting to grasp what European citizenship both actually is and could be, to adopt a viewpoint adapted to the very newness of the European project (this 'original political object' as M. Abélès (1996: 13) defines it) and on the other hand to suggest places and topics for empirical observations and analysis. My main argument is that while history forces us, to a certain extent, to refer ourselves to a model of national citizenship, any discussion of European citizenship requires us to fully take into account the originality of Europe, and to closely analyze the representations to which it gives birth. In considering the many ways through which institutions and/or citizens are already involved in political and social processes from which a European form (or forms) of citizenship could evolve, an anthropological approach can contribute to the more global debates about citizenship, especially concerning new practices being articulated and linked at different scales.

National Citizenship as Yardstick

Generally speaking, much of the debate going on about European citizenship takes national citizenship as the starting point, an unsurprising feature since such a reference to the 'national model' is also to be found in analysis of other dimensions of the European building process. However, 'to grasp precisely both the obstacles and stakes of Community building, one has to emancipate oneself from the Nation-State paradigm which still commands much of the readings of this historical process' (Abélès 1996: 11). With the national reference as a yardstick, some scholars conclude that the nation state is the only legitimate political entity and guarantee for democracy. Still others elaborate a new stage for citizenship, usually qualified as post-national. Debates about European citizenship indeed raise two series of questions, which while they are strongly related, nevertheless need to be distinguished, not the least because notions like 'nationality' and 'citizenship' are 'socially and politically constructed, so that the issues raised are not just about normative or logical theory. They depend on the processes through which the available cognitive capital has been constructed in a given society' (Leca 1991). I will turn back later to issues of 'cultural translation' in the European institutions' uses and constructions of citizenship, but it seems necessary here to try and clarify what is meant in this chapter by nationality and citizenship.

By nationality, I mean a legal status, according to which an individual owes allegiance to a state and obtains a passport. Citizenship (contrary to a common English use of the term) refers not to that status but to membership in a political community; in some European countries, you can thus be a citizen without being a national, i.e. you can enjoy political rights, like voting rights, without being a national (what in French is called '*un ressortissant*'). This is the case for instance for Pakistani or Indian nationals residing in Britain, who while not having a British passport can nevertheless, under certain conditions, vote and be elected in local or general elections. Interestingly enough, and I will return to this latter, the very use of the term 'citizenship' in English often leads to confusion between these two notions, since it sometimes refers to membership in the polity, and sometimes it is used as if it is synonymous with nationality (i.e. a different legal status). These two notions are again distinct from that of national identity. Indeed one's legal nationality and citizenship do not necessarily correlate with national identity (Gilroy 1987). In Europe, the degree of correlation between these three notions varies greatly according to political and cultural histories, France being a case of high correlation between membership in the political community (citizenship), nationality and national identity ('nationness' to refer to Anderson's proposal (1983) to distinguish national identity from nationality as a status; see also Borneman 1992). Paradoxically though, it is also in France that scholars stress so often the purely political nature of citizenship, i.e. the fact that membership in the political community has nothing to do with national identity. Such distinctions are more important to the on-going debates about European citizenship, which must also concern itself with the purely political nature of citizenship, along with the relationships this notion has with that of identity(ies), and especially that of national identity. Indeed one could subsume much of the discussions under the following question: 'is it possible (or feasible, or desirable) to build a political community (a polity) distinct from national identities?'

In answer, one line of argument is well represented by Schnapper, who offers a definition of 'national (or classical) citizenship', according to which 'the political dimension is clearly paramount' to the extent that the very principle of citizenship relies on the use of politics to transcend particularisms (1997: 200). According to her, on-going processes of European citizenship building weaken, if not totally suppress, this central political dimension, replacing it with social and economic claims. Commenting on writings by authors according to whom socio-economic participation in civil society today would be a more relevant criterion to define citizenship than political membership, she considers that the building of Europe 'should not call into question the fundamental fact that the principle of citizenship is the basis of a political society . . . and that citizenship must always be based on a distinction between the citizen and the concrete individual. Allegiance to a political community must by nature be kept distinct from participation in concrete society' (Schnapper 1997: 212, 216).

She is therefore very suspicious of any attempt to separate access to citizenship from nationality, be it in the name of a 'new citizenship' or of 'post-national citizenship', and suggests that the emergence of a true European citizenship would first need to establish a European public sphere in which individuals would consider themselves as fully-fledged citizens. However she considers it will be extremely difficult for that kind of public sphere to emerge since proponents of a post-national citizenship 'tend to underestimate not only the ethnic realities of any concrete society but above all the necessity to integrate these ethnic realities in the concrete political organization, even the one calling on the principle of citizenship' (Schnapper 1997: 219). Indeed according to her the Nation is not just a civic project based on the abstraction of citizenship. Participation in a national society can be founded on many elements that can be called ethnic, such as a common language, a common culture, a particular historical memory shared by all nationals, and participation in the same institutions (1997: 214). One could here strongly question the propensity of some political scientists and sociologists to 'ethnicize' societies by calling some processes 'ethnic' that would better come under an analysis in terms of political cultures. Such a tendency is all the more surprising when one considers the critical reappraisal anthropologists themselves have made recently of the very theorizing about ethnic groups (see Amselle and M'Bokolo 1985).

Other authors offer less elaborate arguments which point to the unfeasibility of European citizenship, if they are not openly against European citizenship. Their main argument is that political traditions and feelings of belonging and identity in Europe are too heterogeneous to be ever superseded by any European identity or common political sphere, except by coercive means which would be contrary to the democratic ideal. In this vein, the only possible basis for a community would be ethnic, or some kind of cultural homogeneity (Smith 1992). As noted by Meehan (1996: 121):

> Too often the arguments about European integration and citizenship are put in terms of the feasibility or desirability of a transformation of national citizenship as we have known it on to a grander scale – as though it would be the same but in a new state, a superstate called Europe. When based on a need for homogeneity, this way of understanding or explaining the argumentation about Europe conceals an implicit assumption that successful politics are communautarian (1996: 121).

In criticizing analysis still steeped in the nation-state model, proponents of a 'new citizenship' put forward their own vision of European citizenship. They stress on the one hand the fact that recent evolution within European society, and especially the settlement of third-states nationals, call into question traditional definitions of the limits of citizenship. By enjoying social and economic rights and formulating claims and demands, these residents tend to blur the classical limits of membership in society, which should therefore be readapted to the new situation (Soysal 1994). On the other hand, some of these authors consider that beyond normative considerations, it is the actual evolution induced by the European building process that renders a new definition of citizenship necessary. Thus according to Meehan for instance, the notion of European citizen in the Maastricht Treaty offers a substantial breakthrough by providing a formal recognition that the links between citizenship, nationality and the nation state are not as necessary as it was previously thought: 'Although the Maastricht Treaty preserves the right of Nation-States to determine who are their nationals and, thus, eligible for Union citizenship, it introduces the idea that "place" [of residence] is equally important.' (1996: 102). Such a 'new citizenship' would thus be based on shared conceptions of solidarity and social justice, membership in the community being no longer defined by membership of the political community, but by economic and social participation in the civil society, thus questioning the classical Hegelian distinction between political society and civil society.

There exists of course a large variety of opinion as to the sources for new or post-national forms of citizenship in Europe, ranging from the need to stress social and economic citizenship instead of a purely political one (Kofman 1995), to the disqualification of the national level of citizenship through the implementation of universal human rights (Soysal 1994), or to the project of using the process of European building to replace the historically-contingent model of national citizenship linking nationality, citizenship and territory (the Westphalian model) with one in which identity and politics would at last be separated (Tassin 1994). This last project would make the Europe-building process into a unique experiment in '*Gesellschaft* building' (Meehan 1996).

But if some authors are keen to base their analysis on empirical facts, trying to grasp the consequences of the definition of citizenship, it has to be said that most tend to situate their reflections on a purely normative ground. If such a viewpoint has its own legitimacy, I would argue that issues of European building and imagining are better grasped, because of their originality, by 'observing the actual functioning of community institutions without reducing them to a pre-existing model they would have as an aim to realize' (Abélès 1996). As far as the more precise issue of citizenship is concerned, I would suggest that such an observation of representations, discourses and practices at work in institutions should be related to representations and practices in civil society itself. The conception of citizenship should take into account both its vertical and horizontal dimensions, i.e. where the polity is conceived as the set of relationships both of the individual citizens with the state and amongst citizens themselves (see Neveu 1997).

Representations, Discourses, Policies and Participation

The issue of European citizenship seems to be a particularly complex one, in that not only does it engage several levels of political integration, but also because it relates to a very peculiar political object. First of all, as has already been mentioned, it questions the historical relationship between nationality and citizenship, and thus both the legitimacy of the nation state as a relevant and unique level for membership in a polity or for allegiance and loyalty, and the definitions of citizenship itself. But it is the very complexity of the European project itself, in terms of institutions and functioning as well as in terms of representation and imagination, that makes for a particularly complex object. Many observers of the EU stress the fact that right from the beginning, member states have always hesitated or looked for a compromise between four conceptions of citizenship: to assert a common identity, and/or a single values system; to create specific rights for the citizen as producer; to extend such rights to the citizen as a consumer; or to assert a more political citizenship, thus recognizing at last the new democratic legitimacy created by the Union. The 'common identity option' was the first one to be launched, through legal and formal decisions taken in the 1970s, endowing member state nationals with special rights and a Union passport, decisions flowing from the will of European politicians to create a European identity (Wiener and Della Sala 1997). After a period during which it was the citizen as worker, then as consumer who was the main target of European policies, Shore and Black (1994) stress the development after 1985 of policies emphasizing the symbolic and cultural dimensions of citizenship, through education, training and consciousness-raising campaigns relying on self-consciously constructed Euro-symbols.

Through the ratification of the Maastricht Treaty, the notion of 'Citizen of the Union' has more recently gained a formal basis endowing individual citizens with concrete rights: the right to move and reside freely within the territory of the Community; to vote and be eligible in local and European Parliamentary elections; to formulate a petition to the European Parliament; to apply to a Union Ombudsman and to have access to diplomatic representation abroad from one of the member states. Such a series of rights creates new opportunities for direct relationships between these individual citizens and Europe, bypassing the national level (Meehan 1996) or 'representing' it in the European Parliament. Thus European citizenship is a direct relationship between citizens and European institutions, but certain aspects of this relationship are only activated when these citizens are outside of their own states. Thus European citizenship in terms of voting rights is only open to those nationals settled in another member state. European citizenship is at the same time a mediated relationship between citizens and European institutions, through the implementation of European directives by national governments and because only member-states nationals are Union citizens.

If European citizenship allows for imagining a new type of citizenship in which 'residence' would be the (only?) basis for membership, thus problematizing the territorial dimension of politics, it restricts at the same time such a move by denying residence is a relevant criterion for non-member-states nationals. Europe can thus be seen as a political space for the exclusion of those not endowed with one of the member-state's nationality (for example, in Schengen Europe), but the Commission in Brussels has also been trying to give them access to the European political agenda through such instances as the Migrants Forum, where third-country nationals settled in Europe can voice recommendations and claims.

Such complexity in levels and content pleads for a multi-faceted observation of citizenship as it is defined and discussed in representations and discourses, and as it is practiced and contested in politics and participation, among European institutions, civil servants and citizens themselves.

Citizenship in a Multilingual and Multicultural Context

Despite its legal dimension, citizenship, like nationality, is also an arbitrary social construct, that carries historical and ideological dimensions with which actors endow it (Leca 1991; Neveu 1997). Thus depending on the political culture(s) of different societies, and of the relative centrality given to the notion of citizenship in them, one can observe relevant variations on the definition of European citizenship, the effects of which have to be examined carefully, especially since the structures in charge of implementing and/or fostering such a citizenship are themselves places where cultures and languages are contested issues. As noted by Bellier (1995: 242), two phenomena are linked to the multilingual situation of European institutions. A 'European jargon' has evolved which has been built up through borrowings from national linguistic registers and has given rise to the creation of new vocabularies. Moreover, an institutional universe of mutual understanding has also evolved, in which civil servants of different nationalities and languages are not only able to understand each other and to express themselves according to several registers, but are also sensitive to the cultural differences separating or linking them along large geographical zones or along political and religious affinities (Bellier 1995: 242). Such a multilingual and multicultural environment thus creates many opportunities to develop mutual (mis)understandings as to the meaning of the notion of citizenship, as well as to create new meanings or to reinforce certain national models.

An example of such variation can be found in the often found confusion between two meanings of citizenship in English. While it is sometimes used to convey what in French is meant by *citoyenneté*, i.e. membership in a political community, in other instances it is used as synonymous to nationality, i.e. the legal status linking an individual to a state (cf. Kofman 1995; see also Close 1995). The confusion between the two meanings is understandable to the extent that in many cases only nationals are granted full citizenship rights; but it seems nevertheless important to maintain the distinction between nationality and citizenship, especially so since it is this very distinction which provides for the possibility of thinking of forms of citizenship not linked to the national level.

But translation raises here other questions. Not only is citizenship only sometimes synonymous to nationality, it is also conceived of differently according to political cultures in each society. Most analysts agree on the existence of at least three 'traditions' of citizenship: the American one, mostly concerned with issues of relationships between minorities and the state; the French one, marked by the Revolution and stressing its political dimension; and the British one, rooted in the development of the welfare state and socio-economic traits (Schnapper 1997). Complicating these three models is their own variation over time, which is often dependent on whether the emphasis is on the individual's freedom and responsibility or on rights and the state's duty to look after its citizens. For instance, the Thatcherite conception of 'the active citizen' stresses charitable giving, voluntary service and denigration of taxation as a means of discharging the obligations of citizenship (see Lister 1987). Steeped as they are in specific histories and political traditions, such general conceptions of citizenship also pretend to some universality, and the building of European citizenship can be seen as one of the arenas for competition between these different conceptions. A close analysis of the potential discrepancies between such models and the actual history and conceptions in each society can thus allow for a better understanding both of the way contemporary definitions of European citizenship are perceived in the different member states, and of alternative definitions and practices being circulated.

Thus, Garcia (1994: 257–8) reminds us that 'the challenge of building European Union citizenship forces us to consider the diverse paths towards modernity experienced by different West European societies' and considers that the paths followed by Southern European societies represent a different version altogether in which, at least in Spain's case, the British classical model advanced by T.H. Marshall is only partially relevant to understanding citizenship. Indeed Garcia stresses the fact that the Spanish Civil War left deep wounds in the society, with the victory of the Franco regime marking an end to civil and political rights through its promotion of patriotism under authoritarian rule rather than the building of a political community in which citizenship would have evolved. Contrary to most Western European societies where the welfare state developed in the 1950s with the participation of civil society, the Spanish experience is one of welfare policies being decided without such participation. In fact, the Franco regime forged specific types of relationship between civil society and the state, which still have concrete consequences on the vision Spanish citizens have of citizenship, including at the European level. In a similar way, in her analysis of Spanish and Catalan youth attitudes towards citizenship, Feixa Pampols concludes that the notion of citizenship within the framework of the Spanish state is still conditioned by the relatively recent experience of dictatorship, which explains in part the resistance today to the notion of 'education to citizenship' (1998: 56).

Similar analysis could be made of the specific experiences of each member state, in terms of social citizenship and of relationships between civil society and the state. Soysal frames this sort of analysis in terms of 'membership models and incorporation patterns', that is 'the institutionalized scripts and understandings of the relationship between individuals, the State, and the polity, as well as the organizational structures and practices that maintain this relationship' (1994: 36). If according to Soysal, the French membership model can be described as 'statist' (i.e. a model in which the state as a bureaucratic administrative unit constitutes the locus of sovereignty and, to a great extent, organizes the polity), one could add that according to some, such a model would also have included 'ethnic' traits in its concrete political organization (see Schnapper 1997). It is thus necessary to carefully analyze, in discourses developed by European institutions and civil servants, how different political cultures and historical traditions contribute to the definition of European citizenship, and how they are questioned and contested by new avenues challenging such representations. These analyses will have to include negotiations and compromises on translations and meanings, so as to highlight discrepancies or variations according to the political, social and cultural rights and issues at stake.

Building European Citizenship

One should not forget that if it is important to better understand the ways structural backgrounds and models inform definitions and conceptions of European citizenship, this citizenship is also already being enacted through policies and programmes, demonstrating the impact of institutional practices in creating Europe (see Bellier and Wilson, introduction to this volume). Therefore, when considering issues of identity and of how they relate to citizenship, modalities of access to European institutions should constitute an important line for observation. The issue here is to understand the kind of political and social resources necessary to gain access to the many different programmes and forums launched by European institutions. By considering closely what kind of associations or voluntary groups (in terms of national backgrounds as well as in terms of functioning patterns) succeed in having access to instances where European policies are elaborated and enacted, one could see more precisely the types of resources which are valuable in such settings, and thus derive from that the membership patterns and practices which are implicitly encouraged.

Conversely, this approach allows us to grasp more precisely how potentially different conceptions of citizenship percolate in European societies. The aim would be to discern on the one hand the kind of competencies that are useful to gain access to different European policy-making levels or to capture subsidies, and on the other hand, to see the extent to which such efficiency produces effects on the way participants in such groups define citizenship, and whether such effects are instrumental or reflect deeper changes at the national or regional level. It has to be noted here that evolution at the local, regional or national levels can also affect participation in or perceptions of European programmes. Thus Feixa Pampols (1998: 59) notes that Catalan associations were integrated within European institutional structures (such as the Youth Forum and the European Coordination of National Youth Committees) before the region achieved autonomy in Spain in 1979, and before many of their Spanish counterparts. Attitudes to citizenship among Catalan youth have changed over the years accordingly, especially in reaction to Catalan political autonomy and the development of a nationalist discourse. As Feixa Pampols clearly explains, as long as citizenship was not identified with state power (i.e. as long as it was conceived as active participation in associations at different levels, without being linked to a state), it could be positively perceived by youth. But when the nation became official, there developed among Catalan youth a double tendency towards independentist radicalization and "pasotismo" (a damn-all attitude) (Feixa Pampols 1998: 59).

Understanding the building of European citizenship from an anthropological point of view thus implies that particular attention must be paid to the many different ways through which background models and representations regarding citizenship are invoked by European officials and lobbies, and then negotiated when they decide, implement and evaluate policies and programmes. This has to be seen as a self-producing process, in that on the one hand, new frameworks are phrased as compromises between diverse conceptions and objectives, and on the other hand the ways such frameworks are used and interpreted by those they are aimed at can influence both the construction of European citizenship and actual practices of citizenship at other levels. In such an approach, those variations should be taken for what they are, i.e. political cultures, informed both by historical traditions and political evolution, and not some kind of 'ethnic' traits.

Defining European Citizens

A second dimension which has to be studied concerning European citizenship is that of the definition of a community of Europeans. What elements will link people(s) with a variety of histories, references or aspirations, whether between European societies or within them (Lagrée 1998)? Answers to the question 'What does it take for Europeans to feel European?' range from proposals deriving from nation-building processes to liberal considerations as to the civic qualities required to be recognized as members of the same community. On the whole, such discussions all relate to a central issue, that of the relationships between identity or identities and citizenship.

Confronted with the on-going process of Europe-building from a policy point of view, some observers consider a feeling of belonging to Europe will flow quite naturally from the attachment of 'state-like qualities' to the EU. Thus according to Howe, tangible homogeneity is not among the prerequisites for a community of Europeans. Considering that what constitutes the basis for any 'modern liberal community' is some kind of 'generous disposition' towards co-citizens, Howe concludes that progress will not flow from exercising European citizenship rights, but from recognizing such rights:

> As the European Union acquires some important trapping of statehood – in particular, as it starts to confer rights that define people as European citizens – there gradually will develop a more dominant sense of Europeaness and a concomitant willingness on the part of the average Europeans to make sacrifices for the sake of that community . . . The belief that others are of the same community can provide the social cement for a diverse population. This, more than anything, is the prerequisite underpinning for the modern liberal community. (Howe 1995: 34, 43)

The striking aspect of this kind of liberal argumentation is that it largely under-estimates justification and legitimation processes in membership building (i.e. how does one reach such a belief in others' membership in the same community), leaving them either to some kind of inevitable end-result, or falling back once more on the old recipes of nation-building, like shrouding the barren instrumentality of common interests in some dim notion of community (Howe 1995). Yet it is essential to clearly understand the actual basis of recognition and acknowledgement of membership which are defined and practiced within society itself, wherein 'society creates an image of itself in which it agrees to recognize itself' (Poche 1992). Here again it seems important to adopt a more thomist approach, and to observe precisely actual processes or attempts aiming at creating some feeling of commonality amongst Europeans. Such an approach implies close observation of already on-going European practices of citizenship and practices of European citizenship. Such a distinction is essential in that understanding European citizenship implies in my view to observe and analyze both how European citizens act *qua* European citizens (i.e. individuals endowed with specific legal rights by the Maastricht Treaty), and how Europeans act as citizens at the European level and/or by articulating different levels of citizenship practices (i.e. local, regional, national and European levels). It requires to once again consider closely the links between citizenship and identity(ies).

A fragmented citizenship?

One of the main criticisms voiced against the actual forms taken by European citizenship is that it depoliticizes the very notion by creating a fragmented series of groups according to specialized interests. 'EC/EU citizenship policy that evolved from the idea of special rights and passport policy in order to create a European identity, has developed a fragmented citizenship policy establishing special rights, not for Europeans as a people, but for special groups of Europeans ... Rights were thus literally specialized' (Wiener and Della Sala 1997: 605). If it is important to relate such developments to issues of political cultures explored earlier, one has also to fully take on board the effects such a fragmented citizenship practice would have on individual and collective representations of membership.

Thus similar processes of categories created by public policies, when analyzed at the national level, sometimes point to the paradoxical effects such categorization can have. Research lead in France on youth policies has shown that a significant number of young people tend to reject the categories (such as unemployed, marginalized, or under-trained youth) on which these policies are usually based, since on the one hand youth perceive them as stigmatizing and on the other hand they are not the terms according to which these youth primarily define themselves (Raymond 1999). If one can consider that involvement in European programmes cannot be fully paralleled with involvement in national public policies, the first ones clearly implying a voluntary move which the second ones do not necessarily require, it is nevertheless important to go beyond the first statement of a categorized citizenship. One should try and understand more precisely firstly how such specialization affects people's own perception of their belonging and citizenship, and secondly, how such practices, beyond instrumental dimensions (to apply for European programmes in order to have access to funding national governments cannot or would not deliver), can be seen as starting points to re-evaluate relationships between identity(ies) and involvement. For instance, when benefiting from European programmes as students (Erasmus or Tempus programmes), is it this dimension of their identities young people tend to stress, or is such an instrumental opportunity used to develop new kinds of networks and resources which will be reinvested in turn at the regional, national or European level, and in spheres of action or gathering which would not primarily be defined by their 'studentness'?

But one should also be aware that such potential or actual 'fragmenting effects', dividing Europeans in as many groups having specialized interests, do not automatically create homogeneous groups. In other words, fragmentation does not only occur between students, workers, consumers, youth or women, it can also take place within each of the so-defined groups, along socio-economic lines, according to the access fractions of these groups have to opportunities created by European programmes. Analysing European youth's attitudes towards Europe as collected by Eurobarometers, Lagrée insists on the profound differences between aspirations of 'Nordic' and 'Mediterranean' youth, but also within each country according to their levels of education, training, or income. He thus notices that it is in societies where new technologies of communication are already well developed that this factor ranks high in young people's definitions of European priorities, while youth in poorer societies will stress first of all employment policies as a priority. He then concludes that 'Saint Matthew's principle, "to whom who has received a lot, a lot will be given" is thus confirmed'. This is an important dimension to bear in mind when studying European citizenship, i.e. the emergence of an 'elite' or a 'two-tears' citizenship, dividing within each society those who can 'make the most of it' and the others.

One must then be aware that debates about European citizenship, if they are in part due to the very uniqueness of the European project itself, should nevertheless be contextualized and placed within the larger framework of contemporary discussions about the changing practices of citizenship. Thus worries as to the fragmenting effect contemporary public policies have on the polity are also expressed by authors analyzing processes at the national level. According to Bonny (1995), in France contemporary national political changes could be seen as the emergence of 'a new system of pragmatic integration' based on operational regulations, through the development of local and sectoral bargaining. In the process politics as a transcendent sphere might be replaced by an inflation of norms and juridical categories, with efficiency as the only integration principle. This would be the triumph of policies and the end of politics. The on-going construction of a European common sphere could be read according to such a framework, with its fragmented citizenship based on specific status or situations targeted by European policies and programmes, where citizens seem to be replaced by workers, employees, employers, students or academics (Wiener and Della Sala 1997). Such a reading is in tune with comments pointing to the absence of any strong political dimension to European building, a dimension which would be the necessary antidote to the risks carried by generalized bargaining along specific interests (see Bellier's chapter in this volume).

I would argue that in order to contribute to such a debate, one should take as our starting point citizens and their practices and the multiple interpretations of citizenship by citizens themselves (MacKian 1995). This acknowledges that while it seems to be an established fact that European citizenship does not seem for the time being to mobilize significant portions of EU societies, there are nevertheless places and times where people act as citizens at the European level. Fieldwork observation can then be pursued in one or the other of the NGO forum or umbrella groups, like ECAS (Euro Citizen Action Service) or VOICE (Voluntary Organizations in a Citizens' Europe), or in many of the places where European programmes (like URBAN or INTERREG) are enacted. Indeed, observations made in such places could provide illuminating material as to the way groups of citizens use or adapt themselves to institutional policies, languages and procedures, as well as to the diverse effects such involvement has on their practices and conceptions 'back home', at the national or regional level. Observing the implementation of programmes like INTERREG or URBAN could also allow for a better grasping of the multiple interactions and evolutions induced not only by the confrontation between local and regional authorities and European institutions, but also between these authorities across borders (see Wilson's chapter in this volume).

Conclusion

The analysis of European citizenship must challenge classical notions of binary logic which oppose polity and society, or civil society and the state, or which refer once again to the nation-state model in order to evaluate Europe-building or imagining. As Kofman (1995: 134) suggests, 'it is not simply the disparity between the normative and the real that lies at the heart of some of the problems, but . . . we also need to rethink the relationship between civil society and the state, the public and the private, and the mechanisms of exclusion and inclusion that regulate membership of socio-cultural and political communities'.

Arguments in favour of such a critical perspective depend on the fact that civil society and its roles in policy making and politics have been constructed differently across Europe according to the different histories of European societies. An anthropological critique of European citizenship is clearly rendered necessary by the global questioning of citizenship, whether in relation to issues of identities or to issues of changes in the relative weight of representative and participatory forms of democracy. In this turn in anthropology, one must be careful to distinguish and to relate top-down and bottom-up processes, that is, how European policies and programmes can be used by European institutions themselves to bypass the national level or contribute to the weakening of political citizenship, and how initiatives taken by local authorities or groups of citizens can modify political participation patterns. Again, this means that we need to explore how different levels of citizenship, both as practices and as representations, and different types of identity are mobilized or stimulated, how they interrelate and how they contradict or reinforce each other. For instance, while some see in Europe-building a unique opportunity for the creation of a post-national polity, others stress the persistent role and relevance of nation states in European integration and Europeanization. Using Eurobarometers, Deflem and Pampel show that 'popular support for unification of Europe' only exists to the extent that citizens perceive their own country's likelihood of benefiting (1996: 138), a point supported elsewhere in an analysis of Ireland's relations with Europe (Ruane 1994). Others argue that Europe-building could follow the same pattern as nation-state building, a sense of Europeaness being brought about by the Commission activities themselves and by the rise of an élite cadre. Thus just as the national élite was 'equipped with a new and distinctive "national" self-consciousness and with a vested interest in promoting the idea of nationhood', the new European élite would promote an idea of Europeaness (Shore and Black 1994).

Of importance to the anthropology of citizenship and identities are the initiatives taken by local authorities to link local and European levels. Thus in a document on *La citoyenneté européenne*, Barcelona local authorities consider that European citizenship can be a field of intervention for local authorities. To support this idea, they stress the fact that the crisis of citizenship concerns most urban Europeans, that local authorities are in the best position to face such a crisis and that they already have a legitimate position at the European level through such organs as the Committee of Regions and the establishment of Eurocities. But their main argument is that local and regional authorities have an incontestable advantage in their efforts to foster European policies, namely their direct relationship with the territory and the economic, social and cultural dimensions which constitute the space for life and activity of Europeans. In this view the worst policies are those which, because of their distant origin, their sectoral implementation, and their evaluation based only on market results, separate peoples instead of uniting them (Mairie de Barcelone 1996). But authors analyzing the effect of the EU on border regions also point to the very mixed impact it has had on local and provincial politics. According to Wilson, at least in the Northern Irish situation (1996: 210) 'this is largely due to the ethnonationalist politics of border life, which clearly take precedence over any other type of identity politics'.

To explore the effects of new kinds of relationship, in both conception and implementation, between different levels of citizenship practices at different territorial levels is one of the more stimulating challenges of European citizenship for anthropologists and other observers. A number of research questions arise from the issues reviewed in this chapter. Will European practices of citizenship and practices of European citizenship modify relationships to territory? Will such changes flow from citizenship being based on a different set of references, for instance access to rights flowing from universal human rights or from residence, and not any more from belonging to a national community? Do Europeans need some kind of common identity to feel and act as Europeans, or do they mainly need to develop networks and common practices to be Europeans in the European Union model? And what are the shared values that could link together groups of citizens and their diverse interests?

An anthropological approach to European citizenship can thus contribute to a better understanding of essential processes long omitted by political anthropological literature, those linked to state and popular sovereignty, to 'citizenship and its relation to a variety of social and political identities' (Wilson 1996: 202). Indeed, investigations into Europe-building, experiencing and imagining provide anthropologists with unique opportunities to explore alternatives to the nation-state model, to understand how people(s) or institutions build the complex and always evolving relationships between social and political identities, legal status, loyalty to a state, legitimacy, access to rights and services, and territorial scales. To approach such issues by exploring discourses, representations and practices of citizenship is then all the more important because the modern notion of political community (the polity) is based on the idea of citizenship. To that extent, 'citizenship' is a very 'anthropological' object since its analysis in a European perspective must take into account the variety of histories (including external and internal colonialism in Europe) which are lived and/or told by European people(s), the variety of political cultures, traditions, and ideologies which are related to the state and civil society, and the relative weight of the individual and of the 'community' in politics. By interrogating how, when, why, and by whom different conceptions of citizenship are voiced and practiced, an anthropological approach can contribute to research on long underestimated topics and issues in political anthropology, and renew the definitions of supposedly well-understood notions (see Hann 1996).

Notes

1. This chapter reflects work which will contribute to an on-going comparative research project between the EU and the Indian Union, under the direction of I. Bellier (LAIOS-CNRS, France), which has been subsidized by the EU.

References

Abélès, M. (1996), *En attente d'Europe*, Paris: Hachette.

Amselle, J.L. and M'Bokolo, E. (eds) (1985), *Au cœur de l'ethnie*, Paris: La Découverte.

Anderson, B. (1983), *Imagined Communities. Reflections on the Origin and Spread of Nationalism*, London: Verso.

Bellier, I. (1995), 'Moralité, langue et pouvoirs dans les institutions européennes', *Social Anthropology*, 3(3): 235–50.

Bonny, Y. (1995), 'Les formes contemporaines de participation: citoyenneté située ou fin du politique?' in P. Merle and F. Vatin (eds), *La citoyenneté aujourd'hui, extension ou régression?* Rennes: Presses Universitaires de Rennes.

Borneman, J. (1992), *Belonging in the Two Berlins: Kin, State, Nation*, Cambridge: Cambridge University Press.

Close, P. (1995), *Citizenship, Europe and Change*, London: Macmillan.

Deflem, M. and Pampel, F.C. (1996), 'The Myth of Postnational Identity: Popular Support for European Unification', *Social Forces*, 75(1): 119–43.

Feixa Pampols, C. (1998), 'Identités sociales, identités citoyennes en Espagne et en Catalogne: du franquisme à nos jours', *Agora Débats Jeunesses*, 12: 53–68.

Garcia, S. (1994), 'The Spanish Experience and Its Implication for a Citizen's Europe', in V.A. Goddard, J.R. Llobera and C. Shore (eds), *The Anthropology of Europe, Identities and Boundaries in Conflict*, Oxford: Berg.

Gilroy, P. (1987), *There ain't no black in the Union Jack*, London: Hutchinson.

Hann, C. (1996), 'Introduction. Political Society and Civil Anthropology', in C. Hann and E. Dunn (eds), *Civil Society. Challenging Western Models*, London: EASA-Routledge.

Howe, P. (1995), 'A Community of Europeans. The Requisite Underpinnings', *Journal of Common Market Studies*, 33(1): 27–46.

Kofman, E. (1995), 'Citizenship for Some but not for Others: Spaces of Citizenship in Contemporary Europe', *Political Geography*, 14(2): 121–37.

Lagrée, J.C. (1998), 'Jeunesse nordique, jeunesse méditerranéenne, les jeunes européens et l'Europe', *Agora Débats Jeunesses*, 12: 99-116.

Leca, J. (1991), 'Citoyenneté et individualisme', in P. Birnbaum and J. Leca (eds), *Sur l'individualisme*, Paris: Presses de la FNSP.

Lister, R. (1987), *The Exclusive Society: Citizenship and the Poor*, London: Child Poverty Action Group.

MacKian, S. (1995), 'That Great Dust-heap Called History: Recovering the Multiple Spaces of Citizenship', *Political Geography*, 14(2): 209–16.

Mairie de Barcelone (avec le soutien d'Eurocités) (1996), *La citoyenneté européenne. Éléments d'introduction à une contribution des villes et des pouvoirs locaux à la définition, à la protection et au développement de la citoyenneté européenne*, Document de travail.

Meehan, E. (1996), 'European integration and citizens' rights : a comparative perspective', *Publius*, 26(4): 99–121.

Neveu, C. (1997), 'Anthropologie de la citoyenneté', in M. Abélés and H.P. Jeudy (eds), *Anthropologie du politique*, Paris: Armand Colin, Collection U.

Poche, B. (1992), 'Citoyenneté et représentation de l'appartenance' *Espaces et Sociétés*, 68(1): 15–35.

Raymond, R. (1999), 'La politique associative de la ville à l'épreuve de l'informel' in C. Neveu (ed.), *Espace public et engagement politique. Enjeux et logiques de la citoyenneté locale*, Paris: L'Harmattan, Collection Logiques Politiques.

Ruane, J. (1994), 'Nationalism and European Community Integration: the Republic of Ireland', in V.A. Goddard, J.R. Llobera and C. Shore (eds), *The Anthropology of Europe, Identities and Boundaries in Conflict*, Oxford: Berg.

Schnapper, D. (1997), 'The European Debate on Citizenship', *Daedalus*, 126(3): 199–222.

Shore, C. and Black, A. (1994), 'Citizens' Europe and the Construction of European Identity', in V.A. Goddard, J.R. Llobera and C. Shore (eds), *The Anthropology of Europe, Identities and Boundaries in Conflict*, Oxford: Berg.

Smith, A. (1992), 'National Identity and the Idea of European Unity', *International Affairs*, 68(1): 55–76.

Soysal, Y.N. (1994), *Limits of Citizenship. Migrants and Postnational Membership in Europe*, Chicago: University of Chicago Press.

Tassin, É. (1994), 'Identités nationales et citoyenneté politique', *Esprit*, January: 97–111.

Wiener, A. and Della Sala, V. (1997), 'Constitution-making and Citizenship Practice. Bridging the democracy gap in the European Union', *Journal of Common Market Studies*, 35(4): 595–613.

Wilson, T.M. (1996), 'Sovereignty, Identity and Borders: Political Anthropology and European Integration', in L. O'Dowd and T.M. Wilson (eds), *Borders, Nations and States. Frontiers of Sovereignty in the New Europe*, Aldershot: Avebury.

−7−

Agendas in Conflict: Nation, State and Europe in the Northern Ireland Borderlands

Thomas M. Wilson

In an address to the Irish Institute for European Affairs in Dublin on 3 November 1997, the British Foreign Secretary Robin Cook MP warned that

> political leaders must be careful that as we build supranational structures, we do not lose contact with the people. We need to reconnect the peoples of Europe with the European Union which their governments are trying to create. They need to know that the EU is relevant to their lives. The EU seems to spend too much of its time discussing things that do not touch the people's lives, abstractions and institutions rather than a concrete agenda. The people need to believe that their agenda is our agenda. Britain has a mission as President of the European Union − to give Europe back to the people.[1]

Rhetoric like this has become increasingly common in popular, governmental and scholarly debates on the relationships between European residents and citizens and the institutions and processes of 'European', i.e. European Union (EU), integration. Scholars are beginning to focus on the growing gap between, on the one hand, the initiatives of economic and political elites in fostering post-Maastricht programmes of economic and monetary union, common European citizenship, and common security and defence policies, and, on the other hand, the social understanding and acceptance of such initiatives in the localities of Europe, among non-elites. Although such scholarly inquiries often focus on the EU's so-called 'democratic deficit', there has been a marked recent turn to what may be termed the 'cultural deficit', a lack of fit between diverse European cultures and the elite cultures of member states' governments, multinational corporations, and the institutions of the EU, i.e. those people, institutions, and ideologies which give impetus to the European project.

The words of the British Foreign Secretary provide a useful frame to the issues of culture and integration which are the concerns of this chapter. 'Giving Europe back to the people' makes the Europe of the EU into an object, which presumably should be returned to its rightful owners. But who are these people? If they are the citizens of the member states, are they also Europe's immigrants? If they are

Europeans by birth, or culture, or residence, are they also Europeans who do not live within the boundaries of the EU? In a 'Europe without frontiers', as the EU has called itself because of its great strides to achieve a common market, what are the political and social borders of inclusion and exclusion? What are the boundaries of identity which delimit those who are the Europeans to whom Europe must be returned?

Anthropologists have much to add to our understanding of a possibly widening 'culture gap' between those who seek to build a New Europe, and those who experience such changes in their everyday lives but who are often absent in official and scholarly discourse. The potential role of anthropologists in the study of European cultural integration has been recognized recently by other social scientists. As Sidney Tarrow points out, Eurobarometer surveys chronicle Europeans' attitudes, but do little to help us to predict action based on such attitudes (1994:17). Anthony Smith specifically called for more scholarly attention to 'questions of meaning, value and symbolism' in the processes of European unification (1992: 57). Ulf Hedetoft suggests, in his analysis (1994a) of Danish, German and British attitudes towards European integration, that social scientists in the past have concentrated on the match or mismatch between social attitudes, as gleaned from survey data, and the objectives of political integration at any one point in time, but they have all but ignored the study of national identities in their own right. While there have been a number of intriguing attempts to relate the development of European identity to wider processes of transnationalism, post-nationalism and globalization (see, for example, Delanty 1995; Hedetoft 1994a, 1994b, 1995), the interplay among local, regional, and national identities to be found within member states is seldom related to the wider issues of European identity and integration (Borneman and Fowler 1997).

It is perhaps ironic to note that despite these calls for more anthropological interest in the EU there has been considerable attention paid by social and cultural anthropologists, on both sides of the Atlantic, to issues of EU culture and society for some time now (Wilson 1998; Hedetoft 1994b). A great deal of this anthropological interest in the EU has been in the roles which national culture plays in the creation of a new sense of Europeaness, both among the policy makers and the bureaucrats of such places as Brussels and Strasbourg (see, for example, Bellier 1997; McDonald 1997; Shore 1993), and among people throughout the Union who have been affected by efforts to build a sense of European identity as one way to ensure their participation in the greater European agenda of political and economic integration (see, for example, Zabusky 1995; Wilson 1996). This process of creating a new European consciousness may very well affect just about everyone who lives and works in the EU, but this needs to be empirically demonstrated rather than just stipulated. This issue might be usefully rephrased as a question, namely, to what extent and in what ways have the peoples of the Union been affected by various attempts by European elites, working in EU jobs, national governments, corporate headquarters, or in universities, to either create a new European identity, or to modify and adapt notions of common European heritage and identity already held by various groups of people in different ways?

While long-term case studies of local, regional, and national identities as they relate to European integration have been few, there has been increasing attention paid throughout social science to ways in which various cultural identities change through interaction with agents and institutions of European integration. Hedetoft (1997: 17–19) categorizes the general concerns with the future of European cultural identity within the EU as perspectives of 'threat' and 'opportunity'. In the former view, social scientists and others see European integration as a threat to a wide range of identities in Europe, but most importantly to national identity, especially in regard to the presumed essential fit between nation, territory and sovereignty. Others see the EU as an opportunity to forge a new common European identity, either based on those aspects of culture shared by most Europeans, or based on the new forms of institutional and ideological culture which is being shaped in the integration process.

'Identity' is a concept whose usefulness is increasingly apparent in the general social science of the EU, and it is certainly important to anthropological approaches to the building, imagining, and experiencing of the New Europe, perhaps better expressed as the new Europes, of the EU. But 'identity' is also a rather chameleon-like concept. It is perhaps useful, then, to give better definition to the concept of European identity by referring to its related roles as *a condition and a process*. While it is clear that European integration is a process, which is often seen to be synonymous with Europeanization, its objective or end result is obscure. So too European identity is about both *'being'* European and *'becoming'* European, in that surveys, ethnographic research, inferences from a variety of scholarly studies, and just plain common sense all agree that the people of the EU recognize that they are European by culture, tradition and heritage, but they are also in the process of becoming something new, also European, depending on the course which the EU takes, and the path which their member state takes in reaction and adaptation. It is in this latter way that *European identity* can be seen usefully as both a political agenda (i.e. something to be forged within the EU by national and supranational elites), and a political tactic (i.e. to support or oppose aspects of common European identity and culture in order to gain power or other advantage in local, regional, national and international arenas). Both of these functions can be discerned in the midst of European regional policy in Northern Ireland, at the border between the Republic of Ireland and the United Kingdom.

Borderlands

Not surprisingly, perhaps, the 'European project' as it is being directed from Brussels and elsewhere is coming into conflict with a number of the old, tried and true political spaces of the nation state, and is stimulating new alternative political spaces, such as regions. Borderlands are areas of cultural contest and integration, in which national identity and citizenship are often not the same thing, and where states and many of their people dispute widely held beliefs about state sovereignty. Borderlands are productive arenas for the study of both old and new political entities in the EU. Border frontiers have been changed but not removed in the EU's drive to a common market, and the identities of the people of the borderlands reflect these changes, but only in part.

Anthropological attention to the meanings people ascribe to national cultures has particular salience at international frontiers and borders, in areas where the state has invested a great deal in order to impose its definitions of boundary (for a review of the anthropology of international borders, see Donnan and Wilson 1999). The anthropological investigation of culture at international borders highlights many ways in which state-building and nation-building are two very different processes, in which the state's projection of its 'own' national culture may be at odds with the lived experiences of many of its people. In fact, anthropological studies of borders often highlight an extremely problematic area for any new Europe: the construction of local, regional and national identities (Wilson 1996; see also Wilson and Donnan 1998). For too long the cultural and political importance of minority identities have been of secondary concern to EU elites in their efforts to integrate European 'national' (i.e. nation-state) cultures through the wonders of free market forces, which are presumed by architects of policy to be simultaneously levelling and uplifting. On the surface this process parallels that of 'nation-building' in each of the states, in which the cultures (presumed to be) internal to the state are to be homogenized into a national culture. Here too borderlands have often proved to be difficult for the state, precisely because the cultural landscapes of border zones transcend the borderline. But the twin and simultaneous processes of cultural integration in both EU-building and nation-building sit uneasily with each other because the state has historically concerned itself with strengthening the definition of the national 'we' versus 'them'. Thus, while EU elites promote European citizenship and a common European identity, the borders of states, like the external borders of the EU itself, still stand as markers of difference and heterogeneity. Moreover, in some views, social differences outmatch similarities within the EU, making unity in diversity a difficult goal to achieve. The perceived rights and needs of EU minorities (i.e. races, classes, women, workers, interest groups, and nations striving for self-determination, among others) are powerful forces that the legislators of the EU must address.

Celebrations of a 'Europe without frontiers' notwithstanding, at the Northern Ireland border,[2] as perhaps at other European borders, many strong social barriers to European integration remain. EU drives towards a world of free market capitalism have differential effects on local communities, regions, or entire nations, who sometimes experience economic integration as the exaggeration of cultural difference, a reinforcement of class distinctions, or the accentuation of nationalism. Because EU-building creates opportunities to accumulate wealth, power and prestige for many groups of people throughout the fifteen member states, it is certain that at every stage of the completion of the EU agenda that there will be economic and political "winners" and "losers", just as there has been since the formation of a Common Market. Many of these people identify, rightly and wrongly, the EU as the source of their good fortune or their decline. EU-Northern Ireland relations since 1973, when the United Kingdom acceded to membership, have resulted in a borderlands where the EU is judged almost entirely in terms of its local economic impact. This situation is partly a result of the EU's own marketing of its initiatives to provide much-needed injections of capital to the region, but it is also a product of the projections by some local and other United Kingdom elites, who have elicited local support for European integration by emphasizing the economic gains to be had.

This concentration by local European and British elites on the EU's role in economic development in the province has predominated over the social and political interpretations of the same process put forward by EU elites. As Jacques Delors, former President of the European Commission, suggested in an address to a cross-border development conference in Ireland, the EU can aid the people of Northern Ireland and the Irish border region in general by continuing 'to make a valuable contribution, which goes beyond financial support, by adding an essential extra dimension' (1997: 25). According to Delors, the EU can give Northern Ireland a neutral focus by encouraging its people to seek some external solutions to their problems. The EU also provides a model and framework for international co-operation and partnership, which are essential to the successful integration of economies and societies in Ireland. The EU, however, has even more to offer in Delors' view. 'Perhaps most importantly, it provides a model whereby diversity is seen as a strength rather than a weakness' (Delors 1997: 25).

While economic aid through the EU's Structural Funds and in special pro-grammes such as INTERREG and the European Union Special Support Programme for Peace and Reconciliation are welcome in Northern Ireland, suggestions that the EU can provide models and frameworks for social and political accommodation between the two major communities in Northern Ireland very often fall on deaf ears there, not only among local populations but also among politicians and civil servants who see 'The Troubles' of Northern Ireland as an exclusively internal British concern. This ideological contest over the role of the EU in Northern Ireland, between European elites on the one hand, and Irish, Northern Irish, and British elites on the other, reinforces an important point in the overall study of culture and integration within the EU. The new political and cultural space of the EU will act as a battleground between and among states and the EU over the limits to power and sovereignty. The economics of integration result in the reconfiguration of nation-state politics, another aspect of 'Europeanization'. But even when the EU's role in political restructuring is not evident, the wider processes of integration remain factors in the maintenance or decline of local, regional and state power.

The long-predicted break-up of Britain may be the end result of the current moves to devolution in Scotland, Wales and Northern Ireland. Irrespective of the final arrangements of governance in the British Isles, however, scholars among many other concerned participants and observers will debate the role of the EU, and in particular the rhetoric and realities of a Europe of the Regions, in the outcome. In Northern Ireland one way to observe the critical relations between and among nation, state and Europe, especially in terms of their often divergent agendas which are certain to affect their future relationships, is to investigate the organization and implementation of precisely those programmes of economic development which are so highly touted as the lifeblood of the corpus of European integration. At the Northern Ireland border, one of the most important of these special development programmes over the last decade has been INTERREG.

Design and Organization

The Regional Policy of the EU has increased in importance since its initiation in 1975, a consequence of the EU's recognition of the economic disparities which existed between the core and peripheral regions throughout the new European Community (EC) of nine members (formed when Denmark, Ireland and the United Kingdom joined the original six members: Belgium, France, Germany, Italy, Luxembourg, and the Netherlands). But the EU's Regional Policy was never simply about the righting of economic wrongs. From the beginning a Regional Policy was also conceived as an instrument to shore up regional and national support for the European agenda (Keating 1995), to provide cohesion to the EU as much as, if not more so, to its regions (Jones 1995). The European Regional Development Fund (ERDF) was established in 1975 to act as the financial instrument for the new EC Regional Policy, which also set up measures designed to improve the co-ordination of regional development between and among the EU, member states, and regional and local authorities. At the outset, however, the Regional Policy was a modest one. Its budget for the first three years was £540 million, the equivalent to .04 per cent of the combined GDP of the nine member states (Armstrong 1995: 38), and its allocation was restricted by country and by project.

Reforms over the next decade liberated the Policy from past constraints, and made ERDF reform an integral part of the overall reform of the EU Structural Funds. In terms of regions, these reforms established five EU-wide priority objectives which were not tied directly to member state quotas. The EU's goal was to concentrate financial assistance in those regions most disadvantaged, which were labelled in these new initiatives in 1989 as 'Objective One' regions, i.e. those with GDP per capita under 75 per cent of the EU average (a category in which Northern Ireland was included, albeit as a special case because its GDP was higher than the agreed threshold). These Objective One regions were scheduled to receive fully 80 per cent of regional funds, leaving the remainder to be divided among those regions in the four other categories.

In the 1990s further amendments were made to the Regional Policy, and others are sure to follow in each subsequent step towards economic and political union in what is now a community of fifteen states, with the addition of Greece, Spain, Portugal, Austria, Finland, and Sweden. By 1993 the EU Structural Funds, which co-ordinated the funding to the regions, had grown to £9.2 billion (Armstrong 1995: 46). While there have been a number of problems associated with the EU's Regional Policy in general, including those of level and type of funding, co-ordination with member states and the thorny issues of whether EU funds are simply replacing the meagre national funds allocated to their regions, debates over the targeting of only economic projects, such as infrastructure, at the expense of social and cultural development, and the lack of a plan by the EU to identify clear objectives for the Policy on the whole (for a detailed review of the evolution and critique of this Regional Policy, see Armstrong 1995), it is also clear that it has injected substantial capital into peripheral European regions. Since the 1970s one of these has been Northern Ireland. Among its most disadvantaged areas are its borderlands, which share the conditions of economic underdevelopment with contiguous areas in the Irish Republic.

For funding purposes the Irish border region encompasses most of four of the six Northern Ireland counties and six counties in the Republic. This area is equal to 20 per cent of the total land area of the island, and it is home to over 15 per cent of its total population (approximately 750,00 people) (Kilmurray 1997). Since the creation of the border in 1920, which imposed an international barrier on the economic and political lives of many towns, villages and communities at and in some cases actually straddling the new borderline, the region has been marked by the economic and social conditions of peripheralization, marginalization, under-development and exclusion.

In Northern Ireland the terrible economic and social conditions which resulted from the creation of the border have been heightened since 1969 and the return of 'The Troubles', the local term used to describe the civil and terrorist war in the province which, since the recent ceasefires, may be at an end. During the war, however, the violence perpetrated by paramilitaries and security forces contributed to the local sense of despair and marginality. In addition, most parts of the Northern Ireland border region are also marginal because they are distant from the metropolitan centres of economic and political decision-making in Belfast and Dublin, and all of the borderlands are distant from Westminster, in London, from where the British government until recently had ruled Northern Ireland directly.

Until the 1980s there was little formalized cross-border co-operation in Ireland, and almost no officially co-ordinated cross-border economic activity. As part of its new interest in Regional Policy, the European Commission established the INTERREG Initiative, specifically geared to address the problems of border regions throughout the EU, in part by attempting to foster cross-border economic co-operation. This led, in Ireland, to the Ireland/Northern Ireland INTERREG Programme (1991–93), which was targeted at all of Northern Ireland (except Belfast) and six border counties in the Irish Republic. This programme had a budget of £55 million, which was third highest of the thirty-one programmes begun by the EU. The programme's objectives in Ireland were to assist the border areas in Northern Ireland and in the Republic to encourage economic development and cross-border co-operation in order to maximize the economic impact of the projected '1992' completion of the single market in the EU.

From the outset it was agreed by the two central governments that the programme would be jointly managed by government departments in Belfast and Dublin, and would be monitored by a central monitoring committee and a number of sectoral committees. In the Northern Ireland border region it was quickly recognized by many local community groups that this plan to administer and implement the programme did not support the specific regional and cross-border aims of INTERREG. In fact, the centralized nature of INTERREG became apparent during the consultation phase when a hastily organized process excluded many local interests and community groups. Local organisations complained that they had not received sufficient information on the programme and were thus being prevented from taking advantage of it. As a result, most of the applications for INTERREG funds came from government bodies rather than local community organizations and voluntary trusts. In 1994, the European Court of Auditors concluded that INTERREG in Ireland had performed poorly in developing cross-border projects, and they recommended that there be a strengthening of cross-border partnerships and an improved definition of the transfrontier nature of the programme's various measures (Coopers and Lybrand 1997).

This review body's analysis made clear that many of the aims of INTERREG were not met in the initial programme in Northern Ireland, an opinion echoed on the ground throughout the border region. Nevertheless, the programme was touted as a success, as a preliminary to the implementation of the second initiative, INTERREG II, scheduled for 1994–99. Its aims were essentially those of the first programme (INTERREG Development Office 1994): (1) to promote networks of cross-border co-operation and the linking of these networks to wider community networks, within the context of the completion of the single market, and (2) to assist the eligible region to overcome the problems arising from its isolation within national economies and within the EU as a whole, in the interests of the local people and the environment. The specific sub-programmes were in (1) regional development, (2) human resources development, (3) infrastructure, (4) agriculture/ fisheries/forestry, and (5) environmental protection. The EU's allocation to the Ireland/Northern Ireland INTERREG Programme was almost 157 million ecus, the equivalent of £131 million sterling, but its impact was expected to be more significant because INTERREG would only fund up to 75 per cent of total project costs. All proposals needed to raise at least a quarter of their costs from state and private funding sources in order to be eligible for INTERREG aid. As one senior administrator of INTERREG assessed, the £131 million was expected to generate at least one pound for every two pounds spent. At this stage (1999) of the second INTERREG, funded projects have averaged almost 40 per cent capital support from non-EU sources.[3] Among the most important sub-programmes of INTERREG II in Northern Ireland has been its first, regional development. Its budgetary allocation of approximately £35 million sterling was second only to the £41 million assigned to the sub-programme on infrastructure. However, the regional develop-ment sub-programme was considered a centrepiece of INTERREG, which in official views had proved to be 'highly effective in stimulating development in the border regions and in stimulating cross-border linkages' (INTERREG Develop-ment Office 1994: 4).

INTERREG is, in fact, a European community initiative which lies at the heart of Regional Policy and the overall EU agenda for economic and political union. Community Initiatives are European Commission proposals which are endorsed by the Council of Ministers and set out in concrete and finite ways to achieve specific objectives which further the aims of integration (Simpson 1996). They are intended to be innovative, complementary to other Structural Fund agendas, and stimulating, in terms of public and private capital investment in member states, in ways which lead to greater support for the goals of the EU. These initiatives inject capital, expertise and extra-national support into specific places and among communities which are in clear need. INTERREG is designed to support cross-border co-operation, which to be funded must be based on various forms of horizontal co-operation, i.e. between and among the government, voluntary and private sectors, and vertical co-operation, i.e. between and among political and administrative levels of the EU, member states, regions and localities (Quinlivan 1997). Such co-operation is in fact the ideal form of Europe-building, in which political institutions and other societal structures learn to co-operate across all barriers in order to forge a New Europe. INTERREG II was intended to support three types of cross-border co-operation: joint planning and implementation of specific cross-border actions; the improvement of communication between agencies within border regions and across borders; and the establishment of new structures to continue and to promote co-operation (Quinlivan 1997: 64). Central to the success of this programme, at least as perceived from the vantage point of its architects in the EU, was its reliance on the building of political, administrative, economic and social partners, horizontally and vertically, in border regions. It was also to adhere both to *subsidiarity*, the principle at work in EU integration which requires that problems solved at the lowest level of governance, i.e. the one closest to the problem, and to *additionality*, the principle that member states must use EU Structural Funds in addition to their previous national expenditure on the projects or the problem in question.

It is clear from the programme's origin and guidelines that INTERREG seeks to foster innovative and sustainable partnerships in cross-border co-operation which will link government, business, local community organizations, and voluntary sector bodies. 'Stand-alone' projects, i.e. local projects which support economic development in a peripheral region but do little to promote cross-border co-operation, are not the targets of INTERREG funding, although they may be fundable under other initiatives or programmes.

The rhetoric does not quite match the facts, however. Whereas the first INTERREG was lauded for its achievements in stimulating cross-border linkages, in fact very little cross-border partnership was established under this programme beyond ties at governmental levels. Most projects which received funding in the first INTERREG were government-sponsored border region projects which aided one side of the border or the other, but did little to improve cross-border co-operation. The mid-term report of INTERREG II concurs (Coopers and Lybrand 1997). Up to 1996 the target spending of EU funds through INTERREG was behind schedule in all sub-programmes except that of environmental protection. Administrators and applicants throughout Northern Ireland agreed that there were more joint cross-border applications, and more were funded than in the first INTERREG, but that they were by no means the dominant type of application in all of the sub-programmes. In fact one researcher concluded that in 1997 fully 76 per cent of all approved projects in INTERREG II were 'stand-alone' projects, which are development projects for one side of the border (Quinlivan 1997: 89). While the official mid-term evaluation concluded that the potential for cross-border co-operation was still high for INTERREG II in 1997, the report had to admit that there were a number of factors which inhibited such co-operation (Coopers and Lybrand 1997). Most of these were noted in the report as problems of administration and implementation. However, there are a number of other factors which impede border regional development which are of a more long-standing nature.

Problems for INTERREG and the European Agenda

The most important administrative barrier to the enhancement of cross-border co-operation and the development of cross-border projects is the centralization of the Irish and British states. From 1972 to 1999 Northern Ireland was ruled directly from Westminster by the British government. All economic development programmes were administered by the civil service in Belfast and elsewhere in the UK. The Republic of Ireland is also notable for its high degree of political and administrative centralization, in which there may be local government in the form of county councils, but where there is very little political power below the level of the state, and no real governance in a state formally without regions (see Laffan 1996 for a review of regional policy in Ireland; Bache et al. 1996 for a review of the EU and regions in the UK). This centralization of Irish and British policy and political administration resulted in a dearth of effective regional structures for cross-border co-operation. Centralization also meant a fair degree of mismatch and disagreement in terms of local and national economic and political priorities, and relatively little development planning of a cross-border nature.

The limited role of local authorities on both sides of the border constrained formal local government cross-border co-operation, which in some cases was already hampered by other more volatile factors in borderlands life. At the least it is fair to say that the structure of local government in both Northern Ireland and Ireland, in combination with the social and cultural barriers which have developed over seventy years of political divergence between the two, has seriously weakened the political infrastructure and will to co-operate across the borderline between the states (O'Dowd and Corrigan 1995). Regardless of the degree of political will to co-operate, however, finances were controlled by central government. All national economic planning was done at the centre and not the border peripheries of the two states. This situation only began to change, in Northern Ireland at least, with the advent of the money available from the International Fund for Ireland since its inception in 1986. But even since then, and in terms of EU funding and initiatives, the purse strings have been controlled by national governments and their bureaucracies. As a result, local district councils did little to facilitate the overall implementation of INTERREG, especially in terms of helping to develop cross-border co-operation, except in the projects which they had designed themselves, most of which as the figures above betray had very little cross-border content. Nevertheless, local government councils had important roles to play in INTERREG precisely because they applied for funds from central government under the initiative, in particular under such sub-programmes as infrastructure and tourism. These local authorities, in fact, became the most successful participants under the scheme, a fact which made them not only key agents in the economic development of the border areas on their side of the borderline, but also simultaneously made them appear to be competitors to other bodies in the private community and voluntary sectors.

The centralization of the INTERREG Programme was perceived to be a problem across a wide range of voluntary body and community groups in the eastern border region of Northern Ireland. From the beginning of the programme there have been many strong and oft-repeated complaints about the lack of initial information, the difficulty in obtaining and filling out the relevant forms, the confusion over application procedures and the secrecy about programme decisions and responsibility. In interviews I conducted with people who have applied for INTERREG funding, some of whom were successful, a number of themes emerged which focus on the role of the civil service and information brokerage. Among local applicants the government departments in Belfast were seen as distant and relatively uninterested in their local concerns. While many realized that individuals in these departments were sensitive and often sympathetic, the intricacies of the application procedure, along with the complexities of the programme measures, many of which are administered by different government departments, all seemed to suggest a bureaucratic maze which conspired to make the whole process unfathomable and unmanageable. This situation was exacerbated in the earlier days of INTERREG when there was no local office to consult regarding the programme, a problem partially solved with the establishment of an INTERREG Development Officer based in the border region.

Not only do local people complain of a lack of adequate support regarding the application procedures, some also perceive that their efforts will go unrewarded because in their view local government councils are complicit in efforts to keep INTERREG funding within central and local government domain, to meet the needs of their agendas. Thus many border people have concluded that central government's control of the application process and local government's close partnership with central authorities make it difficult for community and voluntary sector groups to get a fair review in their attempts to get INTERREG money. These people often point to the requirement to get at least 25 per cent matching funds in order to qualify for EU money as evidence of governmental weighting in favour of local government bodies, for the latter have little difficulty in getting the necessary matching funds. And even those locals who believe that there is a level playing field recognize that the centralization of the EU programme makes the funding process more difficult because of its administrative division among many government departments which were already understaffed.

The warlike conditions which marked the region for over a generation, and which may be terminated if the Good Friday Agreement of 1998 ultimately succeeds, have affected all aspects of borderlands life, and they present particular obstacles to cross-border social and cultural integration. Many of the political differences over such co-operation in Northern Ireland have their roots in Irish and British nationalism. In fact, the Irish border is both a symbol and an arena for the national and international conflicts which have defined 'The Troubles' since 1969. This has had an important effect on the ways that INTERREG has been organized and perceived in Northern Ireland.

EU attempts to establish a 'Europe Without Frontiers' have only been partially successful in Northern Ireland. At the border aspects of shared and of disputed culture both facilitate and impede cross-border commerce and communication, in ways which may very well have many parallels elsewhere in Europe, and not just in peripheral border regions. In the border areas of Northern Ireland one's national identity, i.e. whether one is Irish or British, predominates over other political identities. Like all other ethnic and national identities, Irish and British identities in Northern Ireland have ascriptive and elected aspects, in which certain forms of behaviour and beliefs are generally agreed and accepted among those people of like identity, while at the same time other behaviours and values are ascribed to that same group by outsiders, their 'others'. These two sets of actions and beliefs may overlap, but seldom if ever do so entirely. Nevertheless, in Northern Ireland, where almost everyone who was born there either elects or is forced into some identification with either major 'side' in the conflict, national identities may not always be good prescriptive models for certain types of behaviour, but they are very good indicators of notions of community and belonging – notions moulded by a generation if not more of sectarianism, war and prejudice – which also provide keys to the problems facing European integration in the region. In fact, national identities so dominate the cultural identifications of border people, of all people, in Northern Ireland that, to the extent that it is acknowledged as a possible alternative, European identity is often scoffed at as little more than a tactic to get funding, or to support the European stance of a local political party.

It is this primacy of national identity which supports, and in some cases motivates, attempts to develop cross-border co-operation in the region, and which is also responsible for attempts to thwart it at almost all costs. The cultural barriers to co-operation are clear between the two main 'communities' of nationalists (i.e. those Northern Ireland people who are Catholic, and whose culture and politics are sympathetic to the goal of the reunification of the Irish nation) and unionists (i.e. those Northern Ireland people who are Protestant, and whose culture and politics support Northern Ireland's continued role in the United Kingdom). These barriers inhibit cross-community relations at all levels of local society, and in most aspects of the daily discourse of work, sport, religion and politics. Cultural divergence also presents a barrier to communication and commerce between the Republic of Ireland and nationalists in Northern Ireland. This is because Irish nationalism in the Republic has evolved along some different axes from its northern variant. As a result two separate political cultures have arisen, those of Ireland

and Northern Ireland, which place important if seldom-addressed barriers before both international and intra-national co-operation on the island.

The Irish and British governments also have different approaches to Europe and European funding. Each state has an agenda which may well be perceived as supportive or hostile to local communities. Each of the states seeks to use the EU and its funds to achieve what they believe to be the policy priorities within their jurisdictions, and these priorities may very well be at odds with local ones, especially when there has been little local consultation and when government agencies are competing with local private and voluntary bodies for the limited funds.

Finally, it is important to note that British political and economic elites have had ambivalent views of the UK's role in the EU, views which have been one feature in the often contradictory policies which the British state has instituted in Northern Ireland. For example, while the UK is on record as a firm supporter of a 'Europe Without Frontiers' in terms of the removal of international barriers to workers, capital, services, and products, British governments have also opted out of a number of moves towards integration which might have supported and enhanced these freedoms. At the Northern Ireland border, it is also ironic to note that in the midst of the efforts to facilitate the implementation of the 1992 programme for a single European market, the British government actually strengthened and increased military fortifications along that borderline, which as O'Dowd (1994; see also O'Dowd and Corrigan 1996; Wilson 1996) has pointed out enhances the border's role as both the symbol and the reality of the state's sovereignty. This sovereignty is a crucial plank in both the state's and Unionists' agendas in Northern Ireland. Thus even state agendas shift dramatically over time, and in some instances appear Janus-like, at the Northern Ireland border.

Rhetoric and Agenda

The various political identities of Northern Ireland reflect ideologies and movements which have created atmospheres of mistrust and fear, regimes of patronage and clientelism, and beliefs in conspiracy and hidden agendas. In the border region it is no wonder that cross-border co-operation is scarce given the political and economic climate. Unionists distrust local government councils with Catholic majorities and a central government seemingly intent on betraying Ulster loyalism through the British government's insistence on their present peace agenda. Nationalists in Northern Ireland have traditionally distrusted most British government initiatives. Nationalists on either side of the border seem to have different agendas for the future of Ireland, while republicans (i.e. nationalists who seek an island-wide Republic of Ireland, and who in the past have supported the use of violence to achieve this aim), until their political party's recent return to constitutional politics, seemed intent on achieving a united Ireland at all costs.

Loyalists (i.e. more radical and traditional unionists) decry unionist politicians who sit down in government with 'terrorists'. And in the midst of all of this the Irish and British states see particular need for the economic support of their versions of the EU, within their states and in the EU as a whole.

One point needs to be stressed here. There is no evidence that the British government or civil service in Belfast or elsewhere have done anything wrong in their application of INTERREG. But the fact is that in the Northern Ireland borderlands, especially among nationalists, these actions can be and often are perceived to be discriminatory. This reflects seventy years of political development in Northern Ireland which did a great deal to prevent cross-border co-operation, a process which is difficult to stop and reverse, whatever the financial incentives proffered by the EU. Thus the various agendas of the British state are suspect among nationalists in the Northern Ireland border region. This is true even when they involve European funding. Nationalists are not alone with their suspicions. Many unionists are wary of what the EU means to them, to the UK, and to Europe in general. For example, one unionist leader has expressed his concern over the EU-wide papist conspiracy, as symbolized in the aptly titled Treaty of Rome which gave birth to the Common Market.

The politics of Northern Ireland revolve around the popular association of nation with state. In this perspective, a weakening of the sovereignty of the state is a loss to the nation, and in some cases also a threat to citizens' national identity. The EU is perceived by some to mount such a threat in Northern Ireland because its institutions and ideas will diminish nation-state sovereignty, and will seek to create some form of alternative identity which is seen to be at odds with national identities. In Northern Ireland, for example, resistance to the EU is high among unionists because any agency which dilutes sovereignty of the British state is seen to be a threat to the Union of the United Kingdom. Nonetheless, the role of Northern Ireland as a region in Europe has increasingly become part of the Irish and British agendas, and will undoubtedly be a principal concern of the new Northern Ireland Assembly.

The relationships between national identities and national and European political agendas are problematical, and in need of much more empirical research than has been done to date. My research at the Northern Ireland border has revealed that many Irish and British people in Northern Ireland are anti-EU, just as great numbers of each are supporters of the EU. It is probably also fair to say that when they are for or against the EU, it depends on what is being discussed, or what is at stake. 'Irish' and 'British' identity can both be seen as important reasons for supporting or opposing any, or many, or even all aspects of Europeanization. Just as in the Danish case discussed by Jenkins in his contribution to this volume, national identity can be articulated as the rationale for diametrically opposed political actions. 'European identity', for that matter, is also both rationale and weapon. To some in Northern Ireland it is but one of many identities which can constitute an individual or group's consciousness and political self. To others, in zero-sum gamesmanship, it is perceived as an insidious tactic to undermine nation and state. In fact, 'being' European, or 'becoming' European, are tactics and strategies which are openly, though not widely, discussed in Northern Ireland as ways to bolster or weaken economic, political, and social standing.

Irrespective of national identity, few people in Northern Ireland, or in Ireland, oppose the EU's role as a source of funds, or as the watchdog of prices, trade, competition, and social welfare. In other words, the economic benefits of the EU are rarely disputed. But its roles in the politics and society of Northern Ireland, if openly debated at all, are matters of concern and contest. Support for and opposition to the EU are not easily predicted by religion, locality, and national identity, but support for its individual programmes can be much more easily traced, especially in a region like that of the Northern Ireland borderlands where the EU's initiatives are seen to be so closely allied to those of government.

As I have discussed elsewhere (Wilson 1996) the support for and the opposition to the EU in Northern Ireland are part of the dialectics of European integration, wherein building the new Europe through the creation of alternative identities of citizen, worker, and consumer, along with the provision of alternative means of subnational governance and policy making, may very well be weakening the identification of the citizen with the state. The EU offers alternatives to the nation state which are perceived by some people to be plausible and attainable, even if that alternative is little more than a transformed nation state. This creates a tension between member states and the EU, which is exacerbated by a lack of fit between and among local, national and European agendas. This is why the Foreign Minister's words with which this essay began are so ironic, because it is unclear whose agenda is 'theirs' and 'ours'.

In this case, at least, the British agenda in the EU is clearly not the same as that of the EU itself. The EU's agenda seems to be much more than the sum of the member states' parts, as evidenced in each compromise which allows the integration process to proceed. In fact, the whole notion of a coherent EU agenda, and project, is called into question when seen through the eyes of local communities in Northern Ireland. While EU policy objectives are often clear, the means to attain them often rest squarely on the shoulders of the member states. These shoulders may not be as strong in the United Kingdom as they are elsewhere in the EU, as evidenced in the British government's mixed reception to such mainstays of EU integration as common monetary policy and currency, the Common Agricultural Policy, and tax reform. And the many agendas of the British peoples are often quite distinct from those of their government. So not only is it unclear which Europe or whose Europe needs to be returned to which people, but whose agendas will make this return a successful one?

In Northern Ireland a number of overlapping and contesting political agendas seek to benefit, if not appropriate, the EU's seemingly unambiguous programme of INTERREG. The projects approved so far suggest a lack of commitment by the British government to the development of cross-border co-operation in the public, voluntary and private sectors, in a situation where 'cross-border co-operation becomes merely a rhetorical criterion to be used to take advantage of European monies' (Quinlivan 1997: 84). This situation also clarifies the attitude of both the British government and other local actors to that extra dimension which Delors believes the EU can offer to the people of Northern Ireland, which in this case seems to be the infusion of money.

This confusing articulation of policies also highlights the contradictory nature of EU agendas, which on the one hand seek to fund the cross-border integration of economy and society, but on the other to rely on the principles of subsidiarity and additionality. The former essentially leaves the use of EU funds up to the member-state government, and the latter is supposed to guarantee that EU money is in addition to funds, maintained at least at previous levels, already allocated by the states to the same purpose as the EU. In the Northern Ireland borderlands this amounts, in the view of local populations, to a subsidy for the state, to be used according to its needs and not theirs. As a result the EU also presents its Janus-like visage to the people of Northern Ireland, making suspect any extra dimension it might offer.

Conclusion

The situation at the Northern Ireland border supports the conclusion that in centralized states in the EU the institutions and policy-making functions of the state take precedence over all major EU initiatives, precisely because Europe-building is filtered through state structures. This serves to make the related questions of the imagining and experiencing of the EU also a matter related to competing nationalisms. As a result, in areas of strongly felt nationalism of which Northern Ireland may be an extreme example, but one which puts into sharp relief the often divisive issues of state policy and ethnonational and regional movements, national identities serve as charters for actions which inhibit political and economic integration between states. This is so whether these national identities are those of minority or majority populations, or those of agents of the state or its enemies. Furthermore, in the Northern Ireland border example, the economic advantages which are gained through EU programmes are made meaningful in nationalist terms at local levels. As a result, 'Europe' has been perceived as another agent of state or extra-state political power, helping or hurting Irish nationalists or British loyalists. This has made the general category of European institutions suspect, to some, as an extension of the British state, or at least perhaps a set of institutions, laws and ideas which can be easily pre-empted or co-opted to suit the interests, or maybe just some of the agents, of the state.

Consequences such as these fly in the face of the intentions of EU policy makers, who believe that economic development will be the prime mover in fostering an awareness of both European integration and identity. In Northern Ireland, in fact, the opposite seems to have occurred, in that EU funding has reinforced the predominance of national identities in everyday life in the Irish borderlands, and elsewhere in Northern Ireland for that matter. The pre-eminence of national identities found in Northern Ireland supports the belief in the convergence of the related concepts of nation, state, sovereignty and identity, which does little to further social and political integration within and between the EU's member states.

It is ironic that EU initiatives should be having this effect in a periphery of Europe specifically targeted for funds to bring it closer to the mainstream indices of the core areas of the EU. The strengthening of nationalism anywhere in the EU must be disconcerting to the EU's architects, for as McDonald has pointed out, nationalism is a dirty word among the elites of the EU, where it is seen as a condition that needs to be overcome (1996: 52). In fact, nationalism is being constructed by many leaders of the EU as the antithesis of Europeanism. One point of this chapter is that nationalism is more important to people in Northern Ireland than is 'Europe' and a European identity, and to construct the EU as a social and political arena in which nationalism is not welcome is to make a future life within the EU difficult, if not untenable, for many of Northern Ireland's people, and perhaps as well as for many others elsewhere in the EU.

Anthropologists have a role to play in the scholarship of the EU, especially in the issues of culture, identity, and nationalism (Wilson 1993, 1996). As reviewed in the introduction to this volume, some scholars (see, for example, Shore and Black 1992, 1995) have suggested correctly that in order to integrate theory and practice in their studies of the EU, anthropologists should "study up" and focus on the cultures of EU institutions as well as the institutions of European culture (as done, for example, in Abélès 1992). But this chapter champions a different, perhaps wider, concern. An anthropology of the EU must explore the EU's institutions and processes as they are experienced in everyday life, at every level of society and culture throughout the member states and even beyond the EU's borders. In order to integrate the EU into their lives, as both an idea as well as a set of institutions and laws, people are symbolically constructing the EU in more ways than its leaders may wish. Because the EU also constructs itself, through often complex processes of image-building, it seeks to influence the ways it is perceived in its citizens' daily lives. But the images and their meanings cannot be completely controlled in the public spheres of the EU and the member states. What may appear to be clear-cut images of economic union are being used by national elites to strengthen state borders, as well as bolster or weaken the metaphorical boundaries to identity which figure so prominently among many of the diverse populations of the EU. In Ireland, for example, Irish nationalists use the imagery of integration as a weapon against the British state's notions of its sovereignty in Northern Ireland.

Much of the EU's imaging is consciously aimed at symbols, e.g. 'European' flag, passport, and anthem. Much of the EU's production of the culture of European integration is more implicit, done through its representatives' day-to-day administrative activities. For instance, the EU, through its commissioners and other public servants, goes to great lengths to appear disinterested in the EU's assault on the power of both its nation states and their politicians. They push the concept of 'subsidiarity', which is as much a symbol of decentralization as it is a policy objective of delegated authority. But the implicit message is that there will be some important policy decisions which will inevitably be taken at the centre, in the EU's administrative heartland. This is very much a process of political centralization, and is certainly a challenge to the sovereignty of the state. The basic point of this chapter is to examine the tension between European programmes and European integration as experienced in the border region of Northern Ireland, in order to illustrate some of the ways in which new political and cultural spaces of Europe may be competing in its localities and regions with the old ones of nationalism and the state, where the project of EU building may be faltering.

Notes

This chapter, which expands on some points made in Wilson (2000), is based on intermittent field research, since 1991, at the eastern end of the Irish Border. This research was supported in part by the US National Endowment for the Humanities and the Wenner Gren Foundation for Anthropological Research.

1. British Information Services Press Release, Monday, 3 November 1997.
2. Throughout this chapter, the term 'Northern Ireland border' refers to the territory and people who are on the Northern Ireland side of the land border between the Republic of Ireland and the United Kingdom of Great Britain and Northern Ireland.
3. Interview, August 1998.

References

Abélès, M. (1992), *La Vie Quotidienne au Parlement Européen*, Paris: Hachette.

Armstrong, H.W. (1995), 'The Role and Evolution of European Community Regional Policy', in Barry Jones and Michael Keating (eds), *The European Union and the Regions*, Oxford: Clarendon Press.

Bache, I., George, S. and Rhodes, R.A.W. (1996), 'The European Union, Cohesion Policy, and Subnational Authorities in the United Kingdom', in Liesbet Hooghe (ed.), *Cohesion Policy and European Integration: Building Multi-level Governance*, Oxford: Oxford University Press.

Bellier, I. (1997), 'The Commission as an Actor', in H. Wallace and A. Young (eds), *Participation and Policy Making in Europe*, Oxford: Clarendon Press.

Borneman, J. and Fowler, N. (1997), 'Europeanization', *Annual Review of Anthropology*, 26: 487–514.

Coopers and Lybrand (1997), *INTERREG II Mid-term Evaluation*, Dublin and Belfast: Department of Finance and Department of Finance and Personnel.

Delanty, G. (1995), *Inventing Europe: Idea, Identity, Reality*, London: Macmillan.

Delors, J. (1997), 'A Unique Perspective on Cross-border Development', in *A Shared Vision for the North-West, Report of the Cross-Border Community Development Project Conference*, September 1997, Letterkenny.

Donnan, H. and Wilson, T.M. (1999), *Borders: Frontiers of Identity, Nation and State*, Oxford: Berg.

Hedetoft, U. (1994a), 'National Identities and European Integration "From Below": Bringing People Back In', *Journal of European Integration* 17 (1): 1–28.

—— (1994b), 'The State of Sovereignty in Europe: Political Concept or Cultural Self-Image', in S. Zetterholm (ed.), *National Cultures and European Integration*, Oxford: Berg.

—— (1995), *Signs of Nations. Studies in the Political Semiotics of Self and Other in Contemporary European Nationalism*, Aldershot: Dartmouth.

—— (1997), *The Nation State Meets the World: National Identities in the Context of Transnationality and Cultural Globalisation*, Discussion Paper 2/97, Aalborg University: Centre for International Studies.

INTERREG Development Office (1994), *Programme Summary, INTERREG Programme, Ireland and Northern Ireland, 1994-1999*, Monaghan: INTERREG Development Office.

Jones, B. (1995), 'Conclusion', in Barry Jones and Michael Keating (eds), *The European Union and the Regions*, Oxford: Clarendon Press.

Keating, M. (1995), 'Europeanism and Regionalism', in Barry Jones and Michael Keating (eds), *The European Union and the Regions*, Oxford: Clarendon Press.

Kilmurray, A. (1997), 'A Vision of Cross-Border Community Development', in *A Shared Vision for the North-West, Report of the Cross-Border Community Development Project Conference*, September 1997, Letterkenny.

Laffan, B. (1996), 'Ireland: A Region Without Regions – The Odd Man Out?', In Liesbet Hooghe (ed.), *Cohesion Policy and European Integration: Building Multi-level Governance*, Oxford: Oxford University Press.

McDonald, M. (1996), '"Unity in diversity": Some Tensions in the Construction of Europe', *Social Anthropology* 4 (1): 47–60.

—— (1997), 'Identities in the European Commission', in Neill Nugent (ed.), *At the Heart of the Union*, London: Macmillan.

O'Dowd, L. (1994), *Whither the Irish Border? Sovereignty, Democracy and Economic Integration in Ireland*, Belfast: Centre for Research and Documentation.

O'Dowd, L. and Corrigan, J. (1995), 'Buffer Zone or Bridge: Local Responses to Cross-border Economic Co-operation in the Irish Border Region', *Administration*, 42 (4): 335–51.

—— (1996), 'Securing the Irish Border in a Europe Without Frontiers', in Liam O'Dowd and Thomas M. Wilson (eds), *Borders, Nations and States: Frontiers of Sovereignty in the New Europe*, Aldershot: Avebury.

Quinlivan, E. (1997), *The 'Evil Genius' of European Integration, Co-operation across the Irish Border: A Study of the INTERREG II Initiative*, Unpublished MA Thesis, University College Galway.

Shore, C. (1993), 'Inventing the "People's Europe": Critical Approaches to European Community "Cultural Policy"', *Man* 28: 779–800.

Shore, C. and Black, A. (1992), 'The European Communities and the Construction of Europe', *Anthropology Today* 8 (3): 10–11.

—— (1995), 'Citizens' Europe and the Construction of European Identity', in Victoria A. Goddard, Josep R. Llobera and Cris Shore (eds), *The Anthropology of Europe: Identity and Boundaries in Conflict*, Oxford: Berg.

Simpson, J.V. (1996), *Northern Ireland: A Region of the European Union*, London: Representation of the European Commission in the United Kingdom.

Smith, A. (1992), 'National Identity and the Idea of European Unity', *International Affairs* 68 (1): 55–76.

—— (1995), *Nations and Nationalism in a Global Era*, Cambridge: Polity.

Tarrow, S. (1994), *Rebirth or Stagnation? European Studies after 1989*, New York: Social Science Research Council.

Wilson, T.M. (1993), 'An Anthropology of the European Community', in T.M. Wilson and M.E. Smith (eds), *Cultural Change and the New Europe: Perspectives on the European Community*, Boulder and Oxford: Westview Press.

—— (1996), 'Sovereignty, Identity and Borders: Political Anthropology and European Integration', in L. O'Dowd and T.M. Wilson (eds), *Borders, Nations and States: Frontiers of Sovereignty in the New Europe*, Aldershot: Avebury.

—— (1998), 'An Anthropology of the European Union, From Above and Below', in Susan Parman (ed.), *Europe in the Anthropological Imagination*, Upper Saddle River, NJ: Prentice-Hall.

—— (2000), 'The Obstacles to European Union Regional Policy in the Northern Ireland Borderlands', *Human Organization*, 59 (1): 1–10.

Wilson, T.M. and Donnan, H. (eds), (1998), *Border Identities: Nation and State at International Frontiers*, Cambridge: Cambridge University Press.

Zabusky, S.E. (1995), *Launching Europe: An Ethnography of European Co-operation in Space Science*, Princeton: Princeton University Press.

–8–

Not Simple At All: Danish Identity and the European Union

Richard Jenkins

Denmark is often cited as an example par excellence of the onward march of European unity threatened by national identity. Indeed, our editors, in their introduction to this volume, refer to Hedetoft's suggestion that the Danish rejection of Maastricht in the first (1992) referendum on the Treaty may have first alerted academics to the need for more studies of identity in the EU context. One of the most intriguing things about Denmark in this respect is that while, on the one hand, it has a deserved reputation as a conscientious and co-operative member of the EU with respect to its observance of European legislation and directives, it has, on the other, proved to be politically somewhat 'awkward' in its dogged popular scepticism about the terms and conditions of membership at all.

In this chapter, I will draw upon my research in a small town in Jutland, in an area that has voted '*Ja*' in all three Danish referenda about Europe in the 1990s, to look at what 'Danish identity' might mean in this context, and to unpack some of the complex strands of decision-making that come into play with respect to the European question. Appropriately enough, the paper will focus particularly on local positions during the 1992 referendum about the Maastricht Treaty.

In terms of broader theoretical issues, the local ethnographic focus of this paper is intended to illuminate the relationship between shared interests and shared identity to which the editors allude in their introductory chapter, and to contribute to the discussion of these matters begun by Stephen Cornell, for example (1996; Cornell and Hartmann 1998). What matters more, and under what circumstances: shared identity or perceived shared interests? I suspect that politics is, at least in large part, born of the need to strike a balance between the two, and that realpolitik may be what we call those situations in which there is little in the way of balance to be struck. In the European politics of the second half of the twentieth century, however, and for reasons which there is no time to explore here, 'identity' has acquired a privileged status as a resource or bargaining chip, a card which it is difficult to trump, the defence of which does not have to be justified. And even when people appear to share the same identity but have rather different interests, the argument may be carried on in terms of the former rather than the latter.

Conventional Wisdom

The opening sentence of a recent brief discussion of the impact of European policies and programmes on the Danish regions, emphasizes that 'Denmark has a clear sense of national history and identity, which is reinforced by a common language and culture' (Thomas 1995: 381). These factors are among the most common explanations for Danish scepticism about the European Union (EU), and the Community before that: 'The feeling of losing something immaterial – such as national identity, cultural significance, solidarity' (Sørensen and Væver 1992: 14). And of course, seen from another point of view, these phenomena are anything but immaterial and are certainly substantial:

> Real values are at stake and many Danes fear they will disappear when society, nation and state are no longer identical as has been the case for more than a hundred years. That is why they have been reluctant to participate wholeheartedly in 'the construction of Europe'. (Østergård 1992a: 176)

So, Danish scepticism towards European unity – which ranges from outspoken rejectionism to determined ambivalence – is thought to have something important to do with Danish identity. Following Hedetoft's argument (1991), and indeed the logic of countless other discussions of symbolism and collective identity, one would expect that this is at least in part a gathering reaction to the increasingly strident public symbolization of the European project through flags, songs, and public events. Thus the more European identity is stressed and made visible, the more Danes emphasise their identity.

However, national identity means – or includes – many things. 'National sentiment' in the modern era definitively involves, inter alia, the evocation of 'self-determination' (Jørgensen 1993: 100). This issue is frequently expressed – inside and outside Denmark – in terms of *sovereignty*, and its surrender to the EU. Thus, in the run up to the 1998 referendum on the Amsterdam Treaty, the right-wing populist tabloid that is Denmark's best-selling newspaper launched its *No* campaign by arguing on its front page that 'The undermining of Denmark's sovereignty must stop' (*Ekstra Bladet*, 12 May 1998). The anti-Union position is, in this respect, frequently justified in terms of Danish law and history:

> grass roots resistance to Maastricht – and subsequently to the Treaty of Amsterdam – continues in Denmark, on the grounds that the Danish constitution bars the transfer of sovereignty except in specific areas, whereas these Treaties grant wide-ranging sovereign-type powers to the EU. (Leach 1998: 59)

Sauerberg's analysis of Danish public opinion polls in advance of the 1992 referendum on Maastricht helps us to unpack the issue of self-determination further. He identifies two basic currents of Danish opposition to European unification. One is associated with right-wing political parties which focus on national boundaries and immigration, the other – and, he believes, the more substantial – expresses 'anti-authoritarian and leftist attitudes' in support of progressive, decentralized, eco-friendly, Nordic social democracy (Sauerberg 1992: 70). Each claims a distinctive Danish-ness for its position, and each claims to defend self-determination. Newspaper coverage of the referendum about the Amsterdam Treaty suggests that little has changed since 1992:

> Some on the right want Denmark to keep its own border controls to keep immigrants – and Germans – out. Those on the left believe that the EU's move towards stronger external borders will build a fortress Europe, making it harder for refugees to get in. (*Guardian*, 28 May 1998)

Taking all of these arguments together, the following emerges as the conventional wisdom about Danish scepticism with respect to greater European integration:

- Danes have a relatively clear-cut and homogenous sense of themselves, and of who they are and who they are not (i.e. Danish identity, Danish-ness).
- This consensual national identity has made large numbers of them sceptical and suspicious about increasing European unification.
- This scepticism revolves around issues to do with self-determination.
- Self-determination means: on the right hand, the freedom to preserve Danish cultural and ethnic homogeneity; on the left hand, the freedom to preserve what one might call the Nordic welfare model of participatory social democracy.

In the rest of this chapter I will compare this conventional wisdom to the picture that is revealed by looking in greater depth at the area of mid-Jutland where I have undertaken fieldwork.

Before doing so, however, there is one further and very interesting question which remains to be asked. Why did this conventional-wisdom explanation of the difficulties attendant upon Danish ratification of the Union – for that is what we are talking about – take the shape that it has? One answer which is at least worth taking seriously is that it was convenient for all the other member states. When Denmark rejected the Maastricht Treaty in 1992, the result, regardless of the narrowness of the margin, probably caused relief as well as consternation and relief in equal parts among its fellow EC member states. Support for Maastricht in many of the other countries was less solid than their governmental endorsement of the Treaty might have suggested, and the Danes being 'difficult' allowed cracks in the facade of unanimity elsewhere to be underplayed, at the same time as some of the problems were actually addressed.

Not only that, but putting the Danish difficulty down to 'identity' meant that in some senses it was beyond criticism. In the late twentieth century the imperative demands of identity have to be heeded. In the European context, it is explicit policy that identity – particularly the identities of the small peoples of the Union – should be respected as part of the complex frameworks of give-and-take which hold the whole thing together. Thus, the world did not come to an end following the narrow Danish rejection – despite the obligatory dire warnings from all sides to this effect – and it gave everyone, not least the United Kingdom, an opportunity, at the subsequent Edinburgh summit, to go back and fiddle around with some of the more problematic aspects of the Treaty.

An Ordinary Town

Between September 1996 and July 1997 I carried out fieldwork in mid-Jutland, Denmark, looking at the town of Skive and its hinterland.[1] The *kommune* has approximately 27,000 inhabitants, of whom about 20,000 live in the town itself. Although for many *skibonitter,* as those who can qualify as local by birth call themselves, it is a special place unlike any other, it is also an altogether ordinary Danish small town, not unrepresentative of many other Danish small towns. Since Denmark is – greater Copenhagen and Århus aside – a nation of small towns, it is therefore unlikely to be particularly un-representative of Denmark.

The local economy is mixed, with unemployment at around 5 per cent of the working population. Although the public sector is the largest single employment sector, there are many small-to-medium-sized manufacturing companies and a large private service sector. Skive is also an educational centre, with a teacher-training college, a Folk High School, a Technical College, a Business College, and a *gymnasium* (an élite post-compulsory secondary school). Students of one kind or another are among the most visible inhabitants, as are soldiers, because of the town's large modern artillery garrison.

Since the early 1990s the population of Skive town, in particular, has changed from relative ethnic homogeneity to something more complex. According to local agencies dealing with the situation, as much as 5 per cent of the local population may now be made up of immigrants: largely refugees and mainly Islamic, from various Middle Eastern countries. This is, however, a figure it is not possible to verify definitively, and other local sources doubt that the total is so high. Whichever estimate one accepts, the town now has a visible, and probably permanent, ethnic minority presence. At the municipal elections in November 1997, broadly in line with national trends, the town acquired a Conservative mayor, after more than sixty years of Social Democrat control. The anti-immigrant Danish People's

Party (*Dansk Folkeparti*) increased its representation from one to two council members.

In the 1992 referendum, Denmark as a whole voted against Danish endorsement of the Maastricht Treaty by the narrowest of margins: 50.7 per cent voting 'no', and 49.3 per cent 'yes'. Within Denmark, Jutland voted 'yes', the islands voted 'no' (narrowly) and greater Copenhagen returned a definite 'no' (Thomas 1995: 283). In the Skive parliamentary constituency (*kreds*) all five of the constituent local government areas – Skive, Spøttrup, Sallingsund, Sundsøre and Fjends *kommuner* – voted for the Treaty. In Skive *kommune*, 53.6 per cent of the votes were for the 'yes' option; in rural Spøttrup, Sallingsund, and Fjends the percentage was slightly higher; in Sundsøre, which is equally rural, it was very slightly lower. In Viborg *amt* – the county of which Skive forms a part – the percentage of 'yes' votes was 53.6 per cent (see Skive Kommune 1994: 132, Table 124). In the subsequent referenda – 1993 on the Edinburgh adjustments to Maastricht, and 1998 on the Amsterdam Treaty – the difference between the local and national pictures remained, with Skive returning a higher percentage vote 'for' than the overall national figure.

The 1992 Referendum Campaign

I am going to focus on the first six months of 1992, the period leading up to, and immediately after, the referendum on 2 June 1992. It was a period of intense campaigning and public debate, on both sides of the argument. This period has been chosen for that reason. The subsequent referenda, in 1993 and 1998, seem to have been attended locally – although there was a considerable amount of conflict elsewhere in 1993 – by less discord and public position-taking. Despite the continued presence of a rump of opposition, membership of the EU had settled down by the time of my fieldwork to become a relatively unproblematic aspect of the paradigm of 'normal politics'. Locally the battle has, effectively, been won.

The data comes from the local newspaper, *Skive* Folkeblad,[2] which publishes six days a week, plus a weekly supplement 'Middle of the Week' (*Midt på Ugen*). The paper has a basic political orientation towards the Radical (*Radikale Venstre*) Party, a small centre party, with a history of pacifism and anti-establishment positions, which has participated in many Danish governments since the War. The Radicals began 1992 opposed to the Union; by the time of referendum, however, they were more or less supporting it. The paper's editorial line was in favour of the Union throughout this period. Indeed, in an editorial on 24 March the editor congratulated the Radical Party on finally beginning to change its European policy, towards support for the Union and the Treaty.

During this period two main political issues generated not only news and editorial comment, but also readers' letters, The first was the EU and the referendum, the second, immigration and refugees (the local area had recently seen the arrival of its first refugees). The volume of readers' letters during this period, and their use by parties and pressure groups as a medium of communication, prompted an editorial in *Midt på Ugen* (26 February) about 'false readers' letters': standard texts prepared by interest groups and organisations and sent, masquerading as genuine personal communications, to a number of newspapers. Where discovered, the paper said, these would not be published.

Now, the reader's letter is almost an art form in the Danish local press. Every locality has a number of assiduous contributors to the genre – 'readers' letter terrorists', as I have heard them called – generally with particular axes to grind. They can be seen hard at work in this period. I have tried to minimize my use in this chapter of their contributions to the debate, in order to avoid privileging a noisy and often extreme minority. Most people in Skive do not write at all to the newspaper, let alone regularly.

All of which suggests that the readers' letters, which are among the most colourful of the data which the newspaper offers, should be read with at least some caution. I have certainly tried to avoid the temptation to *rely* on them as a source of material. The prudence of this approach is underlined by the comments of one of the persistent letter-writers himself, a local priest and an opponent of the Union, who, in a letter headed 'Think with the heart' (29 May), bemoaned the fact that the referendum campaign had been played out in 'Enormous advertisements from the yes-sayers, but only readers' letters from the no-sayers.' Thus the preponderance of readers' letters supporting a 'no' vote should not be taken to indicate the balance of local opinion. A formal content analysis of the letters pages of the newspaper would therefore be a futile task.

Nonetheless, this letter is a useful reminder that the 1992 'yes' campaign was supported enthusiastically – and expensively – by nearly every major political party in Denmark. The major opponents of Union and the Treaty were the Progress Party, on the right (*Fremskridtspartiet,* which in 1995 split and gave birth to *Dansk Folkeparti*), and, on the left, the Socialist People's Party (*Socialistisk Folkeparti,* the *SF*) and the Unity List (*Enhedslisten,* a coalition of greens, left-socialists and communists). The change in position of the Radical Party during this period has already been noted. The small centre-oriented *Kristeligt Folkeparti* (Christian People's Party) was utterly split. Nor did the Social Democrats enter the campaign completely united. They may have been publicly agreed on a pro-Union stance but in the aftermath of a viciously-contested leadership campaign, some supporters of the defeated Svend Auken were dissident and disruptive.

In advance of the referendum, however, there was a clear and taken-for-granted presumption on the part of most public commentators that the vote would endorse the Treaty, even if only narrowly. As the day approached this presumption weakened, but it formed an important part of the background and context in which the following material should be read. A 'yes' vote was widely expected.

However, another important aspect of that context was simple lack of interest, if not actual apathy. While the organized parties, and enthusiasts of one hue or another, debated the issues, most local voters seem to have been less bothered. For example, a week before the conference organized in a local hotel by the European Movement (*Europabevægelsen*) and the European Commission, the newspaper reported that, out of a thousand invitations sent out to schools, business folk, politicians, and voluntary organizations, only twenty-eight people had registered. As the headline put it: 'No interest in the EC-union' (18 April).

That may also, however, have reflected a lack of interest in, or enthusiasm for, politics in general. According to an editorial on 16 March, in the wake of a particularly dismal passage of Danish politics – in respect of a range of issues, and on the left and the right – many 'no' votes were likely to be cast simply as a protest against the politicians of Christiansborg (the Danish parliament building). Whatever the truth of that, it is certainly plausible that many voters saw the issues as somewhat distant, and obscured rather than illuminated by the debate. On 16 May, the newspaper did a series of interviews in a local supermarket, asking shoppers whether they felt they had been properly informed about the issues. Most of those asked intended to vote 'yes'. Many thought that it was 'their own fault' that they were so poorly informed, because they had not taken enough interest. But many were also sceptical about politicians. Here is a sergeant from the garrison speaking:

> I will vote yes, but I don't think that the advantages of the union have come forward in the debate yet. Politicians don't really know yet. The spread is too big. Some say very strongly yes, and others no, the middle way is missing.

A *gymnasium* student had this to say:

> It is so uncertain, that it is impossible to find out about. What the politicians say is also different. Nor are they so agreed about what will come out of it.

Consensus and the quest for a 'middle way' are important rhetorical themes and values in Danish politics. While there was considerable agreement across a spectrum on both sides of the political centre, conflict over the European issue extended beyond Party positions. Some members of the Social Democrats in Skive defied their party line to campaign for a 'no' vote. Some local members of the Progress Party did the same thing, in the opposite direction. Nationally, the small Christian People's Party got into a hopeless muddle and publicly collapsed into disagreement on the issue. None of this would have been positively received.

Allowing for these reservations, the voting figures suggest that the presumption of overall support for the Union was realistic in Skive. And that is perhaps the first point to be made. The argument that resistance to the Union is rooted in Danish national identity fails to account adequately for the yes-voters, who are presumably no less authentically Danish then those who voted 'no'. Nor are they necessarily any less concerned about Danish-ness and Danish identity. Witness, for example, the 'day school' on the theme of 'To be Danish' which was held on 22 February in a local boarding school (advertised in the newspaper on 6 February). Organized by *Venstre*, the Danish Liberal Party, who represent farming and business interests and have consistently been pro-Union, it included talks on themes such as 'Yes, but when did the Danes become Danish?', 'The Danes seen from outside' and 'To be Danish in the coming Europe', plus a session of Danish songs.

There is, however, no doubt that 'Danish-ness' was important to the 'no' campaign. This concern was very 'traditionally' expressed, drawing on the symbolism of *Dannebrog*, the national flag — with a swipe at politicians en passant — in one reader's letter on 30 April:

Dear Dannebrog, our much-loved flag, that we always love to see, both here at home and when we are abroad, it is always good to see you flying high. But now that too will soon be over, if people are so foolish as to vote yes on the 2nd June. If there is anyone who can point to a single thing that will benefit us if we vote yes, let us hear it. The one thing that will benefit us is that we can save the pay of the government and the *Folketing* [the Danish parliament] . . . Think about this, so therefore a big no on the 2nd June, if we are to rescue the last remnants of Denmark. Think about your descendants.

A different take on Danish culture, this time from the definitively non-traditional left, came in an article on 6 April, called 'Danish culture in the EC', contributed by Holger K. Nielsen, national leader of the Socialist People's Party (*SF*):

It is often raised in the debate that Danish culture is so strong that it can well survive EC-co-operation. If Danish culture is understood as the Danish language, the High School Songbook, the Southern Jutland coffee table and Danish *hygge* [the conventional, if inadequate, translation of which is 'cosiness'], that is absolutely true. Naturally, Danish culture understood in that way can survive EC-co-operation.

But culture is also a question of the possibilities for self-determination, for being master in one's own house. Among other things, therefore, it is an important part of the new national movements in Europe, that people who have previously lived in federal states wish for self-determination . . . The Union Treaty lays the foundation stone for a European federal state . . . SF is against that development, not least because it would result in bad democracy . . . In this respect, it is part of the Danish tradition that democracy is also a question of popular [*folkelig*] sympathy, and a short distance, between voters and politicians. Unfortunately, the very opposite impression is given by the EC-Union, namely a centralisation of power.

This kind of defence of national democracy and self-determination can easily become something different, an assertion of the superiority of the Danish way of life and system verging on chauvinism, if not xenophobia. A reader's letter of 27 May, which dramatized the cultural and political differences between Northern and Southern Europe in its reference to the 'mafia-style' politics of the EC, ended up by returning to threatened Danish virtues:

> So vote, therefore, no on the 2nd June, and let us keep the little bit of welfare and Danish-ness [*danskhed*] that we have left.

A similar, implicit, distinction between the civilised and uncivilized parts of Europe was also there in a letter on 9 April, pinpointing 'Ireland and the four southern European countries' as potentially capable, in a Union with qualified majority voting, of obstructing the kind of environmental measures that Danish standards would require.

Returning to the *SF*'s reasons for voting 'no', how do they compare with those of the right-wing opponents of the Union? In an article on 11 May, Pia Kjærsgaard of the anti-immigrant Progress Party offered the following arguments for voting 'no': loss of sovereignty, loss of the veto, the risk of direct Union taxation, the interference in the labour market threatened by 'the so-called social dimension', and the fact that 'decision-making processes in the EC are also extremely undemocratic'. In important respects, the two parties – despite the gulf that separated them on nearly every other issue – were saying something very similar, if not actually the same thing. They were even using the same rhetoric. Arguing for the protection of 'popular [*folkelig*] debate such as we know in Denmark', Kjærsgaard's arguments against an 'EC federal state' did not, in this article at least, wave the flag of Danish-ness or conjure up the threat of increased immigration.

That threat was, however, frequently raised during the debate, and not always as an argument *against* Union. Here, for example, is a marketing manager from Skive, a prospective parliamentary candidate for *Venstre*, the Danish Liberal Party, writing to the newspaper on 14 May:

> The rich part of Europe is surrounded by countries in economic, political and social need. There is no doubt that the pressure on Europe from poor, adult populations in North Africa and places in eastern Europe and Asia will increase in the coming years.
>
> The European countries cannot, each for themselves, handle the enormous problem that is piling up outside Europe's borders.
>
> If the European countries' borders are to resist the pressure, it is necessary that we co-operate. . . . I am naturally voting yes on the 2nd June. For many reasons, but first and foremost in order that my children will become good Europeans. They will not become worse Danes because of that.

Being a Dane may be about something other than being a European, however. During the campaign, a picture also emerges of a Nordic sphere which is seen as distinctly *not* European. This idea has its roots in nineteenth-century Nordic romanticism – promoted by social philosophers and authors such as Grundtvig – and remains powerful in everyday discourse and popular sentiment today. One of the regular letter writers had this to say on 11 May, concerning his fear that a 'yes' vote would mean slipping away from the 'Nordic model of society': 'In the Nordic lands there is great economic and cultural homogeneity, and more equality than in the rest of the world.' Following the eventual national vote against Union, the Nordic dimension was trumpeted, in a reader's letter on 9 June, as one of the positive aspects of the decision:

> It is a yes to freedom, and also to co-operation with Norway, Sweden, Iceland and Finland, in a united Nordic world [*Norden*[3]] – a Scandinavian cultural community with points of view.

However, Nordic particularism was also used to justify a 'yes' vote, as in this speech given to a local meeting by a Liberal (*Venstre*) member of parliament, and reported in *Skive Folkeblad* on 6 March:

> Today Denmark is the bridgehead for the EC in the Nordic world . We run the risk that, in the year 2000, Denmark will be the only Nordic country outside the EC. Denmark will not be a more interesting co-operation partner if we are working outside the EC or as a part-time member.

Discussions of the 'Nordic model' often went hand in hand with anxieties about loss of sovereignty and democracy. A local parliamentary candidate for the Unity List, for example, asking, on 2 March, whether the Nordic welfare model could be maintained in an EU, argued that, 'If we say yes to participation in the coming EC-Union, it means that we are at the same time saying no to being master in our own house.' He went to argue that the Union would mean, 'Throwing the baby out with the dirty bathwater. And the baby actually hasn't earned that.'

In the words of a reader's letter on 22 April:

> The vote is not about the economy or Danish membership of the EC, but about who shall decide in Denmark. At the same time opposition is rising among the population of the other Nordic countries . . . We are Danish and want to continue to be Danish, and our independence can be secured by voting no on the 2nd June.

One of the most emotive conflations of national identity with loss of sovereignty and the democratic deficit, comes in appeals to the Constitution, which occupies a central place in the mythology of Danish nationhood and citizenship: 'Let us show the politicians that the Danish people will not tolerate the Constitution being trampled underfoot. Show respect for the Constitution and vote no on the 2nd June' (reader's letter, 21 May).

Another point of view on these issues could, however, be mobilized in support of Danish membership of a European Union. Here the argument was that in order to have proper influence on what the big countries of Europe might decide, which, in or out of the Union, would affect 'a little land' such as Denmark, membership was vital:

> in a modern society one cannot isolate oneself from the surrounding world. We need to go in and influence the other European countries in the correct 'for Denmark' direction in a host of areas. That will happen through close co-operation. (reader's letter, 20 March)

At this point, there is a further thread to be woven into the developing picture of the complexity of local points of view on Europe. The question of control can be directed inward rather than outward. 'Who shall decide *within* Denmark?' speaks to ideals of equality, to class relationships, and to a well-established image of Danish cultural and social homogeneity. It also revisits the general dissatisfaction with politics and the state elite discussed earlier:

> the popularly elected idols, the stars in Christianborg's heaven . . . have the knife ready to take their share . . . The nice men in collars and ties [*slipsemænd*] in Brussels and their followers, who know how to score a jack-pot for themselves, well know that it is not possible for the ordinary man or woman to foresee the consequences of a yes, and are therefore easy in their mind and grateful to be able to threaten with fire and brimstone, and when yes-voters are aboard, click the trap shut and the citizen can later grieve over this development, that he/she did not have an earthly chance of foreseeing. (reader's letter, 11 May)

Politics is here seen as a gravy train, and politicians – most of whom, let us remember, were campaigning for a 'yes' vote – as motivated by self-interest, if not completely corrupt. More in a similar vein was printed on 14 April, in a letter from a priest in one of the rural areas (not the one who has already been quoted, however). Here the theme emerges in potent combination with some of the themes that have already been discussed:

> Do you claim in all seriousness that the EC will expel a member in good standing just because it is exercising its Treaty right to say no to the majority's wishes? . . . If that's the way it is, I think that Denmark should vote no on the 2nd June, not just for Denmark's sake, but for the Nordic world's, yes, for the whole of dear Europe's sake.
>
> If the others cannot understand this, the only explanation is that our understanding of democracy is that politics is a popular [*folkelig*] affair, as I think the understanding of

democracy is in the whole of the Nordic world. But politics under the southern skies of Europe is a specialism of top people [*topfolk*].

Translation is an issue here.[4] It is impossible to do adequate justice in English to the scorn and *ressentiment* that is condensed into words like '*slipsemænd*' and '*topfolk*'. In a country which has a well-developed cultural repertoire and vocabulary for ensuring that people do not get above themselves, they are harsh words indeed. It is equally impossible to communicate fully the historical, cultural and political resonance of the word *folkelig*, here clumsily translated as 'popular'. On the one hand, this alludes to what is seen as a distinctly Danish (or Nordic) tradition of politics – participatory social democracy, in the non-party sense – that is historically grounded in the post-1848 modernization of Denmark (Østergård 1992c: 21–5). On the other, it denotes a distinct way of getting on socially – and sociably – with one's fellows, as equals whom one can look in the eye and talk to, one to another. This is an ideological complex of great power and continuing importance in Denmark, on which politicians of both left and right routinely trade.

Returning to the issue of who shall decide within Denmark, there is – as with nearly all of this – another side to be examined, and a different kind of resentment perhaps. In the last couple of weeks before the referendum, as it became clearer that there might not, after all, be a 'yes' vote, and – perhaps – the volume of local rhetoric against the Union was reaching saturation point, more voices in its favour began to be raised. And there was a measure of irritation evident. Here is a reader from 'out in the country', clearly making a living from agriculture, writing to the newspaper on 29 May. He begins by referring to a recent announcement of the local Committee Against the Union: 'They are mostly priests, teachers and school principals. I dare say that they can call for a no. They will get their salary or pension anyway.' He then asks who will pay the subsidies to the farmers that are necessary to keep the prices that Danish housewives can afford to pay:

> So let the government fire some priests, teachers and school principals. Most churches here in Salling are nearly empty every Sunday anyway . . . They would be able to save a lot of money, which could be used for assistance [i.e. unemployment or welfare benefits] offices.
>
> Think about that, therefore, and vote yes on the 2nd June.

This is not just the self-interested voice of one whose livelihood depends on Europe. He is also expressing two other, not-uncommon local sentiments – anti-intellectualism, and exasperation with the size, cost and decision-making powers of the public sector – both of which appeal to notions about 'real' productive work.

Another correspondent, on the same day, also drew attention to the composition of the Committee Against the Union and to the fact that they were mostly teachers, priests and the like:

It is unbelievable that people who I thought stood with both feet on the ground, are participating, together with many camp followers, in stopping development in Denmark. What are all these people afraid of? It is my conviction that a lot of Danes have lost their senses. All the talk and angst about Turks, our Danish-ness, and so on, is just hot air to confuse them.

No, the real reason (which the no-sayers conceal well) is cowardice. The same cowardice that made Denmark surrender on 9th April 1940.

In 1940 the Danes were cowards. We let others win the war for us, we did not dare to join in from the start. That is also what we are doing now . . . I am 76 years old, so I experienced the war . . . I do not value Germans. A big people are always a danger for a small country, but in this situation we must stand with the big nations for that will help us to help ourselves. Moreover, it is always safer for a dwarf to sit on the giant's knee, than to stand outdoors.

I hope that all Danes who wish for good progress for their children and grandchildren, and not least for Denmark, vote yes on the 2nd June.

Fighting talk, and certainly not a point of view that is often publicly articulated. Be that as it may, this letter brings me to the final theme that I wish to explore in this material. Much of the anxiety about Europe in the run-up the 1992 referendum was, at least in part, anxiety about Germany. This emerges, entangled with concerns about self-determination, resentment of the state elite and the better-off, and Nordic romanticism, in the following letter (24 April):

This may be Denmark's final sale of independence. Let us remember that diverse trade union bosses [*pampere*], financial speculators and business leaders will happily use millions of kroner to propagandise for themselves and the future's EC.

These really are golden times for shopkeepers.

The nation state of Denmark is being sold. King Christian's border of 1920 is being erased. The northern province from the Eider to Skagen is being laid out as a holiday paradise for the master-race [*herrefolket*]!

Yes, so we will keep ourselves busy as sausage sellers and shoe-shiners. This really is the new world order in the year 2000. Our money system is not good enough either.

Will the next thing be our language and our ancient Nordic culture?

One must ask: have we already forgotten the dates, 9th April 1940 [when Denmark was occupied by Germany] and 5th May 1945 [the liberation]? Shall they be forgotten, who that time gave their lives for something that was sacred and precious? Namely Denmark's freedom and independence. Already, twenty years' membership speaks for itself. . . . One must recognise that the pin-striped gentlemen will put everything into the Roman Empire, even if it erodes citizens' rights, when *Folketing* is left carrying the can for EC legislation.

Therefore one must say to oneself: don't be a traitor, save Denmark now and in the future.

Therefore I will be voting no on the 2nd June.

In various forms, anti-German sentiments were regularly mobilized during the campaign, as arguments against the Union and for a 'no' vote. Here, for example, is another reader's letter (14 May) invoking Denmark's experience of occupation by the Germans during the Second World War:

> What we managed to avoid that time was to become Germany's northern *mark* [literally, 'field'; it implies something along the lines of 'province']. Let that not happen now.
>
> If the politicians who today are so busy getting us to vote yes to the EC Union, had been adults and said that then, they would have been called traitors . . .
>
> Let it be enough now. Vote no on the 2nd June, so that we still can live in a free Denmark.

Perhaps even more interesting, however – and in direct response – the spectre of Germany was also regularly conjured up in many appeals for a 'yes' vote, as in the letter, quoted earlier, addressing the sensitive issue of the Danish record during the Second World War. These 'pro-Union-anti-German' arguments did not just find their expression in readers' letters, and they were not straightforward. Here is an extract from an editorial in *Skive Folkeblad*, dated 9 March and written by the paper's parliamentary correspondent in Christianborg:

> One should not be so naive as to doubt that some in the re-united Germany have ambitions and dreams of being a great power . . . Street mobs with neo-Nazi tendencies aside, the belief in, not a militaristic, but such a powerful Germany is particularly found among right-wing popularists and in financial circles. But it is also exactly there that one finds the most substantial resistance to EC plans. . . .
>
> Far and away the majority of Germans, and that goes not least for the younger generation, choose like [Hans-Dietrich] Genscher, a European Germany . . . On the 2nd June, it is a no and not a yes that creates the greatest danger that it will become a *jawohl*.

So: vote yes to make sure that Germany does not return to its bad old ways, and to encourage the good Germans. This extract – with others already quoted – also suggests that concerns about the vulnerability of Danish language were a significant dimension of the perceived threat to identity and culture.

In case my emphasis in closing this section, on anti-German sentiments, appears to accentuate something that is actually not so important, it is worth remembering subsequent events. When the Danish football team beat Germany 2-0 in the European Championship final in Malmö three weeks later, on 26 June, the town centre of Skive, and many other Danish towns, erupted in celebrations, the scale and excitement of which many of my informants – and the terms in which they talk about it are no coincidence – have compared to the liberation celebrations in May 1945. Winning the championship was wonderful; beating the Germans was, it seems, even better.

Less frivolously, the 'yes' vote in the referendum the following year was secured – at least in part – by negotiating an opt-out at the Edinburgh summit meeting, prohibiting non-nationals resident outside Denmark from buying property in Denmark. Although it could not have been openly framed in these terms, this was and is widely understood as preventing Germans from buying up summer houses, particularly on the west coast, an area which experiences/suffers, at the same time as it profits from, an enormous influx of German tourists every summer. Profit is one thing, and the tourist trade as such was not under threat. The symbolization of national identity bound up in the annual summer house idyll is, however, an altogether different thing, and Danish politicians have learned that it is wise to take such matters seriously.

Issues of Identity

It is time to look again at the conventional wisdom about Danish identity and the EU that I outlined earlier. First, do Danes have a relatively clear-cut and homogenous sense of Danish identity and Danish-ness? Certainly, many contributors to the debate in Skive talked *as if they did*. The ease with which many of them obviously felt able to refer to Danish culture, as something with which their readers could understand and identify, is striking. On closer inspection, however, they did not always agree about *what* it was that they had in common. It is the assumption of Danish cultural homogeneity – and the mobilization of that idea as a political and rhetorical resource – that we are talking about here, not its actual existence. Precisely the same point should, of course, be made about the supposed political and cultural homogeneity of the Nordic world. However, that they are both – Danish-ness and Nordic-ness – imagined, does not mean that they are imaginary (Jenkins 1996). Each is a presence in the social world and is consequential in social life. Each means something.

This image of Danish-ness is the cultural allotrope of a general and well-established Danish ideological theme – 'we are all the same' – which runs through politics and social life at all levels.[5] There is little doubt that there is a *sense* of shared and relatively consistent *folkelig* Danish-ness, to which people regularly refer. However, one might also suggest that the heightened public debate about 'Danish-ness' at this time (see, for example, Gabrielsen and Séférian 1991; Østergård 1992b) was a response to an increasing and uncomfortable awareness – in the face of increasing ethnic heterogeneity, on the one hand, and increasing social and economic diversity and distance, on the other – that this was rhetoric. And perhaps always had been.

Scepticism about the 'substance' of this consensual Danish national identity is reinforced by the fact that the vote was finely balanced. Although large numbers of people locally were indeed hostile to, or suspicious of, increasing European unification, larger numbers appear not to have been. Or, if they were, they voted 'yes' anyway. Furthermore, 'yes' voters and 'no' voters seemed to have *at least* as much in common, with respect to ideas about Danish-ness and national identity, as not. It is clear that opposition to the Union, rather than stemming from any straightforward shared culture or identity, seems to have reflected a *range* of factors. There was indeed a sense of a Danish – and a Nordic – culture, way of life and social model under threat, but there were also the following:

- concern about the loss of independence and political self-determination;
- anxiety about immigration (which may involve a perceived threat to Danish culture and identity, but may also reflect racism);
- populist *ressentiment* with respect to diversity, status and hierarchy within Denmark;
- protests against Danish politics and politicians in general; and
- anti-German feelings.

Thus the evidence which I have presented from the 1992 referendum campaign in Skive suggests that, to some extent, anxieties about the loss of national self-determination were influential in determining opposition to the Union. However, discourses about self-determination were (and still are) more complex than a right-wing defence of Danish borders and ethnic homogeneity, on the one hand, or the left's call to arms on behalf of the Nordic welfare state model of democracy, on the other. And they certainly were and are more complex than might be suggested by reference to a relatively clear-cut and homogenous Danish national identity. Furthermore, even if this latter is a defensible understanding of Denmark or Skive – and I do not think that it is – it would be something requiring explanation in its own right, rather than an explanation of anything else.

This analysis is given further weight if we turn to some of the arguments for supporting the Union which were offered locally at this time. A combination of perceived economic self-interest and moderate conformity to existing party loyalties probably explains a good proportion of the yes-voters, in Skive as elsewhere in Denmark. The point about party voting supports Skovgaard-Petersen's argument (1994) that, in some respects, the 1992 debate was only partly about the details of the Maastricht Treaty: it became entangled with other moral and political debates and themes.[6] It is, however, striking that some of the arguments for a 'yes' reflected the same popular concerns as some of the 'no' arguments. The material reviewed in this chapter suggests that this is particularly true with respect to:

- the fear of unchecked immigration;
- an attachment to 'Nordic' society and culture;
- the question of 'who shall decide in Denmark?';

- populist *ressentiment* against cultural and political elites; and
- distrust and hostility towards Germany.

Here we have a set of issues and themes, linked more or less loosely, which spoke loudly to *both* sides of the argument about the Union and the Maastricht treaty. It might actually be said, in fact, that here we have a basic outline of 'Danish identity':

- relations with the rest of the Nordic world or Scandinavia which emphasize co-operation and similarity;
- a relation of differentiation, hostility and conflict with Germany;
- relationships of relative equality within Denmark; and
- the positively valuing of self-determination and ethnic-cultural homogeneity.

However, if these themes did contribute during this period to the on-going construction of the complexity of 'Danish identity', *then they did so in ways that allowed radically different decisions to be made when it came to casting a 'yes' or a 'no' vote in the referendum.* Thus a vote against Maastricht can no more be explained (away) by reference to 'Danish identity' than a vote for the Treaty.

Which returns the discussion to one of its starting points: identity and interests. In terms of their claimed identity, and the arguments and rhetoric they were deploying in its articulation and defence, yes-voters were no less, and no less self-consciously, Danish than no-voters. Although commentators and locals might have taken for granted something fairly straightforward called 'Danish identity' – what it is, and how it works – to talk about 'Danish identity' in this context is, at best, shorthand for a number of complex and interacting axes of identification, which have different histories and may appeal to different constituencies. Nor do they necessarily encourage equivocation or hostility towards Europe.

In addition, it seems quite clear that to talk about identity is to overlook the importance of a range of other interests and factors – economic self-interest and existing party loyalties and habits – which arguably have nothing to do with Danish national identity, however that is understood. The Danish farming vote in favour of Maastricht, for example (and this goes a long way to explaining the regional difference between Jutland and the metropolitan areas) probably has a good deal more to do with markets and subsidies, than with 'Danish identity'. Thus to concentrate on identity can only get you so far in understanding the relationships of individuals, local communities, and states to the EU. Other factors have to be considered too, and the salience of any particular factor – for example, in Cornell's terms (1996) identity, interests or institutions – has to be a matter for local investigation.

Conclusion

Speaking of local investigations, there is a brief point to be made in closing about the role of local-level, ethnographic studies in the social science of modern Europe. Much of what is written about the issues which have been thrown up by the present gradual movement towards greater European unification has necessarily either focused on political elites, or relied on superficialities to which opinion polls, useful as they are, give us access. To return to an issue first identified by anthropologists more than twenty years ago (Boissevain and Friedl 1975; Grillo 1980), there is still much work to be done if we are to connect adequately studies of everyday life in local communities with the large political issues of the day, and vice versa. The timeliness of the present collection is evidence of just how much work.

And anthropology may still offer the research approach which is best poised to achieve this objective. Although this chapter uses data from newspaper files rather than first-hand ethnography, it is a very locally-oriented newspaper, and the material has been interpreted in the context of local knowledge built up in the course of fieldwork. Without local-level studies, and the ethnographic understanding which they make possible, all we have is the kind of conventional wisdom – deriving from taking the most general possible view, and attending more than they perhaps deserve to those, sometimes shrill, voices which make their way into metropolitan and nationwide debates – that this chapter took as its point of departure. It is not that the one is necessarily superior to the other. Not at all. Simply that we need to bring together the fine and complex grain of the local miniature, with the coarser brush strokes of the broad national (and, indeed, supra-national) canvas, if we are to begin to understand properly the complexities and subtleties of the European Union.

Notes

Thanks to Susanne Dybbroe, John Aggergaard Larsen, Jenny Owen, Tracey Warren and the editors of this book for their helpful comments. I alone am responsible for the chapter's remaining faults.

1. As in many other places in Denmark, the fieldworker in Skive does not have the luxury of virgin ground to break. Recent studies of the town and its hinterland include: Højrup 1989; Haastrup and Ottesen 1996; Lindstrøm 1995, Møllgaard 1984; Skive Kommune 1976; Skov- og Naturstyrelsen 1995. As may be easily appreciated, this is a mixed blessing!

2. I am grateful to the editor of *Skive Folkeblad*, Ole Dall, for offering me the luxury of an office for several weeks in order to go through all the papers, and to the paper's staff for their unfailing help and co-operation. I am particularly grateful to my dear friend Bodil Emtkjær.

3. According to my dictionary, *Norden* can be translated as 'the North' (and by implication 'the Nordic world') or 'Scandinavia'. Since Finland was among the countries considering membership at this time, and since there is also a separate word *Scandinavien*, I have opted for the broadest translation.

4. All translations from the Danish are mine.

5. This finds its best-known literary expression in Aksel Sandemose's famous 'Law of Jante' (*Janteloven*), the first rule of which is that 'you shall not think that you *are* something'. The fictional setting is based on Nykøbing Mors, close to Skive, round about 1910 (see Sandemose 1972).

6. This chapter does not offer sufficient space to explore further the local inter-penetration of debates about immigration/refugees and the EU. They did to some extent feed off each other, and each in its own way contributed to debates about, inter alia, Danish-ness and identity.

References

Boissevain, J. and Friedl, J. (eds) (1975), *Beyond the Community: Social Process in Europe,* The Hague: Department of Educational Science of the Netherlands.

Cornell, S. (1996), 'The Variable Ties that Bind: Content and Circumstances in Ethnic Processes', *Ethnic and Racial Studies*, 16: 265–89.

Cornell, S. and Hartmann, D. (1998), *Ethnicity and Race: Making Identities in a Changing World*, Thousand Oaks: Pine Forge Press.

Gabrielsen, T.S. and Séférian, M-A. (eds) (1991), *Hvor Danske er Danskerne?* Copenhagen: Forlaget Amanda.

Grillo, R.D. (ed.) (1980), *'Nation' and 'State' in Europe: Anthropological Perspectives*, London: Academic Press.

Haastrup, L. and Ottesen, L. (1996), *Kultur- og fritidslivet i Salling-Fjends – Statusrapport og idéoplæg op til kulturregionsforsøget*, Gerlev: Center for Idrætsforskning.

Hedetoft, U. (1991), 'Nationale identitet, politiske symboler, politisk kultur', in Ernst-Ullrich Pinkert (ed.), *Politisk Tegnsætning*, Aalborg: Aalborg Universitets-forlag.

Højrup, T. (1989), *Det Glemte Folk: Livsformer og centraldirigering,* 4th. edition, Copenhagen: Institut for Europæisk Folkelivsforskning og Statens Byggeforskningsinstitut.

Jenkins, R. (1996), *Social Identity,* London: Routledge.

Jørgensen, A. (1993), 'Europe in the Wake of the Danish Referendum on European Union', in Ulf Hedetoft (ed.), *Nation or Integration? Perspectives on Europe in the 90s,* Aalborg: Department of Language and Intercultural Studies, Aalborg University.

Leach, R. (1998), *Europe: A Concise Encyclopedia of the European Union from Aachen to Zollverein,* London: Profile Books.

Lindstrøm, B. (1995), *Parcelhusgenerationen bryder op – en boligundersøgelse i Skive,* Skive: Skive Kommune.

Møllgaard, J. (1984), *Byens sociale geografi: Studier af Skive,* SBI-Byplanlægning 47, Copenhagen: Statens Byggeforskningsinstitut.

Sandemose, A. (1972), *En Flygtning Krydser sit Spor,* Copenhagen: Schønberg (first published 1933).

Sauerberg, S. (1992), 'Parties, Voters and the EC', in Lise Lyck (ed.), *Denmark and EC Membership Evaluated,* London: Pinter.

Skive Kommune (1976), *Skive – 650 år,* Skive: Skive Kommune.

—— (1994), *Statistiske oplysninger om Skive Kommune 1994.* Skive: Skive Kommune.

Skovgaard-Petersen, E. (1994), 'Stemmer om Maastricht', in John Liep and Karen Fog-Olwig (eds), *Komplekse liv: Kulturel mangfoldighed i Danmark,* Copenhagen: Akademisk Forlag.

Skov- og Naturstyrelsen (1995), *Skive Kommuneatlas,* Copenhagen: Miljø- og Energiministeriet, Skov- og Naturstyrelsen.

Sørensen, H. and Væver, O. (1992), 'State, Society and Democracy and the Effect of the EC', in Lise Lyck (ed.), *Denmark and EC Membership Evaluated,* London: Pinter.

Thomas, A.H. (1995), 'Danish Policy-Making, Regionalism, and the European Community', in Barry Jones and Micheal Keating (eds), *The European Union and the Regions,* Oxford: Clarendon Press.

Østergård, U. (1992a), 'Danish Identity: European, Nordic or peasant?', in Lise Lyck (ed.), *Denmark and EC Membership Evaluated,* London: Pinter.

—— (ed.) (1992b), *Dansk Identitet?* Århus: Aarhus Universitetsforlaget.

—— (1992c), 'Peasants and Danes: The Danish National Identity and Political Culture', *Comparative Studies in Society and History,* 34, 3–27.

–9–

Boundaries at Work: Discourses and Practices of Belonging in the European Space Agency

Stacia E. Zabusky

There has been undeniable progress in economic and political integration within the European Union (EU). Borders inside the Single Market have dropped, common standards for producing everything from screws to paper are in place, and citizens of all participating states are now subject to common laws on a variety of issues. Young people are growing up in a world structured not by the national antagonisms of the Cold War, but instead by a supra-national European space, represented in part by the common red passport which identifies them as compatriots when they travel beyond the borders of the Single Market. However, even apparently straightforward and mundane efforts to draw people into a shared political and practical space sometimes incite local passions of resistance.

Although the structures of integration were historically intended, at least rhetorically, to prevent further outbreaks of war, now they appear to threaten the very places European nationals have heretofore called home. Rather than feeling any sense of togetherness, in fact, people seem to be continually fighting – over car registration, feta cheese, adulterated chocolate, whose picture should go on the new currency, and mad cows. Moreover, these rows take shape in overtly national terms. When it comes to standardizing and centralizing European policy on a variety of issues, people seem to hold tighter their local identities. Instead of adopting a sense of 'Europeaness' as a meaningful form of identity and a structure of belonging, the general public seems to regard any such assertions of shared identity as artificial creations of political manoeuvring. The EU, it seems, has failed completely to produce an 'imagined community', in Anderson's (1991) familiar phrase, within its wider territorial boundaries. Thus, the question continues to nag at participants in and observers of European integration – are there individuals anywhere who feel that they belong to Europe?

To answer this question, I suggest we consider not only how national interests confront each other in parliamentary treaties, economic policy and industrial contracts, but also how national boundaries are instantiated in the bodies of ordinary people who make their lives and pursue their work in explicitly European contexts. As Bellier and Wilson point out in their introduction to this volume, the contribution anthropology can make in understanding contemporary efforts both to build and to imagine Europe in the era of the euro is to explore the complex symbolic and practical interconnections between macro-political and bureaucratic apparatuses of union and micro-level social and cultural processes.

This cultural work is happening to a significant degree out of sight of those protests and squabbles that repeatedly make the news. Every day, the work of European integration is being industriously carried out by the thousands of office workers, bureaucrats, professionals, businessmen and women who work for and in European regional organizations and businesses. These are the kinds of people (predominantly white bourgeois professionals) in whose interests, many say, Europe is being built, even if they are not the kinds of people anthropologists have typically considered in their explorations of identity in Europe (see Abélès 1992; Holmes 2000).

It is among such 'functionaries' of European unity that the answer to the question raised above is yes, as I learned during an ethnographic study I conducted at the European Space Agency (ESA). I chose to look at issues of national and European identity in this organization precisely because it was dedicated not to the production of European unity per se, but instead to more material outcomes, those of space science and technology. The EU's stated goal is the production of European integration, in one form or another, and those who work in the context of EU institutions are explicitly engaged in that production.[1] I instead chose to examine the dynamics of identity and belonging at a less self-consciously political site. Part of what I wanted to understand was how and whether people infused something called 'Europe' with meaning when that was not explicitly part of their goal, and yet when that same entity (Europe) called into being the institutional context of the very work that brought them together.

Accordingly, I came from the US to ESTEC, the European Space Research and Technology Center, ESA's main research and technology centre which is located in the Netherlands, to carry out fieldwork for a year (1988–9). During that time, I observed the work of European scientists and engineers who were engaged in the daily administrative and technical work of space science mission development. These professionals did not sit around meditating philosophically on issues of identity; they were too busy just 'going on' with their work. After all, these professionals came to ESTEC and to the Netherlands to ply their expertise and not, at least not intentionally, to build Europe or to challenge their national identities. Nonetheless, these functionaries also produced, in addition to space satellites, both an integrated Europe and new idioms of belonging.[2] In this paper, then, I argue that at ESTEC it was precisely in the process of 'going on' that 'Europe' was really being built, as people negotiated multiple boundaries at work, exploring experiences of belonging – to countries of origin, to countries of residence and to organizations which instantiated a European entity – while they went about their daily routines.[3]

Background: ESTEC as Field Site

In order to provide some concrete details through which to pursue this analysis, I begin this exploration by indulging in a bit of Malinowskian 'imagining'.

> Imagine yourself riding the bus through miles of Dutch countryside, admiring the neat rows of red-brick houses, the lush green fields dotted by grazing cows, and the meandering canals. Eventually, you arrive at the gates of the European Space Research and Technology Center. Passing through the gates, you can no longer be certain that you are in the Netherlands. To be sure, there are the requisite grey skies, grassy dunes rising behind the buildings indicating the sea just beyond, and there is the suggestive sign of a security guard pedalling by on a sturdy black bicycle. But there are contrary signs. As you walk down the roadway that winds its way through the complex to the main office building, you pass along a row of fifteen flags whipping in the breeze. The blue and white flag of the European Space Agency begins and ends this array; in between are flags representing different European countries. Around you, people are conversing in many languages – snatches of conversation in English, French, Spanish and Italian float by. Dutch is conspicuous by its absence.

I made this trip every work day during the year I spent doing ethnographic fieldwork at ESTEC. And every day, after passing through the gates of the Center, I remained impressed by this confusion of the national and the international. ESTEC felt like, and represented itself as, a place that existed beyond or despite the political boundaries of the nation state. Every day, I noted this transgression of boundaries with pleasure, finding myself enjoying the presence of all these flags, and the sound of all these languages, at once signifying national distinctiveness but also shared commitments – to co-operation in production most particularly.

In this sense of pleasure, I was just like those who came to work at ESTEC, at least those non-Dutch staff members who found themselves living and working in an adopted country. They repeatedly talked to me about how exciting it was to work in this international organization, where there were so many differences, particularly national differences. They expressed reservations about returning to national environments, worried that they might find it 'narrow' or 'boring'. They liked this work, both intellectually challenging and somehow personally exciting; I say 'somehow', because no one could ever explain fully to me what it was that they found so stimulating. They just knew that it was so.

English anthropologist Maryon McDonald (1987: 121–2), in an article about conducting fieldwork in France, wrote about the way in which the crossing of national boundaries seemed to generate experiences of excitement, an experience which was not also without anxiety. She described the 'attendant thrills' which accompanied the crossing of such boundaries, both physical and symbolic. This excitement was accompanied by the realization of identities which, she suggested, might otherwise lie dormant or at least unarticulated. She described the evocative power of the boundary itself; she wrote of travelling by ferry across the English Channel from England to France, noting that 'This divide has a tried and tested capacity to bring national identities alive.' In other words, it was the sense of the boundary itself which made the national identities (suddenly) real, palpable and noteworthy. At ESTEC, people crossed such boundaries every day, whether physically when passing through the gate, leaving behind the Dutch village of Katwijk, or symbolically in the quotidian conversations in the halls of the Center, where people from different countries crossed such boundaries simply by saying hello. In the crossing was the realization and recognition of nations, not as abstractions but in the form of embodied experience.

It is no surprise to find that national identities are salient at ESTEC. ESA, the umbrella organization, was formed precisely to knit together diverse European nation states in a co-operative venture in space. According to its founding charter, ESA (founded in 1974 with the merging of two progenitor organizations): 'provide[s] for and promote[s], for exclusively peaceful purposes, co-operation among European States in space research and technology and their space applications'. The space missions that ESA undertakes include both commercially-profitable ventures, such as telecommunications and meteorological satellites, as well as pure science research missions. Fourteen nation states are full members of the Agency; these member states contribute funds to the overall administration of the Agency and send national political delegations to the main governing Council.[4] The participation of these states is financially rewarded through the allocation of contracts to national industries for the development and production of space mission technology. The work of the Agency is carried out at four primary sites, located in France, Italy, Germany and the Netherlands; the staff complement at these sites is made up of citizens drawn from all fourteen member states. ESTEC in the Netherlands is the largest ESA site, with 1,600 employees. Personnel policy for the Agency as a whole includes criteria of national distribution as well as technical expertise to insure a balanced distribution of staff across national lines. However, once hired, these employees become members of the international staff, and no longer represent the interests of their nations of origin. In this way, ESA, like the EU, balances both intergovernmental and federal elements in its institutional structures (Bull 1993). Like the EU (see Bellier and Wilson, this volume), ESA is a decentralized organization with a rather diffused set of political actors and institutions. Thus, at ESTEC, local practices and meanings take shape in a context at once dependent on and independent of the larger bureaucratic structure of ESA.[5]

Although ESA is primarily a scientific and commercial venture, high-level business and political leaders view it also as a key player in the political process of European integration. ESA's own public relations material consistently articulates the significance of the European dimension of its activities. For instance, ESA's *Twentieth Anniversary Report* declares that:

> the Agency itself, with its staff and committees made up of representatives of the Member States, constitutes one of the melting pots for the material from which Europe is gradually being forged, and in which nationalist preoccupations have to give way to wider, more promising visions. All who contribute to the life of the Agency have a sense of belonging to a European unity. (Longdon and Guyenne 1984: 229)

It is just this kind of public rhetoric, which implicates and asserts identities of belonging, that requires ethnographic investigation. Is this sense of 'belonging to a European unity' something that participants talked about or valued on the ground, in the local contexts of daily work? Did 'nationalist preoccupations' in fact 'give way', or did they coexist with, or even resist, articulations of international unity?

During the year I spent at ESTEC, I participated in many conversations in which such questions about identity were the topic at hand, whether directly or indirectly. The majority of my informants were located in the Space Science Department, which included at that time about ninety people, although I also talked to people in other departments. My primary informants at ESTEC were drawn from members of the international professional and technical staff of scientists, engineers and technicians. I conducted fieldwork in English (my native language); international staff members, although they were expected to be able to speak both of ESA's two official working languages, English and French, in practice used English nearly exclusively in daily interactions.

National Identity and Belonging Considered

The question of national identity I consider here is not so much a legal, political and practical question (e.g. of citizenship) as it is a cultural one, with emphasis on experiences and expressions of belonging (Smith 1991). I focus, then, on 'nationness', a concept I borrow from Borneman's (1992; see also Anderson 1991) insightful study of identity in East and West Berlin, rather than on 'nationalism'. Borneman argues that a sense of nationness arises out of a 'praxis of belonging' – what people do everyday, how they do it, where they do it, how they talk about it. This belonging is characterized by a feeling of being 'at home, in one place and not in another'. Such an identity of belonging 'is created only when an individual experiences a particular set of lifecourse meanings enabling him or her to belong to a group demarcated from other groups. Over time such everyday relationships become the criteria for national identifications, for a sense of nationness' (1992: 31).

In a similar way, Löfgren (1993, 1996) writes about our everyday interactions with those 'technologies of intimacy' which constitute domestic, daily life (such as the organization of space and time in the household, the way the shapes, sizes and availability of appliances, house decorations, or consumer goods affect our experience in the world). All of these things together help to constitute national identifications, even a national 'habitus' (Hannerz and Löfgren 1994), feelings of belonging to some imagined communities and not others. As 'praxis', moreover, we must be careful not to assume that such identifications take the form of hard and fast objects; belonging is, as Borneman insists, 'more a signification that shifts than a property that adheres' (Borneman 1992: 18). Such national identifications, moreover, are not only *experienced* by social actors, but are also *projected* onto others on the basis of a variety of factors (which I discuss below), such that everyone is presumed to have a national identity.

At ESTEC, people had a variety of ways of talking about the national identities they observed and experienced. A commonly-used term was 'nationality', a term that conflated cultural identity with citizenship. That the emphasis in the term 'nationality' was on the cultural rather than the political, however, could be heard in another term used interchangeably with 'nationality' – that of 'mentality'. When people talked about nationality, they were simultaneously talking about mentality, that is, about an orientation to the world, a value system and a way of behaving that they viewed as characteristic of inhabitants of particular nation states. This mentality was both embodied – it was seen to inhere in the bodies of persons – and essentialized – to be in the nature of things, of physical, human things. People also related 'nationality' to 'culture', a term which participants used to refer especially to clothing, cuisine and custom. These artefacts of culture betrayed or portrayed the essence of the mentality characteristic of nationality. All of this suggested that, in the view of participants, national identity was not something that could be taken off at will; it stuck with a person regardless of circumstance. In this chapter, when I use the term 'nationality', I reflect participants' emic uses and sense of this term, whereas the terms 'national identity' and 'nationness' reflect my own stance as ethnographer towards this problem of belonging.

For the most part, when national identities were invoked at ESTEC, they took the familiar form of stereotypes. Herzfeld (1992: 72–3) argues that 'stereotypes portray national characters as fixed, simple, and unambiguous'. Moreover, 'stereotypes are one of the currencies of social life. They represent long-established prejudices and exclusions [and] they render intimate, and sometimes menacing, the abstraction of otherness.'[6] Indeed, staff members arrived at ESTEC with already well-developed notions of what constituted, in this straightforward, unambiguous way, the various European 'nationalities' represented by their colleagues. In fact, it seemed that the availability of such national stereotypes helped to ease social interaction, especially when colleagues met for the first time or when their professional interactions were few and far between. By classifying others according to the applicable category of 'nationality', with all that it implied, colleagues were spared the difficulties and ambiguities of trying to understand each other and could then get down to work.

Indeed, I found widespread agreement on what constituted different (European) national mentalities and customs. People slipped easily into categorizing others in this way. In interviews, I often asked participants to comment on the international aspect of their work, and although I never asked them to describe specific national 'mentalities', many responded by doing just that, making statements such as: 'the French like to be formal, they call it Cartesian; [whereas] the Italians are flexible, which means anything can happen'; 'if you think of German efficiency, Dr. Schmidt is it'; and 'the British are good leaders, good at taking decisions' (these statements are all made by individuals holding different national identities from the ones they are describing).

It was not only in interviews that people indulged in this kind of easy categorizing. It happened as well in spontaneous commentary, usually in a genre of joking. On one occasion, I was attending a three-day meeting, at which scientists from England, the US, France and Italy were in attendance. One night, after dinner with a group of English scientists, as we all put our money onto the table to pay the bill, one of the scientists commented jokingly: 'It's a good thing the Italians aren't here because it would never work out; with the Italians you either make a profit, or pay more than you should to make up the difference.'

Sometimes someone of the appropriate identity *was* available to contest or agree to such stereotypical propositions, as happened at an office party celebrating the birth of a staff member's new child. Several colleagues, Dutch, English and Swedish, stood around suffering through the eating of the traditional Dutch food served on such occasions – 'beschuit met muisjes', buttered rusks covered with pastel-coloured, anise-flavoured sprinkles. After joking together about how awful it was to eat such things, one English colleague wondered aloud, 'Do the Dutch like them or do they just eat them?' He added, 'I suppose it's something the Dutch do like the Swedes who go out and purposely flagellate themselves with branches.' One of the Swedes said ironically 'We do?'; and turned to his fellow Swede asking 'Do we?'; the other replied 'No, no it's not us, it's the Finns. We are too soft-skinned.'

Here, there was a good-natured demurral – no, we are not like that – and it suggested that the taxonomy of national stereotypes was available for negotiation, although in these negotiations the taxonomy itself was often indirectly legitimated rather than contested (no it's not *us*, but it *is* someone else). Indeed, the legitimacy of this style of categorizing was made particularly clear when, on some occasions, participants even used the available stereotypes to refer to themselves. In an interview, one scientist described himself to me as a 'typical Swiss', and then elaborated on what marked him as such; on another occasion, an ESTEC scientist, in the midst of complaining to his professional colleagues about his difficulties buying a new car in Holland, conceded that 'I didn't plan well; we Spanish are not good at business.'

For the most part, acknowledgement of ambiguity was not a regular part of what I call 'nationality talk' at ESTEC. For instance, staff members did not often recognize the varied journeys in their and others' life histories, which might have led to a challenge of this straightforward categorizing (e.g. a scientist born in one country, but raised or educated in another). They also did not acknowledge intra-state regional or ethnic differences; colleagues were 'Italian', never 'Sicilian', unless they were talking privately with those who were co-citizens of the same nation state. As Herzfeld (1992: 107) notes, 'state ideologies characteristically replace the divisive social universe with a premise of a cultural entity that is at once individualistic and homogeneous'; it is these ideologies which find expression in categories of nationality at ESTEC.

This shared universe of national stereotypes was made vividly clear in a joke I found posted on numerous bulletin boards throughout ESTEC:

> Heaven is where the police are British, the chefs French, the mechanics German, the lovers Italian, and it is all organized by the Swiss. Hell is where the chefs are British, the mechanics French, the lovers Swiss, the police German, and it is all organized by the Italians.

In order to find this joke funny, listeners and readers must share certain assumptions about identity, European nations and work. For one thing, to be able to laugh at this joke, we have to share an understanding of the whole taxonomy of European nations, in both its details and its overall shape. This joke illustrates the way in which, as Löfgren (1993: 167) has argued, nations 'must appear fundamentally different but also complementary'. To be German meant to be not French or not English, along specific lines. Furthermore, to find this joke funny, we have to accept two related premises: one, that people can be meaningfully recognized by their national identities, and two, that these national identities largely determine how people see the world and how they work and act in it. Thus, although the joke also relies on a tacit recognition that there is some set of universal standards by which we recognize the expertise that is required to make someone a 'mechanic', and in particular, that is required to make someone a *good* mechanic, the suggestion here is that national identities interfere with the execution of expertise. The joke says, in effect, that whether we like it or not, our nationness affects the way we do whatever it is we do. This joke comments, too, on international co-operation and the division of labour. It asks us to reflect on the interdependence of nation states in a rather Durkheimian view of the construction of social order. In particular, the joke highlights the utopian possibilities and the dystopian consequences if, in the building of Europe, we inadvertently mix up the component parts.

Despite the apparent essentiality of national identity, this joke shows that an equally significant identity is found in one's occupation. It is beyond the scope of this paper to explore in depth the construction of such occupational identities (see Zabusky (1992) for this analysis); here, I want to point out the way in which occupational categorizing helped to define the meaning and significance of national identity. At ESTEC, national and occupational categories could not be simultaneously present as significant markers of identity; when one was in the ascendant, the other was downplayed. For instance, when I asked participants to talk about the international aspect of their work, their answers revealed a profound sensitivity to context in the articulation of particular identities of difference. One engineering technician indicated: '*privately* I enjoy the international environment but *working* with people from all over [there are] no differences – guys are guys when you come down to it; they just talk with a different accent'. Similarly, a scientist answered: '*professionally* I don't notice the nationality of someone I'm dealing with, [but] *personally* I find it a very nice experience.' In this way, participants self-consciously drew a distinction between work contexts and leisure contexts.

In contexts of work, where the execution of expertise was the focus, nationness was deemed to be irrelevant and participants talked exclusively in terms of occupation – categories of scientist, engineer, technician were the 'common currency' of work contexts and were culturally significant identities (see Zabusky 1992). They repeatedly stressed that although they were aware of national differences, such differences just didn't matter. An engineer who had been at ESTEC for over fifteen years thought that although 'there is a superficial layer that is typical of a nationality', it is not significant; 'people and disciplines are more important'. Said another scientist: 'when we get together in a meeting like this, it's not a question of being British, French, or whatever; we're just a group of scientists doing a job'. What excited their passions in such moments, what generated both heated arguments and collective brainstorming across the meeting table, were differences of occupations related to the technical division of labour.

Nonetheless, the fact remained that outside of work contexts, in domestic domains or leisure moments, 'nationality' asserted itself as the dominant idiom of belonging, an idiom which led both to excitement and despair. National identities mattered both practically and culturally, and presented both obstacles and opportunities to those professionals who came to work at ESTEC.

Working for Europe: Obstacles to and Opportunities for Belonging

The professionals who were the focus of my inquiries left their countries of origin in order to do the work of the supra-national organization that is ESA. Working for *Europe* meant taking up residence in a *different* nation state, albeit one that was also a member of what most understood to be a 'common European home'.

Thus, although employees of ESTEC came to the Netherlands to work, they did not come there with any intention of 'becoming' Dutch. The Netherlands just happened to be the site where the scientific and technical work of European space missions was being carried out. The organization of ESTEC recognized that there were legal, practical and emotional problems associated with entering into the expatriate life; accordingly, it devoted considerable human resource energies toward helping families settle in the Netherlands.

For instance, ESTEC provided a 'Newcomers' Brochure' to all new staff members. The brochure was a thick binder full of information on how to fit in with Dutch life. The first section of the brochure was about 'Taking up Duties at ESTEC'; this referred not to professional responsibilities, but to the legal formalities of moving (e.g. customs regulations on importing household goods and cars). Other sections of the brochure described for these international staff members how things worked in the Netherlands, and covered such topics as housing, banking, medical care, education, religion and sports. There was also a section on 'practical hints', which tried to convey a flavour for daily life in the Netherlands and to give people a sense for what would be expected of them as inhabitants of Dutch municipalities. There was information on owning a car, shopping, television, baby-sitting, public transportation, public holidays, local Dutch customs, home owning and renting, garbage collection and, finally, window cleaning. It was just such practical elements that constituted one's national 'habitus', and which, accordingly, varied across national borders and demanded people's patience, adaptation and accommodation. ESTEC did not simply provide information, however; it also offered direct assistance in dealing with housing, schooling, banking and so on, including providing a bus service to various international schools in The Hague.

By and large, most staff members were appreciative of the information and assistance ESTEC provided, since it made their lives easier, even though it also foregrounded the problems of belonging due to national identifications. What is interesting in a cultural sense is what such help *signifies*. The very recognition on the part of ESTEC that there would be difficulties settling in signified that from the outset, national identities were real, enduring and distinct, and thus posed potential problems for those European professionals coming to work at ESTEC. The Newcomers' Brochure assumed that it was *nationness* that made it hard for new employees to feel 'at home'. By providing such information, ESTEC underscored the view that it was details on the minutiae of daily living that contained the vital resources foreigners needed to develop a sense of belonging to the national community of 'the Netherlands'. Yet most had no intention of shifting their locus of belonging to a new nation. Thus, the direct assistance ESTEC provided was especially significant, in that it meant that their employees could live more easily *without* having to fit in or belong. Such assistance thus had the effect of further inhibiting, rather than facilitating, international staff members' integration into local communities.

National identities presented not only obstacles, however; they presented also opportunities. Specifically, national identities themselves provided the substance for the construction of new experiences of belonging, namely to Europe itself, as instantiated in ESTEC. ESTEC facilitated this development in a variety of practical ways. Perhaps the most basic was the way that it set itself up as a focal point for a wide range of non-work activities. For instance, staff members and their families participated in sports, recreation and arts activities organized under the auspices of ESTEC, which both contributed significant funds to the support of social clubs and provided a substantial recreation facility on the premises open to staff members and their families. This facility, open from early morning till late in the evening, housed a small swimming pool, squash courts, saunas, solarium, fitness room, indoor tennis courts, and a general-purpose sports hall. This centre also included a bar, dance floors and club rooms. Outside the building were a few tennis courts, a soccer field, and a small golf course.

In thus structuring leisure time as well as work time, ESTEC set itself up for both staff members and their families as a 'home away from home'. Most of the international staff and their families appreciated the fact that ESTEC made life comfortable by providing them with a place to socialize without having to explain their (foreign) presence. In fact, many were proud of the multinational character of daily interactions at ESTEC, and they identified this aspect of daily practice as particularly meaningful to them.

It was this kind of arrangement, however, that led most professionals to describe ESTEC as a place set apart, distinct from everything around it. Two metaphors of apartness repeatedly occurred in the remarks of international staff members: ESTEC as an 'island' and as a 'country'. When talking about it as an island, they emphasized ESTEC's separateness from the surrounding communities. Through policies and resources designed to make adjustment to life in the Netherlands easier, the professional staff at ESTEC was effectively cut off from the promises and perversities of local life. At the same time, precisely because it separated people from daily Dutch life, the 'island' of ESTEC operated as a source of alienation, since people felt, in this way, insulated from the local neighbourhoods and national community of the Netherlands where they actually lived. Either way, as one scientist told me, ESTEC was an island because it was something you crossed to in the morning and returned from at night, as if it were not, actually, part of the Netherlands.

An island, however, emphasizes the boundaries without saying anything necessarily about identity or belonging. The frequently enunciated image of ESTEC as a 'country', on the other hand, said something precisely about this since it is 'countries', after all, which strongly influence people's construction of identities of belonging. As Bellier and Wilson note in this volume's introduction, the tenacity of the nation state as the primary model for Europe-building continues to haunt the political and economic development of EU institutions. Here, I am arguing that this same model constrains ordinary citizens' own capacity to imagine new forms of belonging in the emerging Europe. Thus, ESTEC appeared to participants as a rather peculiar country, because it incorporated diverse national identities into its own structure of belonging, rather than offering a singular national identity as a replacement. ESTEC was, in fact, a country in which having a different nationality from your neighbour was the norm. In ESTEC, what united you were your, explicitly national, differences; people were like each other *because* they were, variously, 'French', 'German', 'Spanish', 'Swiss'. In this experience of ESTEC, these employees enjoyed and were excited by their differences.[7]

Preservation and/or Liberation: Talking about National Identity

National identities thus provided both obstacles and opportunities for ESTEC's professional staff. Living as expatriates abroad they were able, on the one hand, to preserve their national differences, and, at the same time, to be engaged in a common European adventure that liberated them from their national differences in the production of a shared European identity. These multiple possibilities of belonging proved also to be sources of tension. These tensions were present as people engaged in the everyday negotiations of difference which were part of living life abroad, in this case, in the Netherlands. These differences were encountered while shopping, eating, dealing with tradespeople, going to the doctor, and so on. No matter how 'at home' people came to feel in their daily routines, most were continually aware that, in some fundamental ways, they did not 'belong' in the host country. These tensions were particularly acute in relation to significant lifecourse decisions, such as marriage, childbearing and child rearing, and retirement. Daily conversation and practice in and out of ESTEC revealed these tensions as staff members puzzled through questions of belonging, questions that were framed in terms of preservation of or liberation from national identities.

ESTEC staff spent an inordinate amount of time, in leisure contexts, focusing on national identities, despite the rhetoric of ESA which emphasized, by contrast, the 'giving way' of 'nationalist preoccupations', as indicated above. For instance, over lunch, it was not uncommon to hear impassioned discussions of events (such as national elections) unfolding in home countries, while similar events in the Netherlands went unnoticed and unremarked. Moreover, in everyday discourse, participants easily referred to themselves and their colleagues by their national affiliations, trading easily in the 'common currency' that was national stereotypes. People not only preserved national identities in their talk, however; they also preserved them through a variety of practical actions. For some this involved joining social groups with a national orientation (e.g. the British Society or the Alliance Française, or more informal networks). Others went 'home' at every chance they got, in order to replenish their supply of native foods and other products and to absorb the local gossip before returning to their 'exile' once again. It was, indeed, a routine part of expatriate life to ask your fellow compatriots if there was anything you could bring them from the home country if you were making a trip there. At holiday time, expatriate staff did their best to practice their own national traditions, even while surrounded by the local community practicing Dutch customs. Preserving national identity was a particular preoccupation for those with children, children who, perhaps, had never really lived in their country of origin. School choice thus played a critical role in strategies to preserve national identities. Some did this by sending their children to national schools in the Netherlands (such as the French, German, or British schools located in The Hague or Amsterdam); others even sent their children to boarding schools in their countries of origin.

At the same time, however, there was evidence that staff members embraced 'wider visions' of belonging to something European; much of what they talked about, and much of what they did, was focused on liberating themselves from national identities. For instance, it was not uncommon to hear people talking about how much they enjoyed having new experiences which widened their sense of identity. At ESTEC, the staff enjoyed learning about and debating the cultural and national differences represented by their colleagues, as I discuss below. Practically, they tried to enter into the spirit of Dutch life on occasion by taking part in local Dutch customs, such as attending the giant national flea market that marked the Queen's birthday celebrations in April. Again, schooling strategies sometimes reflected this quality of liberation from an otherwise narrow national identity. Many chose to send their children to 'international' educational programs, available either in the International School in Amsterdam or The Hague, or in an English-language stream located in selected Dutch schools. Parents talked about how much they enjoyed seeing their children interact with friends from multiple nations, learning multiple languages, and generally gaining a kind of 'flexibility' and 'openness' in their orientation to life.

It was during these moments of liberation that individuals sometimes denied the significance of their own nationness; said one Italian scientist: 'I feel comfortable everywhere, and in that sense I'm not an average Italian, I'm really cosmopolitan.' Indeed, participants articulated a kind of excitement which they derived from the atmosphere of 'internationalism'; in these moments, they asserted with pride an identity of 'European'. For instance, a French engineer, someone who had had some difficulty settling into life in the Netherlands, nonetheless described to me how 'I like this word, "European".' Another Frenchman told me that he felt that working in an international environment 'makes you more tolerant', and that as a result for fifteen years, 'I've felt really European.' Finally, a Spanish scientist who is Jewish talked to me about how exhilarating it had been for him to work for a while in Germany, where fifty years ago he would have been killed for his religion, and how significant he found it to work for a European organization as a European, able to transcend past enmities.

Certainly, it was not always easy to choose between preservation and liberation when it came to national identity. Indeed, for many, questions about belonging posed profound dilemmas, and led to experiences and discourses of alienation from all sources of connection. Participants articulated this alienation in narratives of confusion, where questions about belonging hung in the air, unresolved. This was particularly the case, for instance, when many long-time ESTEC employees talked about the decision they faced about retirement. Not having participated in shared experiences of nationness for a decade and more, these expatriates no longer had a clear sense of belonging, caught between their formative nationness and the more immediately international experiences of their adult working lives. They wondered: where do we go when no longer working 'for' Europe? Where is home, after all? Many at ESTEC articulated a sense of 'homelessness', of not belonging anywhere. One German scientist who had worked at ESTEC for twenty years indicated that despite his long time living as an expatriate: 'I still wouldn't call myself a European.' Similarly, a Spanish scientist who had lived away from Spain for fifteen years said to me, 'I don't feel particularly Spanish any more, but I don't know if I feel European.' Finally, in an expression of utmost despair, an English scientist sighed and told me: 'I feel confused about whether I am English or European.' No expatriate ever talked about being or feeling Dutch.

Cafeteria Conversation

These shifting significations of identity were nowhere more apparent than in the cafeteria, where every day over lunch staff members manipulated the resources of belonging provided by the organization they worked for and the colleagues they worked with. This was a kind of game of which they never seemed to tire, and in which even I, the visiting American, was always conscripted to participate. It was no accident that these kinds of conversations took place in the cafeteria. The experience of having distinct qualities of nationness seemed particularly pronounced where food was concerned. Food seemed to carry national identity with it, such that, figuratively, people were what they ate. But at ESTEC, because there were many varieties of food available, there was also the opportunity to eat what somebody else was. That food and nationness went together was highlighted by the fact that during meals, colleagues regularly remarked on each other's national identities by commenting on the food they were eating.

Sometimes the catering company that ran the cafeteria made this link explicit as well, during their occasional 'nationalities' festivals, when the foods and customs of selected nations were celebrated. Once during my stay, the cafeteria celebrated Scandinavia, each day focusing on the cuisine of a different Scandinavian member state (Norway, Sweden and Denmark). During this week, food and the entire ambience of the cafeteria expressed the distinctiveness of nations. There were appropriate 'traditional' decorations, performances by music and dance groups in 'native' costume, and small kiosks which displayed Scandinavian arts and crafts and provided information about travel to Scandinavia. The people I sat with at lunch remarked on the food, exposing their national identities through their familiarity with or ignorance of particular delicacies. Indeed, on this occasion, some took the opportunity to try on their colleagues' national identities by sharing their 'tastes' for certain foods, in a kind of ritual of transubstantiation.

In this way, nationness, as much as food, became a matter of taste, in the dual sense in which Bourdieu (1984) uses that term. This taste was always open to manipulation. It could mark differences, emphasizing the essentiality of national identity; at the same time, it could also erase differences, pointing to the way in which, at ESTEC, the clarity of national identities was often blurred as people mixed and matched their tastes, ingesting and incorporating each other's essences, leading the way to a kind of unity. This kind of shifting between diversity and unity along the boundaries of national identity is one of the ways in which ESTEC was constituted as a site of belonging in its own right, as a country with its own 'imagined community' in which the freedom to manipulate national tastes was the marker of a shared identity.

That the ESTEC cafeteria was a significant site for such negotiations of identity was apparent to staff members themselves. When I first arrived at ESTEC, my hosts from the Space Science Department, thinking I would find it interesting to see how Europeans interacted during non-work moments, made a point of showing me the 'nationality tables' (as they themselves referred to such tables) in the cafeteria: exclusive groups of French, Italians, Spanish, Germans, Swedes and so on sitting together over lunch. These 'nationality tables' brought together people who were united by common citizenship and a common language, but who during work contexts were divided by occupation, department and tasks. A decision to participate in the social arrangements of 'nationality tables' meant a simultaneous decision to emphasize the very boundaries that people crossed, in contexts of work, with such apparent ease.

But these 'nationality tables', although a distinctive feature of lunchtime social arrangements, were not the only, nor even the primary option. Most staff sat together at lunch with their professional colleagues, and such social arrangements were treated as the norm. Indeed, the people who pointed out the nationality tables to me were doing so in part to pass judgement, as if to say that this was a negative feature of leisure time at ESTEC. They preferred their 'professional tables' (which is a label I gave to this social arrangement, since for participants it had no name), in part because they took pleasure in the fact that here, in a space where work details did not have to dominate discourse or define relationships, colleagues from different countries elected to sit together, to be with each other personally, in their non-occupational selves, talking to each other not about nuts, bolts, gaskets and wires, but about food, sports, politics and relationships.

Conversation at these professional tables, which was where I sat at lunch, often focused attention on nations and nationness. These conversations typically rehearsed the variations among European nation states and their inhabitants, as people traded information about the 'cultural' differences in such things as attitudes towards electoral politics, driving laws and styles, or the ever-popular coffee-drinking customs ('the French never drink milk in their coffee after lunch'; 'Germans don't like cappuccino'; 'why do Americans like their coffee as thin as water?'). These conversations took the form of a mutual exchange in which each member of the table (including me) was an equal and independent contributor to the conversation. In this way, participants came to share the same general, if superficial, knowledge about each other. Despite the social distance that talking about such contrasts generated in its emphasis on boundaries and on personal and national distinctions, the foregrounding of national identity was simultaneously part of an effort to make connections. People, in exchanging information about national and cultural differences, came to share the same general, if superficial, knowledge about each other, incorporating it into their own expertise, as it were, on 'nationalities'. They also bound themselves together in relationships of exchange in the very act of trading information, and so established a common ground. In a sense, it was not so much the contrasts which emerged as significant, but instead the experience of talking together about the same things which was the pre-eminent experience of such conversations 'about' nationality. Furthermore, people were acutely aware that these kinds of conversations never happened 'at home', where everyone was 'the same'. Thus, this genre of speech (Bakhtin 1986) was itself indicative of something new and meaningful, as participants found themselves consistently falling into this pattern of talk in these expatriate contexts and not in others. Those with whom they shared this genre, then, became compatriots of a new type.

In this discursive crossing of boundaries, staff members thus constructed a collectivity, one which incorporated but also transcended the distinctions of nationality. Indeed, latent in this exchange of 'nationality talk' another identity sometimes emerged. Suddenly crystallizing in discursive strategies of othering, the murky elements of a common Europeaness disclosed themselves, as 'Euro-peans' made their appearance around the table. What had been a conversation about diversities in Europe often mutated into one about the unities of Europe. This happened in particular when conversations turned oppositional, and my table partners faced me as a representative of a new, singular other: the American. This 'othering' was a significant mechanism by which participants engaged in a discursive effort to make Europe over lunch.[8]

It is no surprise to find the United States providing such a significant resource in the construction of a European identity in this way. It is indeed impossible to work in the domain of space and not confront things and people American, both literally and abstractly.[9] This is one way in which the macro-political sphere impinged on local dynamics, and became part of the fabric of everyday life. During lunchtime conversations, then, my presence at times conjured up the encompassing political and technical context of global capitalism and technological competition, and I inevitably came to represent for participants their complex network of relationships with American colleagues. So it was that I regularly experienced a shift in frame during lunchtime conversations, as subtly discursive distinctions would shift from a multiplicity to a dichotomy, as what was in common on one side (the European) was pitted against what was different on the other (the American). Now, 'European' became a 'national' identity in its own right, commensurate with 'American', a monolithic category silencing the diversity so significant only moments before. And yet, at the same time, within this monolith, the diversity of European national identities still bubbled beneath the surface. In Europe, my conversation partners would argue insistently, you are always encountering differences; in the words of one scientist: 'It is stimulating and fun to have this possibility of experiencing difference [when travelling in Europe].'

This was, indeed, what characterized Europe, symbolically speaking, in their eyes: the juxtaposition of so many forms and kinds of differences in such a small geographical space. So it was that the supra-national identity of 'being European' was defined by the very presence of the diverse national identities it apparently ignored both in the high-level political world of European politics and also, more critically, in the everyday interactions across the lunch table. In other words, it was directly through their ongoing talk together about what made national identities distinct and what made Europe identifiable, that participants themselves produced not only their own national identities, but also simultaneously, an identity of 'European'.

Conclusion

In the ways that I have sketched here, ESTEC offered expatriates the opportunity to preserve their national differences by helping them negotiate their foreignness without having to give it up. At the same time, it offered people engaged in a common European adventure the opportunity to be liberated from their national differences in the production of a shared identity. The discursive and practical strategies of preservation and liberation involved processes both of boundary making and of boundary unmaking, each in the effort to generate some identity of belonging. The nature of such belonging was, clearly, fluid and ongoing, the 'shifting signification' of which Borneman writes. In the case at hand, this meant that the same people who in one moment talked about how sad they were, for instance, that their children were not growing up to be 'English', might take their children to see the Dutch Sinterklaas arrive in the town square. Or others who talked with excitement about being European might still return home to purchase sorely missed items unavailable in the Netherlands.

What is significant is that few claimed to have lost their national identity altogether, even if its character had somehow changed. There were moments and contexts where national identity was still the most salient one of all, even if at the same time, everyone recognized that working at ESTEC, and socializing in its spaces, had imparted to them some new resources for feeling 'at home'. Thus, becoming, even *being*, 'European' did not mean that people gave up identifying themselves by their 'nationality'. This fact led equally to the pleasures of preservation, the excitements of liberation, and the despair of confusion – practices and discourses available to all.

These shifting categories and experiences of belonging resonate with the observation by historian Peter Sahlins (1989: 164-5) that in the making of France and Spain 'the adoption of national identities did not necessarily displace local ones'. I would argue similarly that the adoption of a 'supra-national' identity such as 'European' does not now mean, and does not have to mean in the future, the displacement of local or national ones. Indeed, in this structural context of European organization, national identity remained important as a category of belonging significant both to the production of unity and to the preservation of differences (this is also a point Herzfeld (1987) makes in his study of European ideology). In other words, having a national identity is a key component of developing a European identity.

Furthermore, it is no surprise to find the development of a European identity taking shape in this structural context. The professionals who work for ESA can be considered, as I argued above, the functionaries of European unity. To understand the significance of this, I turn again to Anderson's (1991) work on the development of the 'imagined community' in the New World. Anderson argued that the 'original shaping' of the American republics came in the form of 'administrative units'. The question he grappled with was 'how administrative units could, over time, come to be conceived as fatherlands' in the sense of 'nations' (1991: 53). After all, '*in themselves*, market-zones, 'natural'-geographic or politico-administrative, do not create attachments. Who will willingly die for Comecon or the EEC?' (1991: 53). For an answer to this question, Anderson suggested we 'look at the ways in which administrative organizations create meaning', and he drew an analogy between the 'journeys' of colonial functionaries in the New World and the 'pilgrimages' of religious believers. In Western Christendom, the pilgrimage took the form of an 'uncoerced flow of faithful seekers from all over Europe' to the monastic centres of Rome, where 'the great Latin-speaking institutions drew together what today we would perhaps regard as Irishmen, Danes, Portuguese, Germans and so forth, in communities whose sacred meaning was every day deciphered from their members' otherwise inexplicable juxtaposition in the refectory' (1991: 54). Likening colonial functionaries to these faithful pilgrims, Anderson argued that as they travelled upwards through the imperial bureaucracy, they became aware of the journeys of other like-minded 'travelling-companions', and 'a consciousness of connectedness emerge[d], above all when all share[d] a single language-of-state' (1991: 55–6). This was a key part of the formation of the 'imagined community' that is the nation.

Anderson's analysis of distant times and places helps clarify the experience of people working today for pan-European and other international organizations, as contemporary functionaries make their journeys through the politico-economic administrative units of Europe. One Spanish scientist I talked to indeed thinks of himself in explicitly such terms; when I asked him how he'd felt about moving to the Netherlands, he said: 'I am a federal civil servant; I'm here because it's my job. All of Europe – anywhere – it's much the same to me. I feel that I work for Europe.' Thus, these journeys are real and meaningful for those who make them; moreover, it is on these journeys that the 'functionaries' of European integration wrestle with questions of identity and belonging, with the significance of 'nationality' and with the meaningfulness of 'Europe' in the context of daily life and work. As a German scientist said emphatically: 'Other people talk about Europe, but we *live* Europe.' They live it not only in the excitements of liberation but in the despair of alienation – this is the emotional and cultural expression of what, in other domains, is a political and legal struggle. Indeed, I would argue that if European identity is made anywhere, it is made here, in the sharing of the most mundane and ordinary activities of daily life, in the practical decisions about and commentary on what to eat, where to go to school and how to live, activities and decisions experienced not at home but away from home, where the challenge is to find a way to belong in a context of continually shifting possibilities.

Notes

1. The precise form of this 'European Union' is uncertain, as Bellier and Wilson point out in their introduction to this volume, because the EU is being imagined even as it is being built. Such uncertainty leads to a fruitful kind of ambiguity,

as people can negotiate and contest the outcome while still participating in this political and social project. Such ambiguity is not lost on the professional staff of ESTEC, whose own status as simultaneous insiders and outsiders to Europe and to their nations of origin is a source of excitement and despair.

2. In *Launching Europe* (1995), I provide an ethnography of the process of space science mission development, focusing particularly on the co-operative practices of working together in the bureaucratic and high-tech context of the European Space Agency. The book focuses less on issues of national identity, and more on the social and cultural processes of co-operation in European science.

3. Similarly, Hannerz and Löfgren (1994: 200) argue that 'people, simply by going about their daily lives, and observing and commenting on one another, set in motion a massive, although largely undeliberate and decentred, flow of meaning, through a variety of institutions and contexts'.

4. Member states are: Austria, Belgium, Denmark, Finland, France, Germany, the United Kingdom, Ireland, Italy, the Netherlands, Norway, Spain, Sweden and Switzerland.

5. For more details on the history and make-up of ESA, see Krige (1992, 1993), Russo (1993) and Zabusky (1995). For a more complete discussion of the complexities of doing ethnography in the decentralized and diffused settings which are characteristic of modernity in many respects, see Zabusky (forthcoming).

6. Herzfeld (1997: 157) expands on the idea of stereotypes as a 'discursive weapon of power'. Here I am not emphasizing the hegemonic aspect of European stereotypes, although this is undoubtedly present; I focus instead on the way that stereotypes can produce order out of difference. See also McDonald (1993) for an insightful account of the role of stereotypes in European identity construction.

7. By contrast, participants described working in national contexts as 'boring' because there everyone was, as they put it, 'the same'. The ideology of the unified and unitary nation state that obscures internal regional, ethnic, racial and religious diversity was here clearly operating in participants' experience of national identity; once removed from national institutional contexts, where such internal diversity may be the more salient experience, their focus becomes the boundary that separates them from their colleagues at ESTEC. This is the segmentary logic inherent in political and cultural life, as Herzfeld (1987: 158ff) points out.

8. Herzfeld notes that this othering has a long history in the construction of a European ideology, whether it is non-Christian peoples in the East or contemporary 'barbarians' from the West (1987: 53). Similarly, Varenne (1993), too, comments on the role that the United States plays in forging a construction of Europe as a quasi-national space.

9. The desire of European states to participate and compete equally with the US and the Soviet Union in the space race played a role in the establishment of ESA itself. See for example Longdon and Guyenne (1984) for ESA's own view of its history. Laqueur 1982 also indicates that pan-European organizations such as ESA were established in part to enable European states to compete with the US.

References

Abélès, M. (1992), *La Vie Quotidienne au Parlement Européen*, Paris: Hachette.

Anderson, B. (1991), *Imagined Communities: Reflections on the Origins and Spread of Nationalism*, rev. ed., London: Verso.

Bakhtin, M. (1986), *Speech Genres and Other Late Essays*, Austin: University of Texas Press.

Borneman, J. (1992), *Belonging in the Two Berlins: Kin, State, Nation*, Cambridge: Cambridge University Press.

Bourdieu, P. (1984), *Distinction – A Social Critique of the Judgement of Taste*, Richard Nice (trans.), Cambridge: Cambridge University Press.

Bull, M. J. (1993), 'Widening versus Deepening the European Community: The Political Dynamics of 1992 in Historical Perspective', in Thomas M. Wilson and M. Estellie Smith (eds), *Cultural Change and the New Europe: Perspectives on the European Community*, Boulder, CO: Westview Press.

Hannerz, U. and Löfgren, O. (1994), 'The Nation in the Global Village', in *Cultural Studies*, special issue: 'Nordic Cultural Studies', Erkki Vainikkala and Katarina Eskola (eds), 8 (2): 198–207.

Herzfeld, M. (1987), *Anthropology Through the Looking-glass: Critical Ethnography in the Margins of Europe*, Cambridge: Cambridge University Press.

—— (1992), *The Social Production of Indifference – Exploring the Symbolic Roots of Western Bureaucracy*, New York: Berg.

—— (1997), *Cultural Intimacy: Social Poetics in the Nation-State*, London: Routledge.

Holmes, D. (2000), *Integral Europe: Fast-Capitalism, Multiculturalism, Neo-fascism*, Princeton: Princeton University Press.

Krige, J. (1992), 'The Prehistory of ESRO 1959/60', *ESA HSR*-1 (July), Noordwijk, the Netherlands: ESA Publications Division.

—— (1993), 'Europe into Space: The Auger Years (1959–1967)', *ESA HSR*-8 (May), Noordwijk, the Netherlands: ESA Publications Division.

Laqueur, W. (1982), *Europe since Hitler – The Rebirth of Europe*, rev. ed., Middlesex, England: Penguin Books.

Löfgren, O. (1993), 'Materializing the Nation in Sweden and America', *Ethnos*, 3–4: 161–96.

—— (1996), 'The Nation as Home or Motel? On the Ethnography of Belonging', *Anthropology Newsletter*, October: 33–4.

Longdon, N. and Guyenne, D. (eds) (1984), *Twenty Years of European Cooperation in Space – An ESA Report*, Noordwijk, the Netherlands: ESA Scientific & Technical Publications Division.

McDonald, M. (1987), 'The politics of fieldwork in Brittany', in Anthony Jackson (ed.), *Anthropology at Home*, ASA Monographs 25, London: Tavistock Publications Ltd.

—— (1993), 'The Construction of Difference: An Anthropological Approach to Stereotypes', in Sharon Macdonald (ed.), *Inside European Identities: Ethnography in Western Europe*, Oxford: Berg.

Russo, A. (1993), 'The Definition of a Scientific Policy: ESRO's Satellite Programme in 1969–1973', *ESA HSR*-6 (March), Noordwijk, the Netherlands: ESA Publications Division.

Sahlins, P. (1989), *Boundaries – The Making of France and Spain in the Pyrenees*, Berkeley: University of California Press.

Smith, A. (1991), *National Identity*, London: Penguin.

Varenne, H. (1993), 'The Question of European Nationalism', in Thomas M. Wilson and M. Estellie Smith (eds), *Cultural Change and the New Europe: Perspectives on the European Community*, Boulder, CO: Westview Press.

Zabusky, S.E. (1992), 'Multiple Meanings, Multiple Contexts: Scientists in the European Space Agency', in David Hess and Linda Layne (eds), *Knowledge and Society: The Anthropology of Science and Technology*, Greenwood, CT: JAI Press.

—— (1995), *Launching Europe: An Ethnography of European Cooperation in Space Science*, Princeton: Princeton University Press.

—— (Forthcoming), 'Ethnography In/Of Transnational Processes: Following Gyres in the Worlds of Big Science and European Integration', in Carol J. Greenhouse, Elizabeth Mertz and Kay Warren (eds), *Altered States, Altered Lives: Ethnography in Contexts of Political Change*, Durham, NC: Duke University Press.

Index

additionality, 146, 153
Adenauer, K, 35, 56, 103
Alsace, 70
Anderson, B., 7, 120, 179, 196–7
Aquinas, Thomas, 104–5
Austria, 3, 16

Bach, M., 76
banana
  case, 64–5
  Common Organization of Banana Market, 65
Benelux, 46, 65
  Belgium, 59, 69, 71
  Luxembourg, 3, 80
  Netherlands, the, 3, 180–99 *passim*
Black, A., 123
Bonny, Y., 136
border(s), 10, 17, 20–1, 37, 39, 64, 69, 71,
  76–7, 132
  borderland(s) 20, 137–55
  boundary (-ies), 8–10, 13, 17, 40, 62–3, 69,
    140, 181–2
Bonn, 61
Borneman, J., 183–4, 196
Bourdieu, P., 193
Brussels, 20, 37, 40, 44, 45, 47, 53–5, 58, 59,
  60–3, 67–71, 124, 138, 140, 169
bureaucracy, 6, 57, 58, 197
business, 20
  firms, 44, 67–69, 87

Catalonia, 126–7
centralization, 6, 20, 107, 147–8, 153, 155
  central authorities, 48, 69, 153
  central government, 63, 153
citizenry, 7
  citizens, 7–9, 12–15
  citizenship, 9,13, 21, 119–33
  European, 9, 21, 22, 36, 37, 41, 51, 58, 69,
    88, 119–33

national, 9, 119–23
post-national, 120–33
supra-national, 21
civil servants; *see also* officials, 2, 7, 124–6
  European, 10, 13, 17, 32–3, 40, 42, 45, 60,
    62–4, 124–5
  national, 19, 20, 32, 44, 57, 60, 63, 141
civil society, 16, 68, 70, 123
Clémentel, E., 97, 99
Clifford, J., 55
commissioner,
  European, 13, 60, 61, 65, 155
  Planning; *see* Commissariat Général au Plan,
    47, 49
committee, 4, 6, 43, 63, 88
  Committee of Institutional Affairs, 36
  Committee of the Regions, 69
  Competitiveness Advisory Group, 75, 80
community, 5, 6, 12, 19, 20, 34, 35, 39, 44, 46,
  128, 149
  action, 32
  culture, 44, 45
  imagined, 55
  interest, 17, 42, 43, 45, 46, 54, 65
  law, 16, 58, 64, 67, 68
  local, 46, 176
  national, 46
  of practice, 15
  political, 36, 58
  regional, 46
competition, 48, 49, 61, 70, 75, 77, 81–2, 86,
  89–90
consumers, 15, 65, 123, 152
Cook, R., 137
Cornell, S., 159, 175
cross border co-operation, 144–55
cultural
  complexity, 44
  diversity, 7, 18, 20, 59, 140–1
  plurality, 43

relativism, 61
culture, 53, 60, 137
  administrative, 57
  European, 1, 2, 4, 7, 33, 42, 58, 60, 81
  institutional, 19, 36
  national, 5, 8, 44, 47, 60
  political, 8, 44, 47–50, 57–8, 67, 128
  regional, 5

decision-making/makers, 58, 68, 71, 75, 76, 79, 81, 88–89
deficit, 33
  'cultural', 137
  'democratic', 19, 70, 71, 137
  symbolic, 19, 38, 39, 51
Deflem, M. and Pampel, F.C., 132
de Gaspari, A., 103
de Gaulle, Ch., 45, 100
Delors, J., 17, 31, 35, 95–7, 141, 153
democracy, 13, 16, 55, 69, 77
Denmark, 3, 20, 159–76
dialogue, 2, 16, 37, 42, 59, 61, 82, 89
  administrative, 18
  consultative, 18
  European, 66, 67
  institutional, 18, 54
  inter-governmental, 55
  political, 16, 18, 71, 77, 78
directorate general, 63
  Agriculture (former DG VI), 65
  Cooperation and Development (former DG VIII), 64
  Culture (former DG X), 36
  External Affairs (former DG I), 64
  Internal Market (former DG III), 46
discourse, 14, 19, 49, 66, 67, 75–9, 89, 119–33
  institutional, 11, 53
  modernist, 20
  official, 15
Duchêne, F., 94

Eurobarometer, 36, 132, 138
Eurocracy, 17
  Eurocrat, 11, 14, 17, 40, 50
Europe, 31, 33, 34, 36
  Council of, 37–8
  Eastern, 66
  institutional, 13, 16, 38, 59

new, 13, 15, 16, 22, 34, 56, 59, 66, 70, 81, 89, 132, 138, 145, 152
  Northern, 43, 64, 65, 66
  political, 36
  Shengen, 124
  Southern, 43, 48, 64, 66, 126
  united, 36, 60
  Western, 13, 66
European Coal and Steel Community (ECSC), 35
European Commission, 5, 7, 11, 13, 17, 18, 32–4, 42, 45–50, 53, 56, 58, 61–8, 70, 75, 102, 141, 144–5, 165
European Council of Ministers, 48, 49, 58, 60, 61, 63, 64
European Court of Auditors, 144
European Court of Justice, 5, 49, 58
European Parliament, 5, 17, 36–8, 40–4, 50, 51, 58, 59, 63, 94, 124
European policy, 127
  Common Agricultural Policy (CAP), 16, 71, 152
  Common Foreign and Security Policy (CFSP), 58
  Justice and Home Affairs, 58
  Regional Policy, 42, 44, 69, 142–6
European Programmes
  ERASMUS, 130
  INTERREG, 131, 137–55
  TEMPUS, 130
European social cohesion, 16, 46, 63, 81–5, 88
European society, 13, 34, 61, 71, 111–2, 154
European Space Agency (ESA), 10, 11, 17, 179–99
European structural funds, 42, 43, 47, 142–5
European symbols, 123, 155, 160
European Union, 1, 3, 6–8, 14, 31, 35, 46, 55, 58, 59, 75, 119, 125, 133, 137, 160, 169, 176, 179, 197
  European Monetary Union, 33
  Economic and Political Union, 4, 75, 89
Europeaness, 11, 132, 138, 179
Europeanism, 7, 154
Europeanization, 1–3, 7, 8, 11, 21, 22, 66, 132, 139, 142, 151
exclusion, 10, 16, 54, 60, 70, 86
expert; *see also* expertise, 17, 19, 44, 59, 66, 75, 76, 84, 86–9

Index

federalism 35, 36, 39, 46
  federal Europe, 34
Feixa Paimpols, C., 126–7
Finland, 3
flexibility, 18, 22, 42, 57, 61, 76–8, 85, 89
  flexible interpretation, 19
food, 185, 192–5
founding fathers, 13, 33, 35, 45, 56
fragmentation, 77
France, 3, 39, 46, 48, 57, 58, 61, 69, 71, 120,
  124, 129, 130, 181–2, 196

Garcia, S., 125–6
Germany, 3, 21, 39, 46, 48, 61, 69, 171–3, 182
Godelier, M., 38
globalization, 8, 12, 61, 65, 75– 82, 88, 89, 138
governance, 11, 13, 65, 69
Greece, 3

Haas, E., 93
Hedetoft, U., 138–9, 160
Herzfeld, M., 184, 186
Hoffman, S., 93
Howe, P., 128
hybrid, 46
  hybridization, 8

identity, 7, 8, 9, 11, 12, 20, 21, 53, 70, 129,
    132–3, 139, 159, 162
  European, 13, 17, 20, 36–9, 43, 50, 61, 75–6,
    80–81, 89–90, 139, 151–2, 154, 160,
    179–99
  ethnic, 149, 162
  minority, 140, 153, 162
  national, 2, 3, 9, 13, 15, 17, 20, 62, 66, 70,
    120, 128, 140, 149, 153–5, 159–76, 180,
    182, 187–99
  political, 66, 70, 150–5
  regional, 140
  social, 81
institution, 2, 8, 9, 12, 80
  bureaucratic, 4
  European (EU), 2–4, 7, 10–20 passim,
    31–34, 42–4, 53–63, 76
  political, 57, 60
  nation state, 58
  supranational, 58, 78, 90
interest(s), 4, 12, 19, 36, 37, 53–71

entrepreneurial, 20,
European; see also common, 3, 16, 42–7,
  54–7, 63–71
general, 47, 48, 50, 57, 63, 69, 70
group, 16, 44, 57, 60, 70, 71
local, 20, 71
national, 9, 16, 19, 20, 55, 57, 62, 63, 67, 71
private, 57, 62, 63, 69, 70
International Fund for Ireland, 147
Ireland, 3, 137–55
Italy, 3, 46, 61, 70, 182

Judt T., 94
Jutland, 159–76 passim

Keohane, R., 93
Kofman, E., 131

Lagrée, J.C., 130
language, 2, 8, 11, 18, 37, 39, 40, 41, 44, 57,
    64, 70, 84, 87, 137–55
  common, 42, 44, 66
  difference, 21, 125
  translation, 40, 58
  working, 88
liberalism (see also liberal), 13, 41, 50, 63, 78
liberalization, 76, 81, 82, 89
Lindberg, L., 93
Lisbon, 6
lobby (ies), 16, 19, 44, 56–9, 65, 69, 70
  lobbyist, 18, 20, 60, 67
local
  authorities, 48, 145–50
  government, 18, 145–50
  level studies, 153–55, 176, 179
Löfgren, O., 183, 186
London, 61

McDonald, M.,154, 181
Madrid, 61
Maritain, J., 103–4
market, 15, 19, 61, 85
  common, 19, 34
  financial, 77–8
  free, 16
  global, 21
  labour, 16, 22, 81, 88
  single, 33, 42, 46, 59, 64, 65, 144–5, 179

Marshall, T. H., 126
Meehan, E., 122
media, 6, 59, 61, 71
Mitrany, D., 93
modernism, 19, 38, 94–112
  social, 19
Monnet, J., 34, 35, 45, 47, 56, 95, 97, 100–103
Mounier, E., 103–104
multiculturalism, 53
  multicultural organization, 68, 76, 124–8
  multicultural environment, 56, 59, 61, 62,
    66, 124–8
Mumby, D.K., 79

nation, 119–35, 151
nation-state, 119–22, 126, 140, 151, 153
national
  affiliation, 43
  difference, 50
  government, 12, 16, 18, 19, 57–71 *passim*, 83
  identity, 120, 128, 140, 149, 151, 154,
    187–9, 199
  politician, 56
  stereotype, 53, 66, 185
nationalism, 2, 7, 13, 20, 21, 141, 149, 153–5
nationality, 119–35 *passim*, 184, 194
nationness, 183, 187, 192–4
post-nationalism, 21, 36, 51, 55, 120–2, 132
negotiation, 36, 38, 39, 42–6, 51, 56, 62, 68
Netherlands, the; *see* Benelux, 3, 180–99
  passim
Nordic
  dimension, 168, 174
  model, 168–74
Northern Ireland, 20, 132, 137–155 *passim*
Nye, J., 93

O'Dowd, L., 150

Paris, 6, 61, 80
Paye, J.-C., 80, 88
pluralism, 18, 19, 20, 40, 43
policy, 18, 43–6
  linguistic policy, 69
  economic and employment, 75, 88
  social, 78
policy-making, 9, 19, 66, 68, 70, 56, 153
politics, 39–41, 44, 51

political centralization, 147–8, 153, 155
political culture, 128, 149
political leaders, 15, 35, 36, 53
political parties, 16, 41, 162–7 *passim*
political representatives, 16, 18, 55, 60, 67
Portugal, 3, 61
power, 93, 153, 155
public, 62–3
  good, 42, 57
  services, 47, 50
  utility, 47

Rabinow, P., 95, 97
rationalism, 38, 39, 88
  rationality, 10, 33, 38, 45, 58, 76, 84
referendum (a), 37, 159–76 *passim*
region(s); *see also* regional, 2, 5, 6, 9, 13–21
  passim, 59, 60, 68–70, 141–55, 160
  regionalism, 20, 21, 160–1, 174
Rousseau, J.-J., 47

Sahlins, P., 196
Santer, J., 80
Sauerberg, S., 161
Schmitter, P., 6
Schnapper, D., 121
Schuman, R., 35, 56, 103
self-determination, 160–1, 174
Sellier, H., 97–8
Sennett, R., 78, 79
Shore, C., 123
Smith, A., 138
Social Catholicism, 46, 94–113
solidarity, 19–21, 22, 46, 75, 107
sovereignty, 9, 12, 13, 90, 150–5, 160, 168
Soysal, Y.N., 126
Spaak, P. H., 35
Spain, 3, 21, 69, 70, 126, 196
Spinelli, A., 35, 46, 56, 106, 108–110
Spinoza, B., 47
states
  British, 20, 137–55 *passim*
  European, 7, 9, 10, 11
  French, 57
  Irish, 20, 137–55 *passim*
  member, 14, 22, 32–6, 42–6, 50–67 *passim*
  nation, 13, 35, 39, 43, 53, 55, 59, 67, 71, 77,
    78, 153

subsidiarity, 14, 19, 42, 43, 46, 47, 96–113
   passim, 146, 153, 155
supra-national (ism), 21, 35, 51, 78
   level, 14, 68, 71, 75
Strasbourg, 37, 40, 59, 138
Sweden, 3
symbols, 4, 5, 12, 21, 37–9, 123, 155, 160

Tarrow, S., 138
Taylor, P., 93
technician, 17, 19
technocrat, 15, 19, 20, 34, 51
Thureau-Dangin, Ph., 75
Tindemans, L., 106–8
territory, 35, 39, 45, 66, 70
trade unions, 81–89 *passim*
transnational, 35, 41, 75
   culture, 19

company, 19
transparency, 18, 19, 37, 57, 69
treaties, 3, 16, 35, 36, 38, 53, 58, 59
   Amsterdam, 36, 59, 160–1
   international, 3
   Maastricht, 33, 35–37, 46, 53, 59, 75, 122–3,
     159, 161
   Rome, 59, 64, 151
Troubles, the, 141, 143

unemployment, 78–81
United Kingdom, 3, 19, 35, 39, 46–48, 55, 57,
   66, 69–70, 79, 137–55 *passim*, 162
United States, 195
universalism, 38, 57, 61, 70

welfare state, 75, 79, 81, 84–85, 88, 125–6
workers, 22, 71, 87, 123, 152